Life, Death
(and everything in between)

Life, Death
(and everything
in between)

Mike Pilavachi
with Craig Borlase

Hodder & Stoughton
LONDON SYDNEY AUCKLAND

Life, Death (and everything in between)
first published in Great Britain in 2001

The four parts of this book, *Walking with a Stranger*, *My First Trousers*,
Weeping Before an Empty Tomb and *Afterlife*, are all copyright
© Mike Pilavachi and Craig Borlase 1999 and were first published
as single volumes in 1999 by Hodder & Stoughton.

British Library Cataloguing in Publication Data
A record for this book is available from the British Library

ISBN 0 340 78592 6

Typeset by Avon Dataset Ltd, Bidford-on-Avon, Warks

Printed and bound in Great Britain by
The Guernsey Press Co. Ltd, Channel Isles

Hodder & Stoughton
A Division of Hodder Headline
338 Euston Road
London NW1 3BH

Acknowledgements

I would like to thank my friends and colleagues at Soul
Survivor who, when I felt like I was sinking, jumped in to
save the drowning man. To Liz, who not only read the
manuscript and made her usual wise comments but also
cancelled my appointments on a couple of days and did not
tell me until the night before. To Martyn Layzell, Carole
Japtha and Neil Pearce, for their helpful suggestions and
comments. To Jonathan Stevens, for his servant heart,
enthusiasm and efficiency. To Andrew Latimer and Andy
Baldwin, who have been such an encouragement to me. To
Chris and Belinda Russell, who came to the rescue in my
hour of need. To J. John, who has once again proved an
invaluable honorary research assistant. There has not yet
been an occasion when I have popped round to the Johns for
coffee and not left with bags full of books, pamphlets and
transcripts of past J. John sermons to help me on my way. To
Matt and Beth Redman, the drama of whose lives keeps me
entertained and anxious in equal measure. Let's hope the
little one gets to lead a quieter life. Some hope! To Ben
Morrison, my 'soultimer', who has been a fantastic research
assistant. To David Moloney, our editor at Hodder – thanks
for your patience and continual flexibility, especially when it
came to the deadlines. Last but by no means least, to Craig

Borlase, whose friendship is a joy to me and whose writing skills never cease to amaze me. Thank you, little ones!

Walking with a Stranger

Discovering God

Mike Pilavachi with Craig Borlase

Hodder & Stoughton
LONDON SYDNEY AUCKLAND

To Rob, Sue, Paul and Mick Taylor,
my South African family.

Contents

1   Is There a God?   .5

2   God is Personal   11

    Bob's Story   19

3   God is Father   23

    Chris's Story   31

4   God is Creator   35

    Craig's Story   41

5   The Scandal of God   45

    Jeannie's Story   53

6   God and the Underdogs   63

    Ken's Story   71

7   The Radical Words of God   75

    Taryn's Story   81

8   God and the Ultimate Sacrifice   85

    Pauline's Story   93

9   God in Me   97

Closing Prayer . . .   103

1

Is There a God?

If you're reading this book the chances are that you're vaguely interested in this question. Of course there's always a chance that you're reading this book because you've somehow got stuck in a cottage in a remote part of Scotland where the weather is terrible and the only choice of reading material is between this, the back of the bleach bottle and a pre-war textbook on urban waste disposal. If that's the case, then thanks for giving us a go and I hope you find it as exciting as the bleach bottle.

Getting back to the first lot of readers, I might be wrong, but I suppose that you might be open-minded about the existence of God. It may be that there have been times when you have sensed that there's something more behind and beyond the material world. You might have been looking at a beautiful sunset and wondered whether something so beautiful could really have come about by chance. If the world is a painting, then maybe you're wondering if there is an artist.

There might be other reasons why you're thinking about God. You may have been in love and wondered whether there is a personal God who makes sense of our ability to love and feel deeply for one another. You might have wondered about love, loyalty and commitment: could they really come about by chance? Then again, you might not be into art or love. You might have come at it from a more scientific angle, wondering as you studied the laws of nature whether there could be a creator who set them up in the first place. If you're looking for an answer to 'Is there a God?', then this book is written for you. I'll tell you what I believe and know, but don't take my word for it, why not ask him yourself?

Until I was fifteen I called myself an atheist. I even wrote an essay in my English class titled 'Why I am not a Christian'. To my mind Christianity was for old people who were scared of dying, for ignorant people who did not realise that Science had the answers and for weak people who needed a crutch. On paper I was steaming: throwing in argument after argument that I thought exposed Christianity as a fake. The trouble was that even while I was writing I had a sense that there must be more. I had a gut feeling that there must be an intelligent power which could make sense of the order and beauty of the universe. Somewhere, I wanted to believe in a power that would explain the sense of purpose that I felt in my own life. Even though I wrote the opposite, I couldn't accept that my existence was the result of a purposeless accident and nothing more.

Then I became friends with two brothers at school. They had 'something about them', something that was so hard to define but that was easy to like. I'm not talking about popularity here or being able to tell good gags; what the Patkai boys had was something extra. They seemed happy and secure, they were interested in people and they didn't have to put people down to feel good themselves. Whenever I spent time with them I felt better about myself.

I decided that I wanted whatever it was that they had. Then I found out they were Christians. I must have forgotten about my future career as a famous atheist because this didn't really bother me that much. They were the first Christians I had stumbled across and they weren't half as bad as I had expected. They knew how to enjoy themselves, they were normal and popular. Their own sense of assurance was something I longed for, and through them I found out that Christianity is not a set of rules and ceremonies, but something far more exciting: a relationship. I found out the truth about what I had always suspected deep inside: that there is a God who created us for a reason. We can get to know him ourselves because he wants to have a relationship with his creatures – but not just as pets: God wants that relationship to be just like a relationship between a Father and his children.

In this book I want to try and show you some of my own discoveries about God. Because you might not believe me I've also asked a few of my friends to help me. They're going to tell their stories and all I ask is that you be open-minded and open-hearted about what we say.

If you're reading this book in the rainy Scottish cottage, you've probably already asked yourself why it is that Christians spend so much time trying to convert people. Wouldn't it all be so much nicer if people like me shut up and kept our beliefs to ourselves, leaving people like you to go about your own life in peace? Undoubtedly there have been times when we Christians have been so keen to tell people about what we believe that we've treated people less like humans and more like grapes; there to be picked, crushed and forced into something that they were not before. Instead of it being the good news of Jesus, we've left people with a bitter aftertaste that has reminded them of every reason why they are not a Christian. Sometimes we have given the impression that we have the monopoly on the truth, that we have no intention of listening to what anyone else has to say.

For all of these things I'm sorry. But I can't be sorry for the fact that we're keen. After all, if you had made a discovery which changed your life and brought you great joy, and you knew that this discovery would do the same for others, wouldn't you want them to know about it?

I'm a fan of a guy called C.S. Lewis. He was a clever bloke whom you've probably heard of as the author of the *Chronicles of Narnia*, especially the second book called *The Lion, the Witch and the Wardrobe*. One of his other books was called *Surprised by Joy*, and in it he describes the times in his early life when he caught glimpses of something beyond the material world. These times when he sensed that there is something more to life than death were unusual, and became the start of his change from being an atheist to a Christian. He called these times *moments of joy* and I'm assuming that they must have been surprising.

Even though he didn't know it at the time, he was actually meeting with God. It took years for him to suss this out, but in time God drew back a curtain to show himself as the source of those moments of joy. When Lewis found God (or should I say when God found him) things fell into place.

After Jesus died on the cross his disciples were totally distressed; their leader had been taken from them and they couldn't decide what to do next. Should they lay low and avoid further persecution at the hands of the Romans, or should they carry on where their master had left off? One day two of them were walking to a village called Emmaus, which was about seven miles from Jerusalem. The Bible continues the story:

> They were talking with each other about everything that had happened. As they talked and discussed these things with each other, Jesus himself came up and walked along with them; but they were kept from recognising him.
>
> He asked them, 'What are you discussing together as you walk along?'
>
> They stood still, their faces downcast. One of them, named Cleopas, asked him, 'Are you only a visitor to

Jerusalem and do not know the things that have happened there in these days?'

'What things?' he asked.

'About Jesus of Nazareth,' they replied. 'He was a prophet, powerful in word and deed before God and all the people. The chief priests and our rulers handed him over to be sentenced to death, and they crucified him; but we had hoped that he was the one who was going to redeem Israel. And what is more, it is the third day since all this took place. In addition, some of our women amazed us. They went to the tomb early this morning but didn't find his body. They came and told us they had seen a vision of angels, who said he was alive. Then some of our companions went to the tomb and found it just as the women had said, but him they did not see.'

He said to them, 'How foolish you are, and how slow of heart to believe all that the prophets have spoken! Did not the Christ have to suffer these things and then enter his glory?' And beginning with Moses and all the Prophets, he explained to them what was said in all the Scriptures concerning himself.

As they approached the village to which they were going, Jesus acted as if he were going further. But they urged him strongly, 'Stay with us, for it is nearly evening; the day is almost over.' So he went in to stay with them.

When he was at the table with them, he took bread, gave thanks, broke it and began to give it to them. Then their eyes were opened and they recognised him, and he disappeared from their sight. They asked each other, 'Were not our hearts burning within us while he talked with us on the road and opened the Scriptures to us?'

(Luke 24:13–32)

These two disciples thought they were walking with a stranger. They were so dosed up on their own pain and assumptions about life, death and the universe that they failed to recognise God walking alongside them. It was only when Jesus revealed himself to them through what he said and what he did that the penny dropped. I love their response: 'Were not our hearts burning within us?' It's one of the classic understatements in the Bible. Just think about it: if you saw someone rise from the dead, having a slightly increased heartbeat would be the least dramatic of your symptoms.

This has been the experience of millions of men and women down the centuries. It was C.S. Lewis's experience. It is my experience. It's the experience of my friends. I thought I was walking through life with a stranger – a world that only half made sense. At some points along the way my heart burned within me as I sensed something out of the ordinary, but I could never put my finger on what it was. Then one day he revealed himself to me.

I've already told you that I want to talk about some of the things I've discovered about God. I suppose, on reflection, it would be more accurate to say that he discovered me. He made himself visible to me. The glimpses of joy, the sense of the heart burning, the desire to see something beyond the material world, all this made sense when I discovered Jesus and Jesus discovered me. I know this is a bit of a cliché, but the lights in my head came on. When I met Jesus I knew that I had come home. It is my hope and prayer that, as you read this book, you will be surprised by joy, that you will recognise the stranger and that you will come to know him as a friend.

2

God is Personal

If I'm right about this whole God thing – if he does exist and is more than just a collection of strange gases or an old bloke with a beard – then doesn't it make sense that he would give us clues about how to find him? I mean, if he is interested in our lives, if he does want to walk alongside us just as Jesus did with the chaps on the way to Emmaus, then it would be kind of stupid if he did all that he could to avoid us. Avoiding people is the sort of thing we do – especially when it comes down to gimpy weirdos who want to tell us about how to farm cockroaches; it is not the kind of thing that God does.

I'm convinced that God speaks to his people. Just like the rest of us, he is into communication. OK, so we may be a little short on booming voices and giant fingers pointing down from the sky, but just take a look around you and you will see the marks of God's communications. Open your eyes and you'll see his mail all over the place: in nature, other people, events and most immediately through the Bible. That book didn't just float down from heaven one day, prepacked, sealed and written on tablets of stone or chunks of wood. The Bible is a history told by many different writers spanning well over two thousand years. It is the ultimate story book, and is stuffed full of tales and sagas, each of which adds a new detail to the greater picture that we see forming throughout. The Bible is history; it is *his* story. We're not talking about some pasty-faced pop star here, but the Creator of heaven and earth: God.

Some of those classic stories that we find on the pages of the Bible tell us about people like Abraham, Isaac, Jacob; three ancient guys whom God blessed and made the fathers of the nation of Israel. There's the tale of Moses: a man who led a nation out of slavery, through the Red Sea and almost into the promised land. There's David, the greatest King of Israel; Solomon, the wise one; and there are even descriptions of the birth of Christianity as the early Church fought oppression and persecution to become established and grow into what it is today. But it's more than that. Mixed in with the stories of these very real characters is the story of God. The Bible is his book: it was written by men, but Christians believe that the people who wrote it were inspired by the Holy Spirit. The result is a true, accurate and fantastic revelation of who God is.

This personal God that we're reading about now decided to inspire the Bible in order that we might have some type of map. It may not tell us which star we need to turn left at to get to heaven, but it does tell us which Son we need to follow to find eternal life. Of course, like any map, just reading it at home is no substitute for taking the journey itself. We need to get on with the job of using the Bible as a tool for understanding God, as a blueprint for how we should live our lives to please him. But if you really are serious about starting out on this journey, having a decent look at the map is a pretty sensible place to start.

Now I don't want you to think that I can't make up my mind, but I've just had another idea. The Bible, as well as being a map, is also a love letter. OK, so it's a pretty long one and has an unusually high proportion of death and famine in it, but it's a love letter nevertheless. Read it and you find out about how God expresses his love for his people through all generations. It clearly shows us all the things that God has done for us, not because he was forced into it, but simply because of his intense love for those he has created.

God is personal and created us to enjoy a relationship with him. In case you hadn't noticed, something's not quite right and we're definitely not living in a free-flowing paradise with God. There's evil around us – wars, oppression and poverty – and the Bible tells us where we went wrong. In giving us free will, God allowed us to make up our own minds, and by doing that he gave us personality. He gave us freedom to make our own choices, even if that meant some of those choices would be mistaken. If he hadn't have done, we would have been no more than robots, responding to his love and expressing devotion simply because we were programmed to. Think about a mother: what would give her more joy – a shop-bought card with a tacky message inside given on Mother's Day or a home-made one with a simple 'I love you', made not because of a marketing ploy but because the child meant it? Like God, we would all rather have love from a person that chose to love us than from a computer that was programmed.

God gave us the knowledge of how to choose between good and evil; it was up to us which one we decided to follow. I'm not talking about the choice between good and evil being like choosing between eating one sweet or eating ten, but choosing whether or not to live in relationship with him. This is precisely what the story of Adam and Eve is about, but it's also something that's going on in our lives today. Right now you can decide to follow good or evil. It really is that black and white. Do we choose to have a relationship with God or do we choose to ignore him? How can I say this? Because life is not about money, power or sex. At the end of it all we were created for one thing – to have relationship with God.

Things do get a little more complicated than this though. After all, if it was a straight choice between God and no God without any consequences or responsibilities then there wouldn't be so much to get quite so worked up about. The truth is that things get messy because of sin. We can define sin as going away from God; as someone old once said, sin is not first of all badness, but awayness. We'll look at it in detail in the next chapter, but Jesus tells a wonderful story about a son who wanders off away from his father. When he goes walkabout he gets involved in some bad things, but the problems didn't all begin when he got high and slept with prostitutes. They started when he decided to part ways with his dad. He broke the natural law of relationship, wishing that his father was dead and putting an end to their relationship. That's exactly what sin is: going away from our Father in heaven; choosing to do our own thing instead of keeping close to him. The son's choice is still on offer to us today: will we live a life of arrogant independence from God or a life of connection with him as our Father?

The Bible tells the story of how the human race decided to turn away from God, to go it alone, and from that moment on the Bible is a heart-wrenching story of God's efforts to woo and win back the human race. It always amazes me when I look at the Bible, no matter how many times I've thought about it, but from every page the message screams that God hasn't given up on us yet. We've turned our back on our Creator – the One who gave us life; we've destroyed one another; we've raped one another; we've oppressed the weak and have chained up the poor. We're not talking about ancient history here, but about places that are just a short flight away from Heathrow; at the beginning of the twenty-first century we're still counting the dead in Bosnia, Kosovo and Rwanda. All of these tragedies have come as a consequence of our decision to turn away from God.

What has he done through all this? He has stayed with us.

Just like we read in the Bible, God today is still full of mercy and forgiveness, still prepared for us to make up our minds to follow him, stumbling along the way. He is full of character and emotions and feelings, and the Bible isn't afraid to show it. At times we read about how he is a joyful God, one who gets jealous over his people – not in a possessive way but because he yearns for them to come back to him. We see how he gets angry when he witnesses injustice, sin, hatred and evil. The Bible tells us how he loves us too. It describes him as being like a mother hen, brooding over us by being tender and compassionate. Ultimately the revelation that we see of God is that he became a human being, that the Creator became like his creation so that we might find our way home.

Most of us today are suspicious of institutions. We've seen the failure of the giants that our grandparents used to trust, and have grown up to be wary and suspicious of people who claim to be right. It started with Watergate: suddenly governments were not squeaky clean, corruption was not beneath them and the most powerful man in the world was unveiled as a cheat and a liar. The assassination of JFK and the death of Marilyn Monroe suggested that those who held the real political power might also have blood on their hands. The truth about Communism was revealed and the Berlin Wall came down – behind it wasn't the proud honesty of a political system that claimed to be 'for the people', but a lot of poor and oppressed people who wanted out. Then they tried to set Capitalism free in Russia, hoping that it would show the whole world that it was the best way forward. What happened? Corruption and greed took over and left the people in an even worse state than when they started. 'Yes, things were bad under Communism,' they said in Moscow, 'but at least we knew where we stood.' The politicians lined their own pockets and the President stocked up his drinks cabinet. In the first ten years that Russia spent out of Communism, the life expectancy of the average man in Moscow reduced from 66 to 56. So much for the great white hope.

Back in America the CIA was linked to killings of anyone from John Lennon (for being 'dangerous') to Martin Luther King (for being right). It has been alleged that they started wars to save political butts and set up dictators that they could control. In the UK three of our Queen's children's marriages have ended up in tatters while prominent politicians were found dead in bondage gear, or receiving back-handers from foreign businessmen or living lies on the greatest of scales.

We've seen the rise and rise of global corporations: Nike, Shell, McDonald's and Nestlé. Each of them has been accused of exploiting the silent thousands in the developing world to make better profits for the people at the top. We cannot trust the media as virtually all publications in the world are owned by one of five multi-national corporations. The media lied to us about the Gulf War, but are we much better: if we hadn't been in the habit of buying the papers to read about her life, would the Princess have been chased by the photographers in Paris?

Whom can you trust? The Church? Many of us see its vast wealth and its reluctance to be anything other than rooted in the past. It's probably the most conservative and cautious institution in the world, the last place where you could expect to find change and progress.

God is not an institution. He's not a liar, cheat or self-centred power fiend. He is personal. It has taken hundreds of years for the Church to grow up, during which time it has managed to do more to hide God's personality than it has to reveal it. The old traditions and political strategies have taken it far away from the original plan.

Look at the Bible and you will see something different. You will see a man, one who came to be vulnerable. One who came to suffer and to serve, to love and have friends as well as to change our lives forever. He was not afraid to stand up to the institutions, and he didn't hold back on telling the people who had turned knowing God into a power struggle that they were wrong and sinful. Jesus was not afraid to deliver one of the most radical political messages of all time in the Sermon on the Mount, and he came as a human being who eventually was killed by other human beings in the most cruel way imaginable.

Looking at the Bible we see a personal God who came to earth and was weak and vulnerable, yet who also triumphed over the institutions. He reached out to people, healing them and giving them hope. Later the Bible shows us the way the early Church did things; they didn't form a clique and decide to function as an institution, instead they were a living organism, a group who were beaten and even killed but who loved each other, who loved the world and who served the people. Before they were called Christians they were called the 'people of the way' because of their lifestyle and commitment to expressing what they understood of our 'personal' God.

Some would say that the worst thing that ever happened to the Christian faith was the conversion of Emperor Constantine. He declared Christianity the official religion of the Roman world and almost overnight it stopped being a subversive society and became a tool for selfish personal advancement – Christianity became a badge to wear that got you into the right clubs. The trouble was that God never went for the right clubs, he always went for the wrong ones that were full of the poor, lost and sick. That's the kind of person he is – the kind who would come as a humble carpenter from Nazareth instead of an influential religious fat cat from Jerusalem.

I'm not inviting you to join a political institution, but a group of people who are trying to follow a man. Although Jesus was rich in the sense that he owned the universe, he became poor. That's who we're looking to for guidance and instructions, to change the world by finishing what he started.

BOB'S STORY

I was born in Wimbledon and brought up in and around South-west London. I came from a dys-functional family and as a result of problems at home I became behaviourally disturbed as a child. I got kicked out of various schools, and at the age of fifteen left school altogether with no qualifications. I couldn't even read or write properly.

When I was sixteen I joined the British Army and became 24589133 Gunner Byrne, Royal Artillery. I was based in the Midlands and visited Gibraltar. The only active service I saw was in bar room brawls with other squaddies and local civvies. I ended up in army prison, serving four short army prison sentences before getting dishonourable discharge because of my violent behaviour.

I had liked the army; it gave vent to my aggression. I thought you were meant to fight, but they were too fussy about who you did it with. I felt hurt and rejected because of my childhood and I felt hurt and rejected by the army. I joined a gang of skinheads, drank too much, got involved with drugs, slept around, lived in squats, and became a thief and drug dealer to pay for my habit, leading me on to frequent trouble with the police.

For several years I lived in a drink and drugs haze. Life was violent and confused. Because I was hurting inside, I tried to be hard on the outside. I've been stabbed in the stomach with a screwdriver. I have ten stitches in my head and five in my mouth from when I got done with an iron bar. I've been stabbed in the wrist with a broken bottle. I've been thrown through two pub windows and been in a coma on two occasions. I have also done these sorts of things to others. I was filled with hate and anger. What I really wanted, but didn't know it, was love.

At the age of twenty-one, I found myself on the run from the police and selling drugs to students in Oxford. I overdosed myself and made myself very ill. A Christian woman got me to the hospital and a Christian doctor pumped my stomach. They didn't know anything about each other, but they both said to me, 'Jesus loves you!' As I was having my stomach pumped out, I had this strange experience that God was real and that he was there with me. I can't make it sound rational because it wasn't – I just knew God was there.

They pump your stomach out, but they can't pump your head. All night long I sat up in bed, stoned out of my brains and all I could hear over and over again was 'Jesus loves you, Jesus loves you'. I wanted to know that love in my life.

The next day when the doctors came on their round, my doctor gave me a little card with a poem printed on it. She said: 'I was praying for you last night and God said to give you this.' Then she left. The poem was 'Footprints in the Sand'. The poem speaks of how when we feel most alone, that's often when God is carrying us.

I read the poem and began to cry. I couldn't remember the last time I'd cried. I just wept and wept and wept. An hour later, the woman who had got me to the hospital came to see how I was doing. I was still crying. She asked what I was going to do and I said I was going to give myself up to the police in London. She said she would drive me there.

We stopped at a petrol station on the M40 and she got out the little book: *Journey into Life*. The book explained what it meant to become a Christian and at the end of the book there was a prayer for those who wanted to ask Jesus into their lives. I prayed the prayer and at that point I believe God forgave me all my sins and gave me a new start.

The police didn't see things quite the way God did and soon I found myself in prison. I did a sentence of two years, two months and one day. I'd been in prison before but this time it was different – God was with me. I learnt to read and write properly and took some exams. When I came out I studied Social Sciences for a couple of years and wanted to be a social worker. However, God had different plans for my life.

I got a job at a church in Battersea that had just been planted by a well-known church called Holy Trinity Brompton. I worked for St Mark's for four years. I did practical work for the church, worked with people with problems, male and female prostitutes and drug addicts. I also led services and preached. I met a girl called Debra who came from a totally different background to me, and we got married in 1991.

I felt God was calling me to ordained ministry in the Church of England, and put myself forward for the long process of selection. I eventually got through that and went on to do a degree at Oak Hill College.

I was ordained in 1995 and served a four-year curacy at St Stephen's Church, Tonbridge, Kent. Recently I have taken up a new post running one church in Coxheath, near Maidstone, and planting another church in a new residential and industrial area called Kings Hill.

We have two children, Ruth aged five and Lily who is nearly three. My life is so very different now. I love working with young people and find great joy in helping them to avoid the mistakes I made. In the years that have passed, God has been faithful to the promise he first made to me that first day: 'Jesus loves you.' He has proved his love to me in so many different ways and his love has set me free from the past.

Rev. Bob Byrne

3

God is Father

For many of us today the word 'father' isn't a very good word. Our experience may have been of a violent or abusive father, or perhaps one that simply wasn't there emotionally – too preoccupied with work or the TV to take any real interest in us. The trouble is that 'father' is a word that is used to describe God. A lot. Throughout the Book, and especially in the New Testament, we read about the Creator of heaven and earth, the most powerful force in the universe, and we're told to call him 'Dad'.

But Jesus made a point of giving us some clues to help us work out what our Father in heaven is like.

> Jesus continued: 'There was a man who had two sons. The younger one said to his father, "Father, give me my share of the estate." So he divided his property between them.'

Jesus was dead keen on using stories to get his point across. Some of them were sad, some happy, but all were about everyday situations that the people he was telling them to would have understood. Kicking off this story with the sentences we've just read was one of the most shocking openings he could have chosen. It was the custom for a father's wealth to be shared out among his sons when he was dead. In asking for his slice of the pie there and then, while the old man was very much still alive and kicking, the subject of the story was delivering a shocker along the lines of 'Oi Pops. I can't wait for you to snuff it . . .' The reaction from the crowd would have been one of utter shock and disgust. But they would have gone even more mental when they heard the next line about the dad dividing things equally between the two boys. Not only did the cheeky son not get what he deserved – which was a quick slap and a kick up the butt – but he got more: he was given something he did not earn.

> 'Not long after that, the younger son got together all he had, set off for a distant country and there squandered his wealth in wild living. After he had spent everything, there was a severe famine in that whole country, and he began to be in need. So he went and hired himself out to a citizen of that country, who sent him to his fields to feed pigs. He longed to fill his stomach with the pods that the pigs were eating, but no one gave him anything.'

So after he got his share he went on a little wander and ended up miles away in a distant country. Perhaps he had only planned on going somewhere close to home, but eventually he found himself far away from anything familiar. Jesus made it clear that the consequences of his decision to live for himself soon caught up with him. The Bible has a word for this: it's sin – living away from our heavenly Father, choosing to go along with our own plans instead of his. Some people think that they only mean to go a little way with sin, but the nature of it means that it doesn't take long for us to end up, like the cheeky son, far away in a distant land.

But it wasn't all bad – he had a laugh. At the start it must have been a bit of a ball, perhaps he was one of the big men in town with a big wad to spend and a desire to have as much fun as possible. Sadly it didn't just end there – his fast living had a payback. It's just the same with sin: of course it's fun (if it wasn't then why would we do it in the first place?), but the fun is always followed by a set of consequences.

If the crowd had been into the story until this point, they would have gone ballistic when they heard what happened next. For a good Jewish lad to end up looking after pigs – an animal so low and unclean that they would not even want to touch, let alone eat it – would have been the ultimate disgrace. As he scrabbled round in the pen, desperate to have whatever leftovers there were after the pigs' dinner, he simply could not have got any lower.

'When he came to his senses, he said, "How many of my father's hired men have food to spare, and here I am starving to death! I will set out and go back to my father and say to him: Father, I have sinned against heaven and against you. I am no longer worthy to be called your son; make me like one of your hired men." So he got up and went to his father.'

When he got to the place of realising that he had nothing, then even the option of living like a servant in his father's house was preferable to the reality of his present situation. As he makes his way back he works on his speech. Like any child he knew how to get round his parents, and his heart-rending words were designed to get the best result – to be allowed back as a servant. You can almost hear him rehearsing his emotional speech: 'Father, I have sinned against heaven and against you [fall to knees]. I am no longer worthy to be called your son [sob heartily], make me like one of your hired men [fling self to dad's feet and kiss them].' He certainly didn't deserve such generosity: after all, in taking his father's inheritance early he had backed out of the family and effectively wished him dead.

'But while he was still a long way off, his father saw him and was filled with compassion for him; he ran to his son, threw his arms around him and kissed him.'

How did his dad see him when he was so far off? I think that the text implies that the father was looking out for him, that he somehow hoped his son would return. Again Jesus followed on by chucking in some social dynamite; no respectable Jewish farmer would have run anywhere, let alone to reach a wayward ex-son. If ever he had needed to have run somewhere he would have had servants to do it for him, but instead he hitched up his long flowing robes and legged it towards his boy. In suggesting that God was capable of forgetting his dignity in favour of getting closer to one of his children Jesus was turning all the traditionally held views of God upside down. He challenged the established order of things and forced people to think again about the boxes into which they had placed God.

Jesus described the dad as being full of compassion. In the original Greek version that reads more like his guts were being ripped out, so intense was the passion he felt for his child. He demonstrated his love through hugs and kisses in a way that no one listening would have expected. Still, the son seems kind of oblivious to this as he starts his speech:

'The son said to him, "Father, I have sinned against heaven and against you. I am no longer worthy to be called your son."

'But the father said to his servants, "Quick! Bring the best robe and put it on him. Put a ring on his finger and sandals on his feet. Bring the fattened calf and kill it. Let's have a feast and celebrate. For this son of mine was dead and is alive again; he was lost and is found." So they began to celebrate.'

I know that I handle things a bit like the son; if I've fallen out with someone and I've got it in mind to try and make it up, then I'll put some work into preparing exactly what I'm going to say. I'll often be so keen to get my words out that I'll forget to pay any attention to what they're doing or saying. In fact, when I was younger and I'd done something wrong I'd often make up two speeches: one for my mum and one for my dad. The one for my mum would involve giving her a hug and telling her how scared I was that Dad would be angry. I'd then go next door and chat with Dad about Mum being on the warpath and suggest we wash the car together. It worked every time.

That's what the son was trying to do – to persuade his dad to take him back. He thought he'd have to work hard to get back in with his father, but he wasn't even allowed to finish his speech. The most surprising thing about the whole story is that the father immediately demands that the son have a robe, ring and sandals. This wasn't because he was looking a little shoddy, but because they were symbols of sonship – the tokens that told everyone you were a valued and much loved son.

And so the celebrations begin, just like they do whenever any of us turn back to God. How do we know this? Again, Jesus told us; he said that there is more rejoicing in heaven over one sinner who repents than over ninety-nine righteous people who don't need to repent. So this is the deal – the son coming back to the loving father is the way it can be for each of us.

'Meanwhile, the older son was in the field. When he came near the house, he heard music and dancing. So he called one of the servants and asked him what was going on. "Your brother has come," he replied, "and your father has killed the fattened calf because he has him back safe and sound."

27

'The older brother became angry and refused to go in. So his father went out and pleaded with him. But he answered his father, "Look! All these years I've been slaving for you and never disobeyed your orders. Yet you never gave me even a young goat so I could celebrate with my friends. But when this son of yours who has squandered your property with prostitutes comes home, you kill the fattened calf for him!"'

It's easy to see that where the younger son didn't understand just how strong and forgiving the father's love was, the elder son was just as confused but in a different way. In his mind he'd earned the right to have a big fuss made of him; he had been working hard for all that time and had never broken the rules in the way his younger brother had. The father soon puts him straight:

'"My son," the father said, "you are always with me, and everything I have is yours. But we had to celebrate and be glad, because this brother of yours was dead and is alive again; he was lost and is found."'

(Luke 15:11–32)

This is a tragedy – the elder son never needed to slave away to earn the good stuff, for as Dad tells him, everything was his already. This is not unusual for us human beings; there are plenty of people who go along thinking that by keeping up a good record of attendance they are earning themselves a decent position in heaven. Jesus' story makes it clear that it's not like this. Just like the father in the story, God loves us even before we start to do good things for him. He loves us when we're bad as well as when we're good. He loves us when we break the rules and when we keep them, but he doesn't love us because of this; God loves us because it's his nature and he cannot help himself.

I'm not saying that we should not put in the hours working for God's purpose – far from it. But all our efforts are meaningless if they're done just to earn his favour. Our obedience to the Father is an act of love, returning the unconditional love he has for us.

There are three sons in this story: the younger one who went away and came back, the elder one who was always there but was away in his heart, and the son who tells the story – Jesus. He knew what it meant to be loved by his Father and he knew what it meant to be accepted and cared for. He wants us to follow his lead and sign up for the same kind of relationship with the Father that he has.

We know more about prodigal fathers in this age than about prodigal sons, and this story makes a huge impact on us, showing exactly what God is like: passionate, forgiving, generous and strong. He doesn't care that he breaks the rules of what we may think a father is like. God doesn't swear at us or cut us down in public. He doesn't drink too much and come home violent. He doesn't get annoyed when we ask him for some time and he doesn't go quiet when we ask him how he's feeling. He doesn't leave, let down or abuse. He won't shy away when you go to hug him and he doesn't have favourites. He doesn't wish we were someone else and he doesn't want out. He's not a cheat, a liar or a slob and he won't push us away.

CHRIS'S STORY

There are two types of vicars' kids: those who are hung up about it and those who aren't. Which one you are depends a lot on the attitude of the old parentals. Fortunately, I was brought up in a family where being part of a church leader's family was no big deal, especially as I was the balanced middle kid with an older sister and younger brother. We were all very different and my parents encouraged us to be ourselves. So when I'd get picked up from parties at the age of six and my mum would be told, 'I thought he would behave better being a vicar's son', she'd usually side with me rather than with them, knowing that just 'cos Dad was a vicar it didn't mean that I was going to be better behaved (it usually means the opposite).

I grew up saying grace at meals, learning how to colour in the disciples and having weird missionaries staying the night. Something about being a missionary meant that they never bothered to lock the bathroom door, so you'd always walk in on them getting ready for bed, and then not be able to look them in the eye at breakfast the next morning.

God was always around. We were taught to call him Father, ask him for help and cry to him when we were scared. We expected that he'd be exactly like Jesus had told us and showed us through the Bible.

I think most people who have parents who lead churches get viewed quite strangely by the rest of the people in the congregation – always being compared to their mum or dad. Many of the people in the church I grew up in thought I would believe the same, act the same and have the same opinions as my dad. But my parents had encouraged us to think, do and believe things for ourselves. I knew that everyone thought I was just doing the church thing because of my dad – but I knew it was all real to me. Anyway, when I was fourteen I went along to a big rally and heard someone explain about Jesus dying for me. I knew about giving your life to God already, but I wanted him to know that I meant it, so I did one of those public up-to-the-front-at-the-end-of-the-meeting-here's-my-life-Jesus things. I went home and told my parents and we were all happy.

As I was going through my teenage years I didn't seriously think about rebelling against God. It never seemed worth it – what was the point when God was so good and wanted the best life for me? But I did rebel against being a vicar's son – I've tried to purge the planet of all photos of me at that time (unfortunately there are a few still out there) – but take it from me, I looked a real sight most of the time. I'd have to sneak out the back door to go to parties because of what my mum would say about how I was dressed. It was always a shock to people I was a vicar's son – but my parents never stopped me or told me dressing like this was wrong. That was a vital lesson – not to get confused between rebelling against the expectations people had of me and sticking two fingers up at God. I rebelled against one and adored the other, and I think the ability to make that distinction helped me thrive.

There was a group of us who were all Christians. We'd go to parties together and try and keep each other in line. They were good, life-wise Christians too and we shared a lot, so much that I don't think I'd have survived on my own.

Worship was an important thing for me. It's not that the church was cool or full of trendies, in fact we often had that service written in 1662 and murdered psalms every week. I can't remember any talks (sorry, Dad), but when I was about fifteen I had heard someone speaking in tongues. I remember being both freaked out and completely intrigued. I knew I wanted it and started praying for it in my room at night. I began to really enjoy being with God – feeling him within touchable distance – and just kept getting overwhelmed. Being loved this much by Jesus did good things to my heart, and I would spend ages praying, reading my Bible and singing (quietly in case anyone should hear) in tongues. This would all happen in my room, and his Spirit would pick me up and take a hold.

At the same time I was doing my A Levels and loving RE. I was a bit worried about this, especially as I thought everyone would tell me that I was going to be a vicar, which was the last thing in the world I wanted to do. Being a vicar's kid means that you've got to be your own person. Still I loved having the opportunity to look into God's stuff, who he was, how we might really know him and what difference it could make. I was also mouthy and loved spouting my opinions, which made RE even more fun. As this was the subject I really enjoyed I applied to study theology – talking about God – at university. Some people started trying to dissuade me, saying how everyone who studies theology loses their faith, but this made me even more determined. I mean, how stupid is it to assume that the Christian faith can't stand up to a detailed look? If it couldn't, I thought, well who wants to believe in something that weak? I knew Jesus was true, but wanted to know more and to be able to tell people more about him.

My faith did stand up, and I even went back for more, completing a second theology degree. I worked at the House of Commons for a while, and then did something that I really wanted to do – trained to become a vicar. Somewhere in the middle of it all I met my most wonderful wife, and have got more and more excited, more and more overwhelmed by how and why this God loves us. I've been more and more inspired to get the news of this God and his Kingdom out there. There's not anything or anyone who is and does as God is and does.

Chris Russell

4

God is Creator

Now I've never had any myself so maybe I'm not one to talk, but it seems clear to me that people have children for all sorts of reasons. Some do it because they're bored, some because they're drunk, some because they want something to play with. But as well as knowing that a child is for life and not just for Christmas, most of the rest of us also know, however deep down, that the best reason behind the urge to create a wee baby is a love between two people which makes them want to create someone whom they can share their love with. Most people see children as an investment – perhaps not financially, but certainly emotionally. Parents tend to be into the idea of lavishing their love on the nippers and seeing them grow over the years, becoming people who in their own right can pass on love and carry on the tradition. Something inside us draws us to this; the need to know love and create is as basic as our need for warmth and shelter.

It's a simple step to take here from talking about children to talking about God. You see, some people believe we are here by chance, the result of a random series of bangs, collisions and slugs crawling out of the sea. But our need to recreate, and the longing for a sense of purpose, are hints that we too were originally created by something or someone

35

else. It was either an accident or part of a plan – and even when I was a fuming atheist I just couldn't get my head around the idea that we existed only by chance. The thought that I might not be anything more than just a simple blip in history – now you see me now you don't – the idea that my life was just another grain of sand in a desert of emptiness was not something that made me happy. There had to be more, I thought; there had to be a reason why.

It was only when I started talking to Christians and reading the Bible that I discovered that we were made for a purpose, that there was a point to it all. I found out that we were made by a Creator who did it not because he was forced to, but because he wanted to have a relationship with us. Just as parents have children so that they can give them love, so God created us so that we could receive and enjoy his love.

The big book for us Christians kicks off with a clear message explaining why we were created in the first place. It says that God made us 'in his image', in other words that we have inherited bits of his character. The whole of the Bible screams out the same story: God is personal. He is interested in us, he loves us and wants us to get closer to him. The Creator cannot therefore be an impersonal force; God cannot be an 'it' that doesn't care for us or a mysterious collection of gases that we can never understand or communicate with. He has got personality and character and we can get to know him. Sure the Bible is full of weird and wonderful stories, of characters and people so varied and unique that one of them even took to burying his underpants in a wall (believe me, it's true), but throughout it all we see God, the star of the show – constant throughout.

In his first letter John describes God perfectly: 'God is love'. The rest of the Bible backs that up, giving us a clear picture of a God who didn't create us as a bizarre experiment only to place us back onto the shelf once he had played with us for a while. As we were made for his pleasure, we were made to have relationship with him. Because of that our hearts will always long to be brought back home to him.

The name of the book of Genesis also means 'beginnings', which seems fairly appropriate seeing as how it starts the whole Bible thing off. This book of beginnings starts out with a chapter titled 'The Beginning', and with the words 'In the beginning God created . . .' The clever ones amongst you will have noticed a common theme there, and we can all be fairly sure that the story of the world – our story – begins with God. But even before we all began God was around. We later find out that he's the kind of guy who's bigger than that whole beginning and ending thing, that he always has been around and always will be around. For us bods who have a very real sense of when we start and when we finish this can be quite confusing, but it is also the solution to an awful lot of head scratching. We've spent centuries wondering how the world started, how the galaxy was formed and how the universe came into existence. Like that game when every answer is met by the question 'why?' we can keep on trying to trace back our beginnings to the nth degree. But with God it's different. Believing that he was there first and that he created it all in the first place gives us the chance to make sense of it all.

In the Bible's telling of the story of how it all began we see that God works through things steadily; first he creates light, then sky and water, land and seas, sun, moon and stars. Then come fish to fill the seas and birds to fill the air, after which come the animals. On the final day of his creative burst he decided to make human beings 'in our image, in our likeness'. Only by creating man and woman can he express the full extent of his beauty, and only when he has shown us just how creative he is can we begin to understand what it means for us to have been created in his image.

After this, so the story goes, God was pleased with what he saw and he rested. I think it's interesting that according to this, our first full day on the planet was a day of rest. This seems odd for us busy people, but perhaps it's another subtle hint about the reason why we're here in the first place; could it be that, instead of our main aim being to earn as much cash as possible or to leave as big an empire as we can, the reason why we are here is to spend time with God, to discover and develop our relationship with him and others?

You might be getting a bit excited by all this talk of God creating everything in six days flat. Surely we grew out of all that stuff years ago? Well, some people believe that it all happened from Monday to Saturday, but many Christians believe that while the proportions are right, it is more likely that this Scripture is talking symbolically of six chunks of time, rather than six blocks of twenty-four hours. I think that science tells us more about creation than the Bible does, and that it can give us a much more detailed picture of how we got here than we can find in Scripture. But, what science cannot answer is the question that could easily be a subtitle of the Bible, *Why Did We Get Here*? Science attempts to tell us how, only the Bible can tell us why. The answer to this is the truth that we all yearn for. It's what gives our lives meaning and purpose, and a life without knowing means missing out.

To see that we were made in the image of a creator God helps us to explain all the creativity that can be found within us. When Michelangelo painted the Sistine Chapel or sculpted the boy David, when Mozart wrote his symphonies or when chart legend Meatloaf penned his 1975 classic 'I Would Do Anything For Love' (yes, I am a fan), each of them was expressing something of the nature of God. The fact that our creativity is inherited from the ultimate Creator goes some way to explaining why we place so much importance and give so much respect to those who can create.

I was fifteen when I became a Christian. I can remember that one of the things that made me so happy was the fact that at last I knew I wasn't alone and adrift in the universe. I wasn't just the product of some hanky-panky late one night in my parents' bed, nor was I Mike Pilavachi just because the right sperm had reached the egg at the right time, beating all the other sperm to it. It wasn't by chance that I was here and I wasn't going to disappear as soon as I was dead. Finally I knew that my life had purpose and I felt great. I knew that while I was in my mother's womb God knit me together, and that even before then, even before Mum and Dad played their part in the whole Mike P story, God had me on his mind.

These are strange days; fear and confusion are top of the bill as we try to make sense of the world around us. One of the biggest reasons that our society today is full of people living with the horror of anorexia, bulimia, alcoholism and drug abuse, as well as those who self-harm and are suicidal, is because, although we're stuffed up to the eyeballs with material wealth and possessions, we're running critically low on a sense of purpose. Are we just here for seventy years and that's it? Is there nothing more to life than the here and now? If this is all we have to live for, then there's no wonder that the strain begins to show.

The thing that certainly puts a smile on my face is the knowledge that we are here for a reason and that we find a reason for living as opposed to a reason for existing when we discover a life with God.

Some old chap named Rousseau said that 'most men live lives of quiet desperation'. I think he had a point; for many of us the weeks drift by, separated only by the snippets of time we get for ourselves at the weekends, and it all blurs together into a mishmash of months, of two-week holidays that are longed for from one end of the year to the next. The decades slip by, grey with memory and low on meaning. We look for things to brighten it up for us, but it is only through getting to know the God who made us for a purpose as a personal friend that we can find freedom.

I used to dream of receiving a knighthood. Sir Craig Borlase had a lovely ring to it. I wasn't kidding myself; I didn't think I'd get it for great works of charity, just for being really, really rich. I'm glad to say things have changed.

My father was unreliable. His relationship with my mum ended when I was in nappies and throughout my first decade any contact we had came when I visited him during school holidays. He married, had a son, and by the time I was eleven our relationship had become so 'non' that it was easier to forget about him than suffer the pain of being continually let down. After one particularly bad visit I said that I didn't want to talk to him. 'He knows where to find me if he wants me' was what he told my mum on the phone when she gave him the news. That was the last I heard from him.

My mum found healing in the church, and I grew up knowing God. Having always loved attention I did a bit of drama at church. People began opening up to the Holy Spirit, and so did I. I began to believe my own hype and to think that my praying, prophesying and shaking made me special. Still, church was good: I felt accepted there, although I hated spending the week at school where no one really understood what I was about. To my mind they were sinners and were to be avoided at all costs.

At the age of nine I had gained a step-dad and a couple of step-brothers. One lived with us and was going through his own troubles which didn't make for a very cosy home-life. Despite that, as I forgot about my dad and concentrated on the good things around me, I was pretty happy with things.

It didn't last. Things seemed to go a bit wrong when I was fifteen. Home was hosting arguments you could set your watch by; I seemed to be losing my status at church (those offers to get on stage were disappearing); I started thinking about my father (whom I hadn't thought about for three years); the buzz of receiving from the Holy Spirit didn't seem to be having any impact on my life.

Actually, not everything was going wrong, for I started to hang around with people from school, getting into the good times and trying to be a little bit naughty. I struggled like this for a few months, trying to get back into church, but eventually it became clear that the world was spoiling my enjoyment of God, and God was spoiling my enjoyment of the world. 'Go,' said my youth leader. 'We'll be here when you want to come back.'

I quit church and found friends, drugs, literature and girls. This carried on when I got to college, but there I was faced with harder drugs, less study and a singled-minded intention to enjoy myself. After a year I felt ill and through a couple of great mates I started being friends with Jesus again.

Strangely enough, it feels as though this was when all the work began – this was when things stopped making sense and I began searching. I felt like this was the wrong way round – aren't you supposed to get low, start searching and then find God? Once I was back at church I realised that I loved the friends I had made in the previous three years and I loved bits of the culture that I had thrown myself into, but my old version of Christianity was telling me that these things were wrong.

The thought of selling up and returning to the Christian Ghetto made me sad: I felt like I had tasted life, I didn't want it to go stale. Thankfully I found a group of friends who hung out on the fringes of church culture who were supportive and loving. They loved to be creative and they valued friendship. It was just what I needed: the chance to be Christian Craig Mk II, a very different model from the teenage prototype. Leaving church brought me closer to God. I lost the interest in hype and being a Holy Spirit junky. Instead of begging God to come down and give me a supernatural fireworks display, or ignoring my hell-bound friends, I found that what I valued most was genuine friendship – with God and others.

The stuff with my father is still the same – perhaps it's the thorn in my flesh – but I've learnt not to try and compensate for the feelings by trying to get people to notice me. Although I was a bit of a fool for a time, hurting myself and others in ways I would never want to repeat, I believe that God, in his mysterious ways, helped me lose my religion. It did me the world of good.

Craig Borlase

5

The Scandal of God

Think of Christianity and I'll bet most people will think about Christmas. In will come mental pictures of gold-embossed cards, carols that make you yawn and some weird story about a bloke on a donkey with stabilisers. Of course, if you've done your homework you will be thinking about Jesus being born in a stable with old and dignified wise men standing next to young and enthusiastic shepherds. You might like to chuck in a few animals, maybe a big-eyed cow and a couple of soft sheep (all odour free, of course). Jesus in his little white nightie would be sleeping soundly, or perhaps staring knowingly about him. There may be a scattering of snow outside, but inside the people, animals and presents are all surrounded by a warming glow that suggests a beautiful family on their way to a beautiful life.

It's true: Jesus was born in a stable, but it wasn't quite like this. The circumstances were kind of different. A few years ago, when I was a youth leader I tried to rediscover the truth about the birth of Jesus. The church was at one end of a reasonably sized village, and each year at Christmas the local shopkeepers helped put on a Christmas night in the high street. Basically this involved them feeding customers with mince pies, burgers and a lethal brew of mulled wine. Feeling full and a bit woozy the happy shoppers would then stroll from shop to shop, merrily purchasing whatever useless tat they didn't need and wouldn't buy when they were sober. It was a stroke of genius on the part of the shopkeepers and was something of a tradition in the village.

On this particular year our church had been asked to do what we could to put on some kind of carol singing and nativity play to entertain the village. It seemed like a great idea, and because I had run out of things to do my vicar gave me the job. Now I'd always fancied myself as a bit of a director, and ever since I had seen Sooty play Prince Charming at the Basildon Palace in *Cinderella* I knew that I wanted to go into the theatre. Working with the likes of Sooty was a long way off, but as I accepted the challenge of putting on the village play, I knew that it was the start of something big.

As the weeks of rehearsal rolled by my plans for the production grew more and more ambitious. I had started with the idea of putting it on as a mime, but when I realised that no one knew how to mime anything other than feeling their way around a glass wall, I binned the idea. Later I thought that it might be nice if we did it in the original Aramaic – the language spoken by Jesus. Again, we hit a bit of a dead end when I found out that the only languages known among the congregation were French, Spanish and enough German to order two Schnitzels and a taxi to the airport. Not one to be deterred, I decided to aim even higher. In a flash of inspiration I remembered the joy of sitting in that theatre in Basildon watching Sooty sweep the beautiful Cinderella off her feet. I decided to do what I knew would be best and went with the 'natural' idea, calling up anyone I knew who had an animal that we could borrow.

On the night of the performance we gathered in the car park of the church and went through our final checks. Instead of a donkey we had only been able to get a horse named Viper for Mary and Joseph to ride, but I was convinced that no one would notice. There had been a bit of trouble trying to track down a flock of sheep, so the three shepherds had to make do with a flock of sheep that consisted of only one goat. Still, I was sure people would get the idea.

The best thing though was the costumes. Someone in the church had made them for all the characters: Mary and Joseph, the three kings, the three shepherds and the angel Gabriel. They all looked excellent, although if you looked hard it wasn't difficult to see what order she had made them in. The three kings were immaculately fitted out in robes that could have come straight from a movie set, while the shepherds were a bit shabbier. This kind of made sense though, apart from the fact that one of them looked as though he was wearing clothes borrowed from a child half his age. What I did notice, however, was the angel Gabriel. All the white muslin had been used up on the kings, so Gabe's outfit had to be made from old material that was going spare. Unfortunately, the only old material that was going spare was an old duvet cover paying homage to Darth Vader. It was a bit of a shame, but as the angel (played by a lovely man named George) walked about the car park with his cape flowing behind him, all I could think of was that I was glad the *Star Wars* villain hadn't worn sandals as well.

It went wrong when I noticed that Mary, Joseph and Gabriel all wore glasses. While I could forgive the odd sandal here and there, glasses were a different thing altogether. It just didn't look right, and despite the fact that Mary told me she was blind without them, I managed to persuade them to do it for the sake of the play.

Being without her glasses made Mary nervous, but not nearly as nervous as being on a horse. As she climbed on the back of Viper, she remembered why it had been years since she had ridden a horse. She shook as though they were galloping even though the horse had not moved an inch.

Still, confidence was high enough and we walked down

the hill towards the high street. I marched on ahead next to the carol singers who were warming up with a bit of 'Good King Wenceslas'. As we prepared to turn left into the high street I looked back to check how things were going. Badly. There were only two shepherds and no flock.

'Stop,' I shouted. 'Where is Shepherd number three?'

Silence. Everyone turned and looked. Eventually, to my horror I saw Shepherd number three at the end of the road pulling the goat's lead as if he were on the losing side in a tug of war. What was worse was that the goat was chewing its way rapidly through a selection of some villager's prized winter pansies. The two other shepherds ran to help and they all pushed the goat as hard as they could towards us at the front. The goat didn't like this too much and trotted ahead making it clear how much he didn't want to be a sheep. Shepherd number three felt likewise and the two were in a strop with each other all night.

Turning the corner into the high street we came to our first stop at the Post Office. Here was a decent crowd of people already enjoying the tray of mince pies and mulled wine that was on offer on the table outside the shop. Our carol singers sang, people looked happy and the horse decided to relieve himself not only up the side of the shop doorway but onto the tray of pies itself. I was embarrassed and the postmaster was angry.

We carried on singing 'Silent Night' as we legged it up the road. Arriving at the butcher's I turned around and noticed that this time it was Shepherd number two who was missing with the goat. I looked across and they were having another argument. Just when things started to get heated Shepherd number two picked up the goat by its legs and slung it around his neck. The goat was not happy. It was not the kind of effect I was after.

At that point I looked around and saw that we were minus two kings.

'Where are Kings number two and three?' I asked King number one.

He looked embarrassed and pointed to the butcher's. Standing in a queue for burgers were Kings two and three. Calmly I walked up to them and enquired as to why they felt it was appropriate for two kings to be queuing for junk food.

'You don't understand, Mike,' said King number two. 'I'm the burger King.'

I didn't laugh.

By this stage I was upset. Everything had gone wrong; Shepherd number three was in a huff at the back of the carol singers, Shepherd number two was wrestling the goat to the ground, Kings number two and three were trying to wipe the ketchup off their robes, Joseph was trying to calm Mary down after the horse had started to walk back towards the mince pies and small children were crying at the sight of the angel Gabriel. I sat down on the bench at the crossroads and turned to the angel.

'George,' I told him. 'This is not how it was supposed to be.' The angel Gabriel looked at me and said, 'Mike, isn't this more like the first Christmas than what you intended it to be?'

I stopped and thought. He was right; what I had planned was a sanitised version of the birth of Jesus, one without the muck and reality that would have been there. According to the Bible the very first Christmas was very different to the one that I had wanted to stage. It happened when a virgin who was engaged to be married was visited by an angel and told that she was pregnant. Joseph was still up for marrying her when he found out, but planned to divorce her quietly after a while as he wasn't really sure that she was telling the truth. Then the angel appeared to him as well and confirmed that it was a miraculous conception. Despite the fact that both believed that she was still a virgin, people not surprisingly would still have questioned Mary's story, and as a result Jesus was born with one of the greatest social handicaps of the day: rumours of illegitimacy.

In the final weeks of her pregnancy Mary had to go with Joseph away from their home town and back to the place of his birth. Bethlehem was over one hundred miles away from Nazareth; no trains, no planes, no automobiles; just lots of walking and a donkey. They were homeless as all the hotels had been comprehensively pre-booked, only able to find a stable for the birth. Perhaps you might think that a palace would have been too obvious a place for a saviour to be born, but surely God could have come up with something better than a stable. Wouldn't a nice semi-detached have been more appropriate?

The only people there to celebrate his birth were the kings (or wise men as they are sometimes known) and the shepherds. At first you could be forgiven for thinking that the wise men might sound like decent sorts, but at that time they would have earned no respect at all for the simple fact that they were foreigners. What's more, in Israel the kind of people who were shepherds were the kind who couldn't do anything else. They were the dregs, but even within their profession there was another hierarchy. Guess who was at the bottom? The night shift. That's what these shepherds were: so inept that they couldn't even get a decent job in the lowest sector of employment. They were muppets of the highest order. The most shocking, amazing and wonderful thing about Christmas is this, however: that in baby Jesus God became a human being.

The story of the first Christmas is that God became like one of us so that we could be rescued from our failure and our sin. God became like those he created, like the most vulnerable ones in his creation. Can you imagine what it must have been like for the Creator and Ruler of the universe to become a baby? Can you imagine the indignity of being dependent on people for everything in your life? Feeding, changing, soiling and vomiting are hardly the sort of things you would expect the Almighty to want to be doing. What's more, can you imagine why God should so value you and me that he would choose to do this?

This is the message of Christianity; it is a mad scandal, one that can only be considered rubbish or truth. It is so extreme that it is impossible to be neutral about it. One of the words we use at Christmas is 'Emmanuel'. This word crops up in the Old Testament book of Isaiah when the writer predicts that one of the names of this miraculous baby would be Emmanuel, meaning 'God with us'. And so we come to the heart of the Christmas story: God with us. When the human race turned away from God, when we made a mess of the whole thing and hurt each other, when our selfishness had become extreme, God didn't stand back and let us suffocate and pay for our own punishment. The message of the stable is that God stepped in, that he made himself accessible to us. God made the first move.

JEANNIE'S STORY

Although my parents were not churchgoers they sent me to Sunday school for a couple of years when I was eight. The only thing I remember was being taught that if I told lies then I would get black spots on my heart, and if I crossed myself before going over a road, I was less likely to get run over. With this helpful spiritual knowledge under my belt, I approached puberty.

When I was a teenager I used to spend hours wondering what was the point of life. I wanted to know what it was all about and why I existed. I used to write morbid poetry to make sense of it all. I remember asking my mum when I was fourteen why hot cross buns had crosses on them and what they had to do with Easter. My mum came from a non-practising Catholic family and my dad came from a Spiritualist background. Neither of them had any answers for me.

I married Ken when I was nineteen and all these questions faded away. I was happy, and even happier when I found out at twenty-two that I was pregnant. It wasn't until I was thirty-six weeks into the pregnancy that, after poor antenatal care, I had an X-ray which showed that the baby was not going to live after it had been born. Our baby was anencephalic, which means that the skull had not formed to the usual size because the brain had not grown. It was impossible for the baby to live with such a tiny brain. No one told me the results of the X-ray and they lied to me about the health of the baby. Only Ken knew the truth, but they told him not to tell me. Instead he had to watch me go through two days of induced labour while student midwives practised their painful examinations of me knowing I would have no baby to hold at the end of it.

The horror of giving birth to a deformed dead baby, of still being a mother but having nothing to show for the thirty-six weeks of loving and nurturing my unborn child threw my mind and emotions into chaos. I didn't fit in with my friends who had no children, and I certainly didn't fit in with those who did have them. I was repulsed by the pictures my imagination conjured up of what our baby must have looked like – we were not allowed to see our baby daughter so my imagination was probably far worse than the actual truth.

Although my concept of God was 'something somewhere', I clearly remember thinking and feeling that I was being punished by an unjust God. I shouted at the top of my voice in anger, 'I never *ever* want to know you.' An interesting statement as I never even realised at that time that anyone could know God.

I swallowed my grief as it was so difficult to grieve for someone I had never met and no one ever gave me permission to speak of my baby – they were too embarrassed. In desperation I quickly became pregnant again. This time around I formed no relationship with my unborn child. In fact, by the time I was thirty-six weeks pregnant again and had the routine X-ray, I reacted in a strange way. Seeing pictures of a perfectly formed head and body I started saying out loud over and over again, 'I'm pregnant – I'm pregnant.'

'Yes, Mrs Morgan,' said the doctors and nurses in

54

calm voices, as if they were talking to someone stupid, 'we can see you're pregnant.'

During the rest of the pregnancy I allowed myself to believe that this baby might live. Although it was a difficult birth I was overjoyed to hold our daughter Alexandra in my arms. After ten days in hospital where I only got one hour of sleep each night as I was so anxious about my baby, I was allowed home.

Even though I was hyperactive and anxious, I was also quite confident in the hospital. As soon as I got home, exhausted, my new responsibility to keep this young baby alive suddenly hit me and threw me into an overanxious state of mind. I can remember trying to care for a screaming baby during our first night home, when nothing I did seemed to help. I slipped over the edge into hysteria as I rushed down the stairs completely out of control screaming, 'Help me – please help me.' I was put into bed where I reverted to the foetal position, sucking my thumb.

There followed a complete nervous breakdown lasting three months. For the first three weeks I was unable to make even the simplest decision. If I was asked whether I wanted a hot drink or a cold one my answer was, 'I don't know.' I was unable to do the simplest of tasks because I had no confidence. It was even impossible for me to change the sterilisation water for Alex's bottles; I was afraid I might do it wrong and she might die. I refused to take any of the medication that was prescribed as I was convinced that Ken and the doctor were trying to poison me. After three weeks the doctor was ready to commit me to a psychiatric hospital but the shock of returning to a hospital environment snapped me out of the manic stage and I started to accept the medication offered me. The doctor introduced me to a Christian who ran courses called 'Relaxation for Living'. I didn't know it at the time, but she belonged to a prayer group that had started to pray for me. Years later I realised that God had used these two Christians to bring me through this time of agony. After three months I gradually became well again and had a positive attitude.

A couple of years later we decided to have another child, and another girl was born – Joanna. Unlike the rest of us in the family she had blonde curly hair, and as far as births go it was great. Due to a medical problem I was sterilised a year later, and as we didn't want any more children this seemed like the best thing to do. When Joanna was two years and three months old tragedy struck. We had a swimming pool in the garden – actually it was more like a concrete hole – four foot deep, unheated and not even filtered. Joanna never went in it – she said it was cold, 'nasty cold'. The weather had been warm at the weekend and the safety net that usually covered it was pulled back. It took two people to secure it back on and we hadn't put it back. Joanna and I had been in the garden for a while and Alex was out at a friend's house. The doorbell rang and I went in from the garden to let Alex in. As Alex and I called out Joanna's name we rushed upstairs thinking she was hiding from us. Halfway up the stairs we looked out of the window to see her body floating in the pool.

When I reached the hospital and they were fighting to save Joanna's life, a big black momma of a nurse held me in her arms to comfort me.

'God is punishing me because I was sterilised,' I told her.

She pulled away from me and looked at me. 'Honey,' she said, 'our God doesn't work that way.' Those words were truth and they went inside me to the depth of my being and took away that lie. I knew she was telling the truth. As the doctors walked in to give us the prognosis I turned around to escape but there was no way out. By the look on their faces I knew it was going to be bad news. They told us that either Joanna would be a vegetable all her life or she would die within the next couple of days. For the first time since I was a little girl I said a prayer. It was simple but I knew that God heard it. 'Please, God, let her die.' If it happened to me now I would pray a different prayer, but at the time I knew what I had prayed was a good and right prayer. Bad things had happened before but nothing had ever been like this.

At that age Joanna was totally dependent on me and needed me for virtually everything throughout the day. Having her with me was like having part of my own body following me around. To be without her was like having a major part of me severed. Although I had a husband and a daughter whom I dearly loved, everything within me cried out for this child that was no longer there.

In a couple of days a vicar arrived from the local church, St Andrew's. His name was David Pytches, and as he stood in the kitchen he said the most unusual thing, 'Let's say a prayer together.' I thought you only prayed in church or at weddings or funerals, but was even more shocked by what he said next. 'Dear Jesus, please come by your presence into this kitchen.' As David reached the front door I said, 'For a vicar I think you're a very nice person, but we don't really want to be bothered with all the stuff you're saying.' He said that it was fine but that there were a lot of people praying for us because they cared about what had happened.

After that the strangest thing happened – whenever I went into the kitchen I could sense this warmth both in me and around me. I couldn't explain it, but I knew that I liked it. As the week went on we started to have some more unusual experiences. We couldn't put into words what was happening – we had no vocabulary to describe it – and all we could come up with was the idea that all these praying Christians must be emitting some kind of electricity that we were feeling. We were being comforted in our pain. I had a distinct impression of hands drawing me along to somewhere. In fact I had so many experiences of what I now know is the Holy Spirit, that if someone had told me about him then I would have immediately said that I know him.

Our closest friends were also affected by this spiritual presence. They told other friends, 'Go and see them, you will feel comforted.' This lasted up to and including Joanna's funeral day. I knew nothing about the Bible and so I didn't realise the significance of what I was saying when I told people that it was Joanna's Wedding Day. I wanted everyone to dress as if they were going to a wedding and it was the most amazing funeral I have ever been to. The crematorium chapel was full of light and lots of people from St Andrew's had come to offer us their support.

The next day I was plunged into despair. Once

more I felt unable to grieve by crying. I felt guilty about what had happened and felt as if my life had no hope whatsoever. David Pytches kept on visiting us and had brought me a Bible. This really annoyed me as I had been brought up to be polite and knew that I would have to pay for it by going to church. I also desperately wanted to know where Joanna was now that she had died. We had never had her christened as we thought it would be hypocritical since we were not believers. David read me a verse from the Bible, 'Unless you change and become as a little child you can never enter the kingdom of heaven.' She was not old enough to choose – she was in the kingdom of heaven. I felt satisfied with this for a few days until I realised that I didn't know about me – was I going to heaven? Did this mean I would never see her again?

I went to church to pay for the Bible. There were so many people there that I recognised from the village but hadn't realised that they were churchgoers. Even though I had never known any, my opinion of Christians was that they were weird and out to get you. As soon as I arrived at the church I immediately felt enclosed in something that I can only describe as being like cotton wool. Later I learnt the language to describe it – it was love, love for Jesus and love from Jesus. At last I had found a place to cry and grieve. I kept coming back to the church, taking communion even though I wasn't a believer. That was where he met me in my pain; I wept and wept and no one interfered. Sometimes I felt a hand on my arm but no one stopped me crying. I felt safe to let it out there, and every Sunday I would go home red and puffy from crying. I still thought the Bible was a fairy tale and that Jesus was just a story, but I knew the Holy Spirit.

On two consecutive weeks there was a sermon about knowing Jesus. Two weeks running I asked Jesus into my life but wasn't sure if I really believed it. On the third week there was another sermon about knowing Jesus and another call to give my life to him. This time around I thought to myself either this Jesus is real or he's a lie. I knew I couldn't keep asking him into my life for the rest of time – I decided to take a risk and ask him in, believing that he would. I felt no different, just relieved that I had made a decision. The next day I woke up and felt very different, but couldn't describe how. As I went outside what I saw was incredible – it was as if all creation had a new vibrancy. It was like the first time that I wore glasses when I found out that without them I was unable to see properly. I knew what I had been missing. Everything had clarity and purpose.

The next major thing that happened in my step towards knowing Jesus was a conversation that I had with a friend of a friend. She wasn't a Christian and as we were talking one day she suggested that I have an operation to reverse my sterilisation. Almost as soon as she had said it she took it back, saying, 'I don't know why I said that; all obstetricians are butchers.' She was a nurse and the wife of an eminent surgeon, and I knew that at that time the reversal operation was only ten per cent successful.

The next day as I was walking home from school I suddenly had these two impressions in my head. One was an audible voice saying, 'Trust in me, trust in me'. The voice was big, strong, warm and kind. The other was a whining voice and I saw the serpent from the film *The Jungle Book* which was also saying, 'Trust in me'. I knew nothing of the significance of the serpent in the Bible, but it was horrible. I made a decision – I wanted to go with the warm voice and turned away from the whining voice. Immediately I was desperate to run all the way home and phone the Consultant who had carried out my operation and ask him to reverse it.

Then came my second prayer. I knelt by the sink in the bathroom and prayed, 'Please God, please give me a baby.' Later, when I talked to the Consultant, I felt hope for the first time. He explained that he had pioneered a new operation that was seventy-five per cent successful. What he didn't tell me was that he hadn't done one for a year and that he had only done four in total.

I had the operation and one year later Elizabeth (Beth) was born. When we chose her name we didn't know that it meant 'gift from God'. Whenever we went to the village shops people would come up to me and ask if this was our miracle baby. So many people had prayed for her to be conceived.

Jesus continued to heal me. At one time the healing was immediate when Alex, who was six at the time, said something that I am sure was from God. It healed all my unresolved grief about Sarah, our first baby. Over the couple of years after I had given my life to Jesus I was significantly healed of many painful memories of Joanna's death. Instead of remembering the doctors working on her, I could see how beautiful and precious she was, how much she was God's child.

In time I was also healed of my massive inferiority complex, huge feelings of insecurity and a lack of self-worth and self-esteem. I became free, not bound.

I fell in love with Jesus and he became the lover of my soul. He took me from the slimy pit of hopelessness and helplessness and tenderly touched me with his love. I will never stop thanking him for all the healing he has done in my life. Through the death of Joanna seven people in our family became Christians. I believe that God used her death to bring glory to himself in a way that would have been impossible without it. I honestly believe that I would not have become a Christian had these things not happened to me. He would have come to me, but I wouldn't have received him.

I've been healed. I am being healed. I will be healed. I give glory to God through Jesus Christ – my Lord and my friend – for all that he has done. His love is the kind that will not let me go.

Jeannie Morgan

6

God and the
Underdogs

So you might have got your head around the idea that Jesus'
birth wasn't too great. You might even have taken on board
that stuff about how God didn't just leave us to suffer the
consequences of our own sin but that he made the first move.
But still you might be wondering what all this Jesus fuss is
about. How can a strange birth mean so much? Well, my
friend, read on.

The point of Christianity is not just that God came down
to earth; it's what he did and how he did it. Through not only
his birth but his life, death and return to heaven Jesus
completely reversed the established order of things. He
changed the way we understood a whole list of things from
success to happiness, poverty to wealth, humans to God. So
forget whatever you might think he stood for and take a look
at the facts of his life; we'll look at his words, his death and
his resurrection over the next few chapters, but for now let's
put his life under the microscope.

The only place in the Bible where we can read about Jesus'
life is in the first four books of the New Testament which are
known as the Gospels. There's no real debate about the fact
that Jesus lived and that he went through the situations as
described in Matthew, Mark, Luke and John. There are even

plenty of other documents from the time that mention Jesus. I'm happy to assume that these four records of Jesus' life can be trusted.

Having got that out of the way it's time to read them. You might like to do it yourself, perhaps starting with the book of John, but before you do it would be good to make a couple of mental notes. First, C.S. Lewis – whom I mentioned in the first chapter – reckoned that reading the Gospels forces you to come to one of three conclusions. You can choose to believe that Jesus was mad. After all anyone who claims to be God, to be able to forgive sin and raise people from the dead seems to have many of the necessary qualifications to secure a place in a psychiatric ward where the furniture is screwed down and the cutlery is plastic. If you don't go for the crazy Jesus option, Mr Lewis thought that you could choose the bad boy option. If he wasn't mad and if he really did know that he wasn't God, that he couldn't forgive sins and that he couldn't raise people from the dead, then it would seem fair to conclude that Jesus was a pretty nasty guy. To deliberately delude and fool people about such important things is certainly not the mark of a gentleman. But if mad or bad doesn't take your fancy, the only option left for you to take is to believe that he was who he said he was: that Jesus believed what he said and was able to do what he offered. It's up to you to decide which one to go for.

But it's not like once you've decided you've got it all sussed: looking at Jesus' life I am constantly surprised. Just like any other human he is unpredictable and spontaneous, but unlike anyone I've ever met he continually does the right thing, even when doing the right thing means doing something new, unexpected and controversial. He acts with such integrity that I think it's impossible not to be impressed.

He was born the son of a carpenter and followed his dad into the family business. Now in those days being a chippie wasn't a bad trade at all, it may not have been the most obvious starting point for a revolutionary, but it wasn't a bad start. Apart from his birth and a trip to the synagogue when he was a boy we don't hear much about him until he hits thirty. Then things get a little crazy. We follow him over an intense three and a half year period where he travels around the country on foot telling people that he is the Son of God, the Saviour they have all been waiting for.

Just like any other rabbi, Jesus made sure that he had a collection of people following him whom he could teach and travel with. He picked twelve of them, and these disciples formed an interesting collective. Perhaps you might think that Jesus would have hand-picked a group of stunning individuals who gelled as a team and could be trusted to carry out his requests with the utmost commitment and reliability. You'd be wrong. Jesus picked a group of half-witted rejects and placed the future of the world in their hands. He didn't opt for the most intelligent, most progressive or the most adaptable bunch to be his crew. He chose a bunch of losers.

One of his key players was Peter, a guy who simply found it impossible to keep his mouth shut. He was always talking without thinking and making promises that he couldn't keep. The two of them met one day when Peter was sitting by the Sea of Galilee repairing his nets after a trip out on the lake (don't ask me why they called it a sea, it is most definitely a lake). Jesus was midway through a sermon by the lake when he decided that, having seen Peter's boat, things would be more comfortable if he preached from the boat which was parked on the shore. After he finished preaching Peter returned from washing his nets to find some bloke taking it easy in his vessel. As if that wasn't cheeky enough, when he approached Jesus, he was told to take him out onto the lake for a quick bit of fishing. Peter must have been utterly gobsmacked by Jesus' bottle, as instead of telling him where to go he made do with some seriously heavy sarcasm.

'Master,' he says, 'we have worked hard all night and haven't caught anything. But because you say so I will let down the nets.'

Imagine the scene: Peter, the fisherman being given fishing advice from Jesus, the carpenter. Peter had been hard at it but was in the slightly embarrassing situation of not having caught anything. To be told what to do by someone who was more used to making ashtrays than reading the waters was a bit of a tough one to swallow. 'We have worked hard . . .' he said, making it clear that he and his two mates were the professionals when it came to fishing. When it came to 'But if you say so . . .' I think it was probably delivered in the kind of tone reserved for humouring small children.

Still, feeling generous Peter took Jesus out on the lake and went through the motions of letting down his nets. Imagine his surprise when by the end of the session they had caught enough fish to fill two boats to sinking point. Not bad for a first timer.

Not only do we read about this time when he had fished all night and come up with nothing, but there's a story later on that seems almost identical; Peter was again empty-handed by the Sea of Galilee after an all-nighter when Jesus (this time having risen from the dead) approaches and tells him to try casting his nets on the other side of the boat. Again he has a result. We suspect that Peter was not the most accomplished of fishermen.

There were another couple of disciples who were brothers, called James and John. They were nicknamed Sons of Thunder, not because of their volatile bowel movements but because of their tempers. If there was a fight brewing you could always rely on them to be the ones stirring it.

Then there was Matthew, a tax collector – the profession which might have guaranteed decent money, but also brought with it hatred and suspicion of virtually all his fellow Jews. Thomas earned the name Doubting Thomas because of his complete inability to see anything other than the negative side of things. He was the ultimate pessimist, refusing even to believe that Jesus had risen from the dead in the way that he said he was going to. In fact the only one of the twelve disciples who seemed to have any ingenuity or intelligence, the only one who had any accounting skills was the guy they allowed to look after the purse, Judas Iscariot. He was taking money for himself for ages and wound up handing Jesus over to the Romans to be tried and killed.

It wasn't the case that these were the best he could get, nor was it a project that went wrong. Jesus loved the disciples; he hand-picked them and made sure they were the ones who got to know him far better than any other person around at the time.

Just look at the sort of things that Jesus did. I love the fact that the first miracle he performed was to turn water into wine at a wedding in Cana. This wasn't a sermon illustration or his part of a deal that meant the guests had to give him their money or attention. It was a disaster; they'd run out of wine – it was a gift, pure and simple. He did it with the sole purpose of letting people have a good time, and he made sure that there was plenty to go round, converting it by the gallon. What's more, the only people who actually knew that the miracle had taken place were the servants, those who were working hard behind the scenes and who weren't soaking up the luxury of the party.

I also love the story of him feeding five thousand people. The preaching had obviously been going down a bomb to have attracted such a large crowd, and when the disciples bring up the subject of food they obviously think it's going to signal the end of the session. They suggest turning people away without even thinking that Jesus may be about to pull a miracle out of the bag. The Bible tells us that Jesus already knew what he was going to do, but that he wanted to test them. He tells his men, 'You feed them,' and we can only assume that they slope off with the worried grumbles of a group of people who are about to end up with a lot of very hungry and very angry people on their backs.

While they're whingeing about how it would take more than eight months' wages to feed them all, Andrew comes back having been on a search. He's nicked some poor kid's packed lunch and offers Jesus the five loaves and two fish. Jesus takes this tiny amount, blesses it, gives thanks and hands it back to the disciples telling them to do the deed and hand it out to the hungry thousands. The miracle actually happens in the disciples' hands as they hand out what seems to be an almost endless supply of food. This is so key to understanding Jesus: that he doesn't hold onto his power and abilities for himself, but that he gets his people to carry out his work too. That doesn't mean he's lazy, it means that like his Father in heaven, he is mad keen on getting us involved. Christianity is about interaction. It's not a passive trip that we sit back on and enjoy the ride – it's a joint venture. Jesus takes the little that we have, he sees what little we can do and multiplies it until it's enough to impact a multitude.

There was the time (you can read it for yourself in John 4) when travelling through Samaria – the territory of the enemies of the Jews – Jesus stopped by a well having sent his disciples into the town to get provisions. He stays back from the town centre just so that he can meet one particular woman. In the heat of the noonday sun she arrived to get her water. The only people who were mad enough to go out at that time of day were those who weren't allowed out when the day was cooler. This Samaritan was obviously excluded from the rest of polite society, and in the conversation that follows between her and Jesus we understand why.

First he asks her for a drink. Shocked, she reminds him of the stupidity of his suggestion; she is a Samaritan and he is a Jew. In that culture a man didn't initiate a conversation with a woman, and he certainly didn't give the time of day to a

Samaritan. He was breaking two rules just so that he could do what happened next. They talk about water and he tells her how he is the living water. They talk about worship and eventually Jesus tells her to go and fetch her husband. She has no husband, she confesses.

'You are right when you say that you have no husband,' says Jesus. 'The fact is you have had five husbands and the man you are with now is not your husband.'

Her reply is the most understated in the whole Bible: 'Sir, I can see you are a prophet.'

Jesus made sure that he met her in the world she lived in every day: an outcast on the edge of society. He spent time with her and showed her the dignity she deserved as a person. She was the wrong sex, the wrong race and the wrong type of person. For this one immoral person Jesus missed out on going into a crowded town full of good Jewish men and women. Eventually she brings along the rest of the towns-people, telling them what had happened to her at the well, and they also believed in him.

Jesus' life has these kinds of patterns in it. He always went with the servants, the underdogs, the disciples and the outcasts. Through them he reached the rest of society, and the plan remains the same today. If you want to get into Christianity you need to know that it's not some private little religion that just goes on in your room. Christianity, following the Christ, means a whole lot more than tacking a little bit of church onto your normal life. It means going where Jesus goes – to the poor, the broken and the outcast, showing them the love of Jesus and joining his work. There were so many other crazy and wonderful things that he did with his life: put them together and you get a message that only Jesus could have preached.

KEN'S STORY

This follows on from Jeannie's story...

I obviously was extremely upset by Joanna's death and did think about the whole question of life, work, family and God. When people said to me that Joanna had gone to heaven I thought he could not have it both ways – to be a God who cared and yet who still allowed Joanna to die and go to heaven.

A few months after Joanna's death I got back into my previous routine of working and not thinking any more about God. When Jeannie started going to church, I thought it was a crutch that she needed and an emotional female response that was not relevant to me. When Jeannie became a Christian and it appeared to me that she was getting more involved with church activities, I started to resent her commitment to the 'church', which seemed more than her commitment to me and the family. As time passed I began to think that Jeannie relied more on God than on me. In the past she had relied on me so much that it definitely felt as if this had changed. I felt that this was coming between us and was even putting our relationship in jeopardy.

It was two and a half years after Joanna died that we went on a winter's holiday in January to Florida for two weeks, which should have been a wonderful time away. However, I was not feeling very happy and seemed to have a lot of anger inside me which I took out on the family. Two weeks after we returned there was a Friday night social with food at St Andrew's Church with a visiting speaker called

Canon Keith de Berry. I went along reluctantly – mainly for the food. Some other non-Christian neighbours were also going. After we had eaten Keith spoke about the dangers in a marriage when one partner was a Christian and the other partner wasn't, and the problems this could cause. I felt as if he was speaking directly to me as what he was saying was a reality to me. He then said that if you wanted to find out the answers to these problems, to come along to church on Sunday when he would be speaking. I thought this was a typical church con to get people like me to go to church.

On that Sunday morning Jeannie went to church and I didn't as I am not an early riser! When she came home she said that I should have gone as he spoke so logically, in a way that I would have appreciated. I said, 'Hard luck, it's too late now.' It was a mild January afternoon and I was doing some gardening. At 6 p.m. I went inside to get changed to go to church. Alex, my eight-year-old daughter said, 'Where are you going?' I replied, 'To church.' She then said, 'No, Daddy, don't be silly. Where are you really going?' I replied, 'Yes, I'm going to church – on my own.'

I did not realise that church got so crowded so early so I crept in and sat at the back. When Keith de Berry spoke he said that for some people their life was like an onion and as you peeled off each layer from the surface you eventually arrived at a centre which is hollow and empty. As I thought about all the material possessions that I had plus my wife and two daughters and friends, I realised that deep inside I was not satisfied and felt hollow and empty. Keith said that the only way to fill that emptiness was to ask Jesus to come into your life and fill you up. He then said it was as easy as the three Rs – Repent, Receive and Rely. I joined in the simple prayer of commitment and asked Jesus into my life as my Lord and Saviour and asked him to fill me up.

I did not particularly feel anything at all but mentioned to Barry Kissell on leaving the service that I had said the prayer of commitment and he seemed genuinely pleased. When I got home I put my arms around Jeannie and told her what had just happened. She was amazed and didn't believe me at first. For the rest of the evening she said she could not look at me because my face had such a radiance and peace that it was a bit awesome and scary. For the first time since we had been married she couldn't speak to me for the rest of the evening because she couldn't believe what she was seeing and hearing.

The next morning as I was walking from the station to my office there was a cold wind and my head was bowed, but suddenly I thought, NO, I have Jesus in my life and I held my head up high.

Ken Morgan

7

The Radical Words
of God

It is impossible to tell the story of Jesus without looking at the things that he said. Like any good teacher of the day Jesus spoke to people and educated them using stories, parables and a big dose of claims so outrageous they shocked a whole nation. To understand some of the scandalous things that he said we need to understand the culture of the day, but many of his claims still have the power to shock today. What his words boiled down to was a brand new way to live, one that challenged all the preconceived ideas about how things should be done. Jesus was a radical, considered so dangerous that they killed him to try and guarantee his silence.

There aren't many better examples of Jesus preaching his message than the lengthy account of his Sermon on the Mount. This was a session when Jesus was on a roll:

'Blessed are you who are poor,
for yours is the kingdom of God.
Blessed are you who hunger now,
for you will be satisfied.
Blessed are you who weep now,
for you will laugh.
Blessed are you when men hate you,

when they exclude you and insult you
and reject your name as evil,
because of the Son of Man.'

(Luke 6:20–2)

The sermon is also recorded in Matthew's telling of Jesus' story. He follows this bit up with an amazing reworking of an old law:

'You have heard that it was said, "Eye for eye and tooth for tooth." But I tell you, Do not resist an evil person. If someone strikes you on the right cheek, turn to him the other also. And if someone wants to sue you and take your tunic, let him have your cloak as well. If someone forces you to go one mile, go with him two miles. Give to the one who asks you and do not turn away from the one who wants to borrow from you.

'You have heard that it was said, "Love your neighbour and hate your enemy." But I tell you: Love your enemies and pray for those who persecute you, that you may be sons of your Father in heaven. He causes his sun to rise on the evil and the good and sends rain on the righteous and the unrighteous.'

(Matthew 5:38–45)

These words have influenced many people throughout time. Mahatma Gandhi, a Hindu, was profoundly affected by Jesus' message of turning the other cheek. These words formed the core of his own message of non-violent resistance that managed to bring an end to British colonial rule in India and Pakistan. Even though I think he failed to understand that there was so much more behind the words of Jesus, he achieved so much.

Then there was that little old Albanian nun who worked in the slums of Calcutta, caring for the dying and the poor who had nowhere else to go. She was a Christian who based her work on the life and words of Jesus. Again, she set an example so powerful that people from world leaders to small children knew that the name of Mother Teresa stood for justice and for the same things that Jesus stood for. Some years ago there was a poll taken among world leaders asking who they thought was the most influential person on the planet. Mother Teresa came out top.

Earlier in history there was an Englishman named William Wilberforce. He was a wealthy MP who played a key role in abolishing slavery not only in the United Kingdom, but also throughout the world. He worked hard to alleviate poverty and was one of the most talked about and respected people of his day. Where did the inspiration come from? Jesus and the words that you've just read above.

The Bible records an incident that happened when Jesus saw some high-ranking religious men lay into a woman who had been caught in adultery (John 8:1–11). They flung her in front of him and tried to trick him asking if she should be stoned there and then. This was the law, and they had it in mind to trap him. What Jesus did was one step ahead. He knelt down and started to write something in the dirt on the ground. We don't know what it was that he wrote – some suggest that it was the secret sins that each of the accusers there was guilty of committing – but after a while he invited whoever thought that they were without sin to step up and take the first shot. No one knows why they did, but one by one the accusers left the scene. Jesus then looked up at the woman who was clearly guilty.

'Woman,' he asked her, 'is there no one left to condemn you?'

'No one, sir,' she replied.

Jesus responded with some amazing words: 'Neither do I condemn you . . . Go and sin no more.' He changed that woman's life for ever; he saved her from death and he saved her from herself. He didn't pretend that what she had been doing wasn't sin, but he revealed to her as he reveals to us the love, mercy and forgiveness of God.

Jesus said things that turned the world on its head. To the people who heard him speak he made it clear that if they acted on his words, they too would play a part in changing the course of history. The offer still stands today.

There are lots of places throughout the Bible that record Jesus claiming to be the Son of God. There's a key passage not long after the incident with the woman caught in adultery. A bunch of Jewish men were arguing with him about whether they were the descendants of Abraham, one of the main figures in the Old Testament. Jesus pulls no punches and has a go at them about disobeying their Father in heaven and they accuse him of being a mixture of demon-possessed and a Samaritan. This calls for Jesus to lay the truth on the line: 'I tell you the truth, if anyone keeps my word, he will never see death' (John 8:51). This makes them all get a tad overexcited and they start falling over themselves to write him off as a nutter. 'Are you greater than our father Abraham? He died, and so did the prophets. Who do you think you are?' I wonder if one day they realised the outrageousness of their question. I mean, who did they think *they* were to ask it?

Jesus replied, 'If I glorify myself, my glory means nothing. My father, whom you claim as your God, is the one who glorifies me. Though you do not know him, I know him. If I said I did not, I would be a liar like you, but I do know him and keep his word. Your father Abraham rejoiced at the thought of seeing my day; he saw it and was glad.'

'You are not yet fifty years old,' the Jews said to him, 'and you have seen Abraham!'

'I tell you the truth,' Jesus answered, 'before Abraham was born, I am.' At this, they picked up stones to stone him, but Jesus hid himself, slipping away from the temple grounds.

(John 8:54–9)

This passage is massively significant, even though it is a little confusing. We understand that Jesus died and rose again, that he was God, but all that stuff about 'I am' can easily go right over our heads. It must have been significant though, just look again at their reaction.

The whole 'I am' thing has its roots way back in the forming of the nation of Israel. God had called Moses out to a place in the desert where he spoke through a burning bush, telling Moses that he was the one who was going to lead his people out of the slavery of Egypt. Cleverly asking for some ID, Moses asked the bush/God who he should tell the people had sent him on such a bold mission.

'Say "I am" has sent you,' came the reply.

'I am' is a name for God, and, as any good Jew would know, when Jesus said that he was 'I am', he was claiming to be God himself.

Later there's an interesting bit of stuff going on in John chapter 20 when Jesus has risen from the dead. As usual it's Thomas who is having a hard time believing the truth behind what's going on, mainly because he is the only one of the disciples who is yet to see the risen Jesus. He knows himself too well to be able to take their word for it, and he tells them that unless he sees the nail marks and the hole in his side, he will not believe that the person the others claim to have seen really is Jesus himself.

Just then, guess what happens? Jesus appears. Not through the door mind you – the disciples knew that it was well and truly bolted for fear of further attacks by the Romans – or through the wall, proper ghost style. He just appears, walks up to Thomas and says to him,

'Put your finger here, see my hands. Reach out your hand and put it into my side. Stop doubting and believe.'

Thomas said to him, 'My Lord and my God.'

Then Jesus told him, 'Because you have seen me, you

have believed; blessed are those who have not seen me and yet have believed.'

(John 20:27–9)

When Thomas saw and called Jesus his God, Jesus didn't rebuke him. Instead he accepted Thomas's declaration that he was God. In a way many of us can sympathise with Tom: there's so much hype around these days that it can be useful for us not to believe everything we see and hear. After all, he was only being cautious, wouldn't you be? There is a difference though between now and then, and Jesus' words picked up on it. Tom was one of the last to see him in the flesh, as from then on he was back in heaven, allowing his Holy Spirit to carry out the work here on earth. Tom was used to seeing God in physical form, but now we have to rely on seeing him in other ways. We can read the Bible and we can ask God, by his Spirit, to make himself known to us. We can pray and listen to what he says. We can take time to meditate on the things that reveal his character, like creation, human people and the Bible. The point is that we have to make a choice either to believe without seeing God in the flesh or not to believe at all. How could Jesus do this? Was this a mistake, the result of him getting bored or cutting corners? No. Jesus had completed his work and had made sure that future believers would have enough to go on, enough to believe that he was exactly who he said he was. Jesus' words were dynamite. They changed everything from how we see the poor, to how we see death, to how we see ourselves. They show us that he was God and they make it clear that we have to grab hold of what he has said for ourselves. Read the Bible and ask God for help; you might not be able to put your fingers in his wounds but you sure can find out what's in his heart.

At the age of two I caught measles, despite having a jab. I didn't recover and after tests I was diagnosed as having Nephritic Syndrome – a kidney disease. This was the beginning of many long stays in hospital. During this time I became increasingly poorly. It was explained to my family that there were three responses to the steroids I was on: steroid responsive, steroid dependent or steroid resistant. I had started off responsive, became dependent and then eventually became resistant. We were warned that unless there was a dramatic change, I would be moved to Great Ormond Street Hospital to try a toxic drug regime. This would have permanent and damaging side-effects.

A prayer chain was immediately set up, with all the Christians we knew (and many we didn't) praying for me. During this time God used a verse in the Bible to speak to us. It came from Psalm 46 (in the King James Version): 'God is in the midst of her; she shall not be moved: God shall help her, and that right early.' This was a promise that God was going to help me, and sure enough there was a dramatic improvement! The doctors were amazed and baffled. That day there was much rejoicing and giving thanks to the Lord for his continuing faithfulness to us.

At around the same time, we moved from Essex to Devon and I was transferred to a hospital in Exeter. I was referred to a specialist at Bristol because the doctors were concerned about my repeated relapses. They wanted to do a renal biopsy with all its related risks. We were given an early morning appointment in Bristol and whilst my parents were contemplating a very early morning start, a Christian doctor spotted a Bible on my locker. He had heard that we hadn't been in the area long and offered us lodgings at his sister's house in Bristol for the night – God's provision again!

Before we went, the Lord gave us another promise: 'You will go out in joy and be led forth in peace' (Isaiah 55:12). Throughout the next day we clung on to these words to try and banish the fears that we were all feeling.

The specialist told us what we had been longing to hear, that he was sure I would grow out of this illness given time. (We had learnt by this stage that the medical profession do not raise false hopes and always point out the worst scenario.) It was another promise from God that he was looking after me. There were many tears of happiness that day and I remember skipping with my mum and dad down the street. We were so happy! God had given us so much joy.

I was baptised at the age of seven. I had no doubt about my faith nor about my reasons for being baptised. I wanted to show everyone that I loved Jesus and wanted to do his will for the rest of my life.

Over the years my relapses became less frequent. I was discharged from hospital at the age of twelve. On my final visit my doctor called in some junior and student doctors to see me. He told them, 'Next time you see a little one very poorly, remember Taryn, she has been there and look at her now!' I had no doubt in my mind that the Lord had made me well again.

From the age of twelve to fifteen I was completely healthy. I relapsed during Christmas 1993 and became very ill again. It was a very painful time for my family and me. I put on about four stone in weight and puffed up like a balloon. I felt like a complete freak and contemplated suicide twice, but something was holding me back and I knew that something was God. Even during the darkest days I knew that I wasn't alone. Slowly but surely the Lord began to soften my heart and really challenged me. He showed me time and time again that if I only trusted in him, he would never let me down. That wasn't to say that there wouldn't be hard times but I had learnt that even in the most despairing hour he can turn things around for the better. Here I am now, five years on, completely well and feeling great!

Taryn Bibby

8

God and the
Ultimate Sacrifice

I once saw a calf being born. I was about ten years old and was excited enough at the fact that I had been allowed to stay up till such a late hour, let alone seeing a cute-looking baby calf take its first stumbling steps in the world. The Pilavachis were staying on a farm in Devon, and the farmer had been talking excitedly ever since we arrived about his prized heifer and her impending labour. I'll never forget the sense of wonder as he calmed the mother down. The anxious excitement as those spindly legs first appeared and the sheer joy of seeing that everything was all right. My dad and I watched intently, and as the mother licked the calf down I plucked up the courage to break the silence. I asked what he would call the new baby.

'Oh, it'll not need a name,' he replied. 'This one will be hamburger by the time it's two.'

It took me weeks to recover. The thought that something could be born just so that it could die sent me into a deep well of confusion. That was probably what started me writing bad poetry, and to be honest I still have trouble forcing down the second double cheeseburger.

At the risk of being irreverent, there is a similarity between a calf born for the table and the Son of God who was born for our sins. Now that all sounds quite nice and pain free, no? I mean 'born for our sins' doesn't exactly send a shiver down your spine – it's preferable to 'dying for our sins' any day of the week. Hold on, though, 'cos the truth is out there. For Jesus, being born for our sins meant paying for our sins. The truth about sin is that it demanded a big payment. The Jews had been paying theirs off in instalments for hundreds of years. Take a look at the first few books of the Bible and you'll see how they were told by God to stick to the rules (you can read them for yourself in Exodus 20 – there are ten of them). When they messed up the deal was that they would pass their sin on to a goat or a pure and perfect lamb offered as a sacrifice to the Lord. These sacrifices all pointed towards the ultimate sacrifice that one day would come and replace their rituals: the perfect and blemish free lamb that would pay for them all.

Throughout the Old Testament this role of Jesus is hidden, but by the time we reach the New he is revealed. As John the Baptist sees him for the first time he cries out, 'Behold, the Lamb of God . . .' He immediately recognised not only who Jesus was, but why he was here. God sent his own Son down to earth so that he could pay the debt of all our sin. This wasn't going to be easy as what was owing wasn't just the sins of the Israelites, but all the rest of the people in the world too. What's more he didn't just stick to the present day, Jesus paid for all the sins that people would commit in the future as well. In terms of doves, sheep and cows that adds up to . . . Well, it actually adds up to far more than can ever be counted. Jesus died once and for all so that we might escape God's judgment.

Jesus' blood had to be shed. In the last chapter we mentioned Moses who was sent by God to bring freedom to his people. It was a struggle and God had to send loads of plagues and stuff to make the Egyptians that were holding his people captive let them go. The last plague was when

God passed over Egypt and killed the first-born son of each Egyptian family. When he did that he told the Israelites to slaughter a lamb beforehand and smear its blood over the doorway of their house so that God would pass over their home and spare their lives. When Jesus died as the ultimate sacrificial lamb, his blood appears on us and we too escape the punishment of God.

The cross is central to Christianity. It may have been just two bits of wood, but Christians believe that when Jesus died on one it changed world history. There were other people who were crucified; criminals, traitors and revolutionaries. It was a particularly barbaric way to kill someone, blending agonising pain with long term exhaustion and an inevitable crawl towards an undignified end. It was to the Romans what a gas chamber was to the Nazis and what the electric chair is to America. It was reserved for the very worst of criminals, but it ended up killing the very best of men.

Understanding that Jesus was born to die is not like saying that Ryan Giggs was born to score *that goal* against Arsenal or that I was born to eat. Jesus was born for something so miraculous yet so costly that his whole life was a build-up to one simple act of barbaric cruelty. He was treated as a common criminal, was mis-tried, falsely accused and left to die, all because the Roman authorities wanted an easy life and the Jewish religious leaders felt threatened by him.

In the book of Romans it says that the pay-back from sin is death. In other words, living away from the source of all life can only lead by itself to one conclusion: separation from God. Just like any other crime, the offence that we humans committed first of all in turning away from God demanded some kind of payment if we are ever to approach God. He is so holy and perfect that he simply cannot look on sin. At the same time the love and mercy of God could not bear to look away from his creations.

Of all the torture that he went through when he was

crucified – of the nails in his hands and feet, the spear in his side and the slow suffocation as his exhaustion made it harder to breathe – I am sure that the worst thing he went through was that for a period of time Jesus was separated from his Father. For the first and only time in all eternity Jesus was alone, crying out at one point, 'My God, my God, why have you forsaken me?' That must have been the worst punishment imaginable for the Son of God. At that moment the sins of all the world were heaped upon him as he bore the punishment for all the things we have done wrong. Taking all our dirt, shame and pain on himself meant that God the Father had to look away, and, if we define hell as 'being totally without God', then for those moments the Son of God was in hell.

In dying Jesus managed to put right all that we had put wrong. When we chose to live apart from God, following our own selfish desires instead of his will, a barrier got erected between us and him. It became impossible for us to break through and reach God but Jesus' death managed to reunite us with him.

Jesus was the ultimate sacrificial lamb, the sacrifice that no human could give. Because he was such a perfect and precious substitute we no longer have to pay a price, all we have to do is ask God to have mercy on us. We know that the punishment we really deserve is death – living away from him and serving our own selfish desires can ultimately lead to nothing else – but we can ask God not to look at our sin, but to remember the cross and all that Jesus did for us, and ask him to have mercy. Through what Jesus did we can again return to having a relationship with God our Father, we can again be adopted by him.

Think of it as being like a shopping trip, one with a full trolley at the end. You approach the till, have your goods swiped and get asked how you intend to pay for what you've loaded up. With Jesus next to you he pipes up 'I'll pay', and promptly gets in the till himself, allowing us to move on.

But to look at the cross without looking at what happened next is like trying to understand quantum physics without a calculator or like trying to sell a diet product by only using the 'before' picture instead of the skinny 'after' shot as well. The cross and the resurrection cannot be separated because they were the final goal of Jesus' time on earth. If there was no resurrection, if Jesus had stayed dead, then Christianity would be nothing more than a collection of decent ideas on how to treat people. Perhaps it might have caught on in the way that odd fashions do, but it would never have had the power needed to keep people going. The truth, on the other hand, is that Jesus did rise from the dead, he did come back to life, so Christianity does have power. Jesus' words and everything he stood for and promised were true.

The fact that Jesus had told them that he would rise again did not stop the disciples from thinking that it was all over once Jesus had been buried. The fact that the Scriptures described what would happen next was not much in the way of comfort, and when we join them at the end of each of the Gospels, we get a clear picture of just how depressed they are. It doesn't stay that way for long though, and looking at their intense reactions when they see Jesus alive and in the flesh after his death teaches us some important lessons.

Mary Magdalene – the prostitute whom Jesus had cared for, respected and treated with dignity – was on her way to look after Jesus' body in the tomb. Having gone back to tell the disciples she returned and stood weeping outside the place where Jesus had been laid to rest.

As she wept, she bent over to look into the tomb and saw two angels in white, seated where Jesus' body had been, one at the head and the other at the foot.

They asked her, 'Woman, why are you crying?'

'They have taken my Lord away,' she said, 'and I don't know where they have put him.' At this, she turned round and saw Jesus standing there, but she did not realise that it was Jesus.

Mary's grief was so intense that she couldn't even recognise the most important man in her life. She had spent time with him, learnt from him and been saved by him yet she couldn't tell him apart from a stranger.

What Jesus said next is interesting. I'm sure that he knew why she was crying but still he asked. Perhaps he wanted her to admit her fears.

'Woman,' he said, 'why are you crying? Who is it you are looking for?'
Thinking he was the gardener, she said, 'Sir, if you have carried him away, tell me where you have put him, and I will get him.'

Perhaps he was having a laugh, as the situation soon descends into a farce with Mary thinking that he has come to trim the hedges. It only took one word to put her straight:

Jesus said to her, 'Mary.'
She turned towards him and cried out in Aramaic, 'Rabboni!' (which means Teacher).

(John 20:11–16)

All that Jesus had to do was say her name, probably in the same way that he had always said it. That was enough for her to know exactly who he was.

Later we read about the wonderful time when Jesus appeared to Thomas. We've already had a quick look, but remember how much of a sceptic Thomas was, how he never believed anything at first? When Jesus showed up and told Thomas to feel his wounds it was exactly the right thing to do. In just the same way that speaking Mary's name allowed her to realise who he was, so letting Thomas see the evidence was enough to allow him to see the truth. 'My Lord and my God!' he said (John 20:28), suddenly aware that Jesus was exactly who he said he was. A ghost wouldn't have been able to convince Thomas: it had to be the real thing, which is exactly what he got. Believe me, this is how it can be with us: one moment of contact when Jesus calls us by name or shows himself to us can be enough to change the way we see him forever.

There were many other people who saw Jesus in the six weeks that he spent on earth after he had been crucified, buried and had risen from the dead, but his resurrection didn't just affect them. Because he rose from the dead Jesus put power into the faith. Because of his own power over death we too are no longer slaves to death or sin; we can also enjoy life after death with God when we die as well as new life here on earth as we enjoy a living relationship with Jesus. Through his death Jesus not only took the punishment for all our sin, he also made it possible for Christians to say 'I know Jesus'. He isn't just a historical figure or a good but dead man, he is around today and available for his people to reach him. Death couldn't beat him, hell couldn't keep him but you and I can meet him.

PAULINE'S STORY

From an early age I showed great promise, both at school and in music. It was no hardship to me to read and study and I suppose I could have accurately been described as a bit of a swot! There were some (including myself at the time) who felt I had everything going for me. Life seemed pretty set and a first class degree from Cambridge was on the horizon.

In my mid-teens I realised that underneath the seemingly competent high-achiever was someone who was distinctly unhappy with herself and with life. I found that my intense pursuit of achievement had left me lonely, unable to relate well to people of my own age; and despite having so much success, I felt inferior to my friends, desperately wanting to be part of the crowd but always feeling 'less than': less fun, less attractive, less popular, less wanted.

Coupled with this, many questions about life were raised when a school friend was tragically killed in a car accident. What is it all about? Where are we going? Who am I? Why am I so empty?

About this time I took a holiday job which was quite physically exerting and without trying I began to lose some weight. As people commented on how good I looked I began to feel a bit more in control. With a bit of effort I could have the figure I wanted, feel less inferior to my friends and, more to the point, feel happier with myself.

Unfortunately I didn't stop there. As I began to lose weight I started to feel a 'high' at having such a control over my body. It was as if another world had begun, full of weight loss plans, exercise plans and calorie counting. My whole mind was obsessed with food and weight. What had begun as a series of choices was fast becoming a life-controlling addiction. I began to feel as if I was the slave of a cruel master, unable to stop the self-destruction that I had begun. I was out of control and unable to let anyone help me. Part of me didn't even want to be helped – what did life have to offer anyway? I began to admit that I had a serious problem, that I was in fact anorexic.

At the end of my first year at Cambridge I was admitted to the eating disorders unit of a London hospital at five stone. Not only did I have no body left, my mind, feelings and personality were dead too. I had no will to live. I didn't feel that there was anyone left inside. Through the hospital programme I gained four stone over nine months and was discharged with everyone hoping that things were 'all better now'. But nothing inside had changed. There was no hope or desire in me for life, and six months later I was five stone again and being re-admitted to hospital for another nine months. The terror of having to eat in hospital was intense and my world remained dominated with fear and food obsession.

A further nine months of treatment ensued, again I left hospital four stone heavier, and again I lost it all over the next six months. By that time a friend of mine mentioned that it would be good for me to talk to a friend of hers from a prayer group. Not particularly keen on the idea but with nothing to lose I met her and told her how I was feeling. Over the next few weeks and months she continued to meet me and began to talk about knowing God. I had always believed in God and even prayed as a young girl, but she was talking about knowing him in a different way. Slowly I began to wonder, would he help me? It seemed that no one else could.

I left hospital for the third time and began attending the prayer group. I loved being there but felt out of it somehow. I watched people as they sang to God and knew that they talked to him and knew him as I didn't. It wasn't long before the old self-destruct feelings and desire to starve came raging up again. I could feel myself losing weight and couldn't bear the thought of going back into hospital, of life being nothing more than this until I died.

One morning, when I thought I could stand no more, I dropped to the floor and cried out to God, 'If you're there, you MUST show me, I'm not leaving this room until I know you exist.' I knew there was nowhere else to turn. Suddenly in the midst of the turmoil and pain it seemed that an intense light, warmth and love broke through on my inside. I could feel him around me and in me and I knew that Jesus was alive. That there in my room, he loved me and accepted me as I came to him, as I was, in all my mess and pain and fear. That he loved me completely and utterly. I was overwhelmed with joy, laughter and tears. 'JESUS IS ALIVE, JESUS IS ALIVE' was all that I could get out of my mouth.

That was the beginning of healing and of real life. Much freedom came in a moment, much more was worked out subsequently. Within four months I was nine stone and, to the amazement of the hospital, never went below that again. More significantly, I knew there was and is a hope. That it is his love and life that changes us, whatever desperate place we are in – thank you, Lord.

Pauline Kirke

9

God in Me

I was sitting in someone's front room just off the Uxbridge Road with my eyes shut tight and my heart beating faster than I thought was probably good for me. Two friends from the church were sat either side, praying in the soft and mellow tones of voice that I had heard Christians use before when they were trying to convince God to do something great. I sneaked a look out of one eye at the clock I had carefully positioned myself opposite. I had been there for two and three-quarter minutes but it felt like years. I tried again to relax.

'Just let God in, Mike,' soothed one of my praying friends.

I tried. I pictured myself opening the doors of my heart to allow his presence to enter gracefully. Nothing. I imagined inviting him in with tea and biscuits and the promise of some telly after we were done. Nothing. I visualised offering him money and a chance to borrow my Simon and Garfunkel records if he would just come in. Still nothing.

Things went on like this for many more minutes. I was supposed to be meeting the Holy Spirit, allowing him to come into my life and do whatever it was he was going to do. I wasn't quite sure what was going to happen, but I was darn sure that it was supposed to be better than this. It was like being constipated only with a chronic case of diarrhoea building up. Why wasn't it working?

My friends carried on praying throughout, thanking God, asking him to meet with me and managing to sound calm and relaxed throughout it all. I was just about to call a halt to it all when I started to feel dizzy. That usually meant that I was hungry, so I decided to keep going. After all, if I broke it off now and disappeared into the kitchen straight away to scoff down a couple of slices of Arctic Roll what would they think of me? I didn't think it was funny, but I started to smile. Pretty soon I felt as though I had drunk the warmest and sweetest drink in the world; I felt a deep happiness and something that I could only describe as joy. I thought it best that I confess and was just about to own up to being an Arctic Roll addict when they both started to clap and thank God for sending me his Spirit.

'That's it, Mike,' one said.

'That's it?' I asked. I was confused for a second but it was soon washed away as I realised that it wasn't my taste buds but it was God who was making me feel great.

Looking back now I'm not surprised that I was confused. Thinking of God as a holy Trinity is hard enough, but breaking it down into the three persons or characteristics of God can be even more of a head-do. OK, so most of us can come up with some kind of idea about what God the Father might be like: we might go with an image or feeling drawn from our ideas of what a perfect father should be like. Thinking of God the Son also tends not to present too many problems as we are all familiar with the form that Jesus took on when he came to earth. Think about God the Spirit though, and we're out of our depth. Do we think of him as some kind of good ghost? A kind force?

The first thing to realise is that the Holy Spirit is not an 'it', he's a 'he'. The Holy Spirit has personality and character just in the same way that the Father and the Son do. We need to know that the Holy Spirit wasn't just called up for action once Jesus returned to heaven: the truth is that he has been part of things since the beginning. Imagine creation: if God the Father had the idea, the Son then spoke the idea into existence and it was the power of the Holy Spirit that brooded over the waters and made it all take shape. The Holy Spirit is the power of God; he is 'God with us' and 'God in us'. When the Bible was translated into one regional dialect in China and they could find no word for spirit or ghost, the translator settled on the phrase 'resident boss'. Someone else once called him 'the go-between God', and both of these can help us understand who he is.

The Holy Spirit is the ultimate in humility. He doesn't exist to make himself known or to raise his own public profile, instead he exists to reveal Jesus to us. The relationship that we can have with him is there simply so that he can teach us more about Jesus, more about who he was, what he did and how we can follow his example. In this way he reveals truth to us, showing the depth of the Scriptures and helping us to apply them to our own lives.

Remember what we were saying in the last chapter about how through Jesus' death we can approach God again? Well it's only possible to do that through the Spirit. Here's the proof:

For you did not receive a spirit that makes you a slave again to fear, but you received the Spirit of sonship. And by him we cry, 'Abba, Father.'

(Romans 8:15)

Don't get bogged down with images of 1970s' Swedes in glitter. *Abba* means 'Daddy'. So through the Holy Spirit we can have a relationship with God that is truly personal and intimate. We don't deserve it, but like small children we can approach him and sit at his feet, all because the Holy Spirit lives in us and draws us back to him.

But how do you get him? Do you catch, snare or win him? Is it a case of needing to earn enough points before we can collect or do some people get better versions of him than others through being good? The answer is that we receive the Holy Spirit when we become Christians. Without him on board it is impossible to know Jesus and say that he is Lord. To want to know God, to feel that you have enough of a vague idea about what he is like to ask him into your life means that the Holy Spirit has already been working in you, revealing Jesus to you. Things don't just end there though, as once we've become Christians we need to be continually refilled. We all fall far short of the standard set by Jesus so it makes sense that we all need to be given regular help to become more like him.

We also need help to be bold and carry out the job of telling others about Jesus. There are loads of verses in the Bible that back this up, and reading them it seems that one of his favourite things is to inspire us to get out and do the business of spreading the word ourselves.

In John we read Jesus' words:

> But the Counsellor, the Holy Spirit, whom the Father will send in my name, will teach you all things, and will remind you of everything I have said to you.
>
> (John 14:26)

And later we find out that the early Church are in on the act too:

> All of them were filled with the Holy Spirit and began to speak in other tongues, as the Spirit enabled them.
>
> (Acts 2:4)

And finally:

This is what we speak, not in words taught us by human wisdom but in words taught by the Spirit, expressing spiritual truths in spiritual words.

(1 Corinthians 2:13)

This power that the early Christians received from the Holy Spirit wasn't just able to inspire them to speak, but it also helped them to be Jesus' witnesses (see Acts 1:8), to get out and do the same things that Jesus did. Reading through the rest of the New Testament we can see that the Holy Spirit gave the first Christians a power that they previously didn't have. We can be sure of this because we saw how useless some of them were when they were following Jesus around as his disciples.

The story about me at the beginning of this chapter happened when I had been a Christian for only a few months. I don't know how, but I knew that I needed to have more of the Holy Spirit inside of me. Looking back now I can see that it was a natural desire, but at the time it was all so hard to pin down. My friends prayed that the Holy Spirit would come and fill me up and after a while I just knew that he had. I felt like I was full up on God's love, inspired and passionate, ready to get on with being the most radical Christian that I could. I knew Jesus and loved him already, but something about that afternoon made it clear that by some miracle God wasn't just in heaven, he was actually living within me too. After that time prayer became so much easier and I felt like what I was saying was really getting through, as well as that I was able to listen to what I thought God was saying. It made sense and seemed to be in line with a verse written to the early Church in Rome:

In the same way the Spirit helps us in our weakness. We do not know what we ought to pray for but the Spirit himself intercedes for us with groans that words cannot express.

And he who searches our hearts knows the mind of the Spirit, because the Spirit intercedes for the saints in accordance with God's will.

(Romans 8:26)

The Holy Spirit actually helps us to pray, joining up with our spirit and helping us to pray to God the Father and God the Son.

If you want to be filled with God's Spirit, the thing to do is to ask. Jesus said to his disciples that if they thought that good parents knew how to give decent gifts to their children, they should check out just how much more the Father in heaven would give the ultimate good gift of the Holy Spirit to those who asked him. We need to ask, and keep on asking and keep on receiving. I know I tend to leak a little bit, so I'm constantly in need of more of him in my life. If we don't do this then we are relying on our own strength to live the Christian life, and that never works.

As you've been reading this book you've heard about some of the different parts that go to make up this mind-blowing phenomenon called Christianity. It changes lives and turns the world upside down. It can be tough sometimes but there's one final thing to note. It's called joy. Jesus didn't die on the cross just so that we could struggle on our own and God didn't just give us a bag-full of commands to make us feel bad. He gave us power so that it wouldn't be a life of frustration, but one fully furnished with all the fullness that comes from God above. We like to think that we know how to live our own lives: take it from God, he's the ultimate Creator of all life and he knows exactly how to get the most out of it.

Closing Prayer...

So, where do we go from here? If you're not sure about the stuff I've said can I ask that you genuinely investigate further? Find people who say that they know this Jesus and look at their lives to see if there's any evidence there for Jesus. Why not examine the Bible for yourself, read the stories in one of the Gospels and see if it makes sense? It may be that you're ready to get to know this Jesus and to be one of his family. If you are it could be helpful for you to say this simple prayer although you can actually use any form of words you want . . .

Dear Jesus,
I thank you that you died on a cross for me. I want the story of my life to be part of your story. I want to be your follower. Would you forgive me for the things I've thought, said and done that have been selfish and have taken me away from you? Jesus, come into my life now; fill me with your Holy Spirit and make me a child of your Father. Help me to become more like you and for the time I'm on this earth to serve you by showing your love to your world.
   Amen.

So that's it then. If you have said this prayer you have not reached the end of a journey but the beginning. It's the same journey my friends and I are on, of going deeper into God and also out to the world he loves. Welcome to the family.

My First Trousers

Growing up with God

Mike Pilavachi with Craig Borlase

Hodder & Stoughton
LONDON SYDNEY AUCKLAND

To Richard, Diana, Emma and David Scott.
You have taught me so much about what servant love
really means.

Contents

	Introduction	109
1	Everybody . . . Needs Somebody	115
2	Getting Intimate	127
3	Just Do It	137
4	Living in the Real World	149
5	The Desert	159
6	Heart for the Lost	171
7	United We Stand	181
8	The Next Step	191

Introduction

I got my first trousers when I was ten. Maybe it was some kind of Greek-Cypriot custom that got brought over when my grandparents arrived before the Second World War, a hangover from the days when they lived in scorching heat nearly all year round. Perhaps it was because my parents wanted me to preserve my childhood innocence. Whatever the reason, it took a decade before my knees were covered with anything other than plasters or scabs, but when it happened, I was the happiest little chap in all of Harrow.

It wasn't as if I had spent my early years naked – I did have shorts to wear; anyway, as far as I could tell, trousers were just a bit of an inconvenience. When I was seven both my heroes wore shorts – Bobby Charlton and George Best – and that was good enough for me. Trousers were for boring sports like golf, darts and bowls. Real men got their knees out, and every other boy I knew did the same. But soon tragedy struck and my mates started to wear long trousers. Of course the first ones were ritually humiliated and con-sidered to be 'a bit odd'. Us windy-kneed boys would stare menacingly at them as they walked into school. We made up stories of how they had wooden legs and avoided getting stuck with them at dinner.

Then the winter came and things got tough. At times it seemed like my boys were defecting on a daily basis, and the group of us that spent our lunch breaks huddled by the wall in the playground gradually became smaller and smaller. By the middle of the spring term, I was alone. All the other boys strolled happily around without needing shelter, while I, with blue knees and a worried look on my face, longed to have something more than just a pair of shorts around my legs.

I spent the next two years dreaming about trousers. I pictured myself collecting milk-bottle tops and sewing them together to make a pair of chinos. I asked my parents to get me out of shorts, but they told me that shorts were for boys.

'But I'm not a boy,' I squeaked.

Eventually I got them – I think it had something to do with me threatening to take them to court – and I was presented with the most magical present I have ever received. As I pulled on the brown, beige and chocolate coloured tartan trousers, my parents watched with pride in their eyes.

'You're a man now, Mike,' said my dad.

I felt like one too. I had finally graduated from boyhood, and it felt great. Strolling down the road to buy some penny chews I knew that I was on my way; people would respect me now, listen to me, even ask my advice about women, money or plumbing. In a couple of years I'd have a girlfriend and soon after that a Ford Capri with a loud exhaust. I was wearing my first trousers; I had made it and the world had better watch out.

A little later on I became a Christian. I was fifteen and thought I knew it all. Starting out back then was like being a child again; every day brought with it something fresh to get excited about, every day I was hungry to find out what would happen next. Instead of being in a playground or woods, my adventure was spiritual, and Jesus was my elder brother. It was just like being back in shorts again – racing around so fast that long trousers would simply get in the way. Just like when I was seven, and my knees were covered in scabs and bruises, the result of having too much energy and not enough wisdom. I made mistakes and fell over, but I was back on my feet straight away and ready to move on.

It makes me happy to think about those early weeks of being a Christian. These days we call it a honeymoon period, just like the time that newlyweds get to allow their love to sink in even deeper away from all the pressures of real life. I don't think I ever wondered if it would last, I guess I just assumed that it would. But of course it didn't. In the same way honeymooners return home and get on with their marriage, and just as children grow up to become the adult that is being formed within them, so I had to move on spiritually. It wasn't that I was forced, but just like when I had got tired of wearing shorts I wanted to move on and grow up.

God's into the idea of our first trousers. And our second, third and fourth. In fact, if each new pair of trousers represents taking a step closer in our relationship with him, I think it's fair to say that God would like us to have as many trousers as possible. God wants us to grow in our relationship with him, not because he hates kids or he prefers not to see our spiritual knees – he loves us at every stage of our Christian life – but he has so much in store for us that he can't wait for us to come and get it.

So this book is about getting your first trousers, moving on in your relationship with God. It's about the how and the why of getting to know God. It doesn't mean that God won't use you until you're snuggly fitted into your pair of 32 longs – God is most certainly into getting us started young – but as you move along in your relationship with him, you'll begin to find out even more about him. Talk to any godly man or woman and they won't tell you that they've made it or that they totally know God. They're much more likely to tell you that they've only just begun and that no matter how long

111

they've known him, he still has fresh things to teach them.

Trousers crop up a lot in the Bible. OK, so you have to look pretty hard, but once you've found one pair, the rest just seem to jump right out at you. Here's a pair, from Paul's letter to the church at Philippi:

> I want to know Christ and the power of his resurrection and the fellowship of sharing in his sufferings, becoming like him in his death, and so, somehow, to attain to the resurrection from the dead.
>
> Not that I have already obtained all this, or have already been made perfect, but I press on to take hold of that for which Christ Jesus took hold of me. Brothers, I do not consider myself yet to have taken hold of it. But one thing I do: Forgetting what is behind and straining towards what is ahead, I press on towards the goal to win the prize for which God has called me heavenwards.
>
> (Philippians 3:10–14)

Now that is one seriously chunky pair of trousers. In kicking off with his thoughts about sharing the sufferings of the man who suffered more than any other man in history, Paul tells us that he is aiming high in his relationship with God. He's not after a Sunday stroll, taking it easy and not working up too much of a sweat. Paul's going for it big time, and judging by the rest of his letters, he means it too. It's something to aim for, don't you think? To be able to stand side by side with Jesus, sharing his pain as well as his power. As Christians – followers of Christ – our aims don't get much higher than that.

But Paul doesn't just leave us feeling bad with our jaws on the floor as we contemplate this superChristian who founded the Church. He goes on to explain how he's not there yet. He's still striving for it, still heading in the direction without having reached the final goal. He's not dwelling on the past, but steaming forward into the future, certain that God has good things in store for him and keen to find out what they are.

This is how we get our first trousers: by saying to God that we want to know more about Jesus, not just for the sake of knowing, but so that it will affect our lives. Moving on with God is about admitting that you're still learning, but instead of worrying about how little you know, concentrating on how much more there is for you to discover of God. It's about progress, that's all.

But, you might be thinking, what's the point of it all anyway, why should we bother moving on just because God wants it? There's one very good reason why we should bother: it's Jesus. Looking at the Bible it becomes clear that Jesus – fully God and fully human – made it his number one priority to keep in touch with his Father. I don't just mean that he spent time alone – although that was important – but that through his relationship with God, he showed what God is like.

If you want to get something out of this book, it would be a great idea to read it with your Bible next to you. There are plenty of stories taken from it and loads of verses quoted that you can look up for yourself. Everything that we believe as Christians is explained and described there, so it's worth getting into the habit of turning to it for inspiration and explanation.

As Christians we have been commanded to do a few things: love God, love our neighbours and get on with the job of telling the world. These are tough orders, but they apply to all of us who call ourselves Christians. It would be foolish to think we can follow them or even properly understand them without a continually deepening relationship with God. Over the years you'll go through plenty of different experiences, some of them good, some of them bad. If you aim to get to know God there are going to be loads of times throughout your Christian life that you feel as though you've taken a big step on in your relationship with him. Hopefully, what we look at here will act as a base on which you can build for many years to come. So what are you waiting for? It's time to try them on.

1

Everybody ... Needs Somebody

THE MEANING OF LIFE

I sometimes think it's kind of strange that I – a swollen-bellied and gently maturing afro-haired bloke from Harrow – know the secret to life itself. Down the centuries men with bizarre names (the Platos, Socrates and Descartes of this world) have spent their lives pondering, musing and arguing about the answer to the eternal Why? I could have saved them the bother.

Before I get too excited, I ought to remind myself that I'm not alone – there are a few billion others who also know the score. You see, life is about just one thing – relationship. The reason why you and I, why all of us are here is to get as deep in with God as possible – soaking up all (and I mean *all*) that it means to be in touch with the Creator of heaven and earth.

Jesus came to earth because we weren't doing too well at getting on with our relationship with God. In some ways things are better now, but there are plenty of people who still have trouble hooking up with the Almighty. Still, so basic is our need for relationship that even if we don't get it from God – the very best source of relationship fulfilment around – we will always look elsewhere for compensation. Wherever you look you see evidence of this – most of the songs around are about relationships, so are the films, videos, magazines and TV shows. As for the soaps, well, where would they be without their constant feed of break-ups, let-downs, heart-aches and back-stabs?

But art imitates life, and all that we see around us is a reflection of what's going on inside each one of us. Relationships are as important to us human beings as oxygen and food. They're part of the 'Must Have' list that we cannot do without.

Back in the fifties someone wondered exactly what would happen if we did try to live without relationships. It seems outrageous now that they were allowed to do it, but a bunch of scientists actually managed to get permission to use twelve newborn babies as goalposts for their extended theoretical kick about. Six of the babies were given to their mothers as soon as they were born, the mothers being encouraged to spend as much time and attention on their new children as possible. Touch, talk, breastfeeding and eye contact were their staple diet. When the babies were asleep, they did so in a cot next to their mothers, so that they could hear them breathing.

Then there were the other six. These ones weren't quite so lucky, as no sooner had they popped their heads out and received a quick slap for their troubles but they were whisked away from their mothers and placed in incubators. Handling was kept to an absolute minimum, and breastfeeding was certainly off limits.

Throughout the month-long experiment, while their emo-tional supplies varied, each of the twelve babies were given exactly the same levels of nutrients. Once the experiment was complete, and the conclusions drawn up, the men in white coats made some startling discoveries. Those babies that were cared for so fully by their mothers had each put on an above average amount of weight for their age. Those who had spent their first thirty days in a sterile and inhuman environment all remained at their birth weight – having put on not a single pound. Yet they all had been pumped full of the same levels of baby-fertiliser. The fact that all the babies who had emotional contact grew so impressively makes it clear that loving relationships are good for us.

The results confirm what we all know instinctively: to grow and to be healthy we need relationships. It may start out as a mother's love, but it doesn't remain there. We need emotional nourishment like we need food – daily, right up to the point of death.

And that's the truth today, we know that this is precisely what lies behind our craving for relationships. I doubt there's a single one of you who read about that experiment who didn't wince at the thought of keeping children away from their mothers for so long. We all recognise how unusual it is for human beings to be starved of relationships. We think it odd for a person to spend a lot of his or her life away from the company of other people, and that's why we are all fascinated by stories of people who have endured prolonged periods of solitude.

On 24 January 1972 hunters near the Talofofo River in Guam made an unusual discovery. Living in a tunnel-like underground cave they discovered Sergeant Shoichi Yokoi, a Japanese imperial army straggler who had lived entirely alone for twenty-eight years. This was not some stunt arranged by a Japanese TV game show, but a result of an attack by American soldiers in the dying months of World War II. Yokoi's unit was located in the Fena Mountain region of the upper reaches of the Talofofo River when the Americans landed on 21 July 1944. The Japanese troops made a night attack on the Americans in Nimitz Bay, but having managed to bring their tanks on shore, the Americans were on the offensive. At this juncture Yokoi's unit already faced a situation in which they would soon be forced to fight until the last man had been killed. Some of them managed to escape to the west shore of Nimitz Bay and ultimately to rejoin the main force in Agana. But Yokoi journeyed to the Talofofo area, and to the bamboo grove that would become his home for nearly three decades.

Yokoi, who had been a tailor's apprentice before being drafted in 1941, made clothing from the fibres of wild hibiscus plants and survived on a diet of coconuts, breadfruit, papayas, snails, eels and rats. 'We Japanese soldiers were told to prefer death to the disgrace of getting captured alive,' Yokoi said afterwards. 'The only thing that gave me the strength and will to survive was my faith in myself and that as a soldier of Japan, it was not a disgrace to continue on living.' No one in the history of humanity has equalled his record. Few have struggled with loneliness, fear, and self for as long as twenty-eight years.

Someone will make a film out of the story one day, but until then there are plenty of others out there that already feed our fascination for the tortures of solitude. Of all the films that have had an impact on me, two of the most significant have to be *Papillon* and *The Shawshank Redemption*, particularly the scenes where the lead characters are put through the horrors of solitary confinement.

Of course, this isn't just a theme that is confined to the movies. Down the centuries solitude has been cropping up in works of literature from all corners of the globe. From *The Count of Monte Cristo* to *Robinson Crusoe*, from western pulp fiction to ancient legend. So deep is our need for relationship that we are often fixated by tales of what happens when we go without. It's like standing inches away from a highly agitated poisonous snake at a zoo; the thrill comes from knowing that if we were inside the enclosure, there is a chance that we might not survive.

Sadly there are times when people don't just exploit our reliance on relationships for entertainment, but do so for

118

personal destruction. During the two recent conflicts in the Balkans, allegations were made that high-ranking military officials used rape as a weapon against the Bosnians and Kosovan-Albanians. The belief is that soldiers were instructed to rape systematically large numbers of women in certain communities. This was not done merely to inflict a horrific evil on individual women, but to undermine the fabric of a whole society. Those who gave the orders did so because they believed that rape was the optimum way of bringing shame, mistrust, secrecy and illness upon entire communities for generations to come.

Christianity is about restored relationships. It is about being reunited with God, about him finding us and us finding him. Christianity is about God having created a people, a human race that would want to be like him, and that human race getting lost from him. He then took the steps necessary to win his creation back by becoming like the people he made. The epic story of the Bible traces God's relationship with his people and his search for them, his wooing of them and his winning of them back.

LOVING EACH OTHER

Christianity is also about our broken relationships being restored with one another as we come to know God. Many of us see that the problems of the human race are often caused by the breakdown of relationships: divorces, hatred, wars and violent crime are all caused by breakdowns in relationship. With all the progress that we have made as a human race, in science, in medicine, in engineering, in numerous other great feats, the one area that we have made no progress in whatsoever is in how to get on with one another.

Now I'm not going to come on all grand and wise here, but I do think that the twentieth century has been host to some fairly horrific things. Not only have we seen the development – and use – of the first weapon ever able to destroy life on a massive scale at the touch of a button, but we have also witnessed genocide more times than at any other point in history. Hitler, Stalin, Mao, Pol Pot, Amin, Hussein, Karadic, Milosevic – these are the names responsible for so much evil. But the hatred isn't limited to these few, as areas from Northern Ireland and Rwanda to North American high schools and the hills of Kashmir have all seen the steady breakdown in human relationships. We don't know how to live together, and the reason we don't know how to live together is because we've lost contact with God who is the source of our life and who is the one who makes sense of our relationships with one another.

When God goes out of the equation, everything else becomes disjointed. As God finds us, peace comes. That's why the Bible speaks so much about peace and justice. That's why John says in his first letter, 'If we say we love God whom we have not seen, but hate our brother whom we have seen we are a liar.' Our relationship with God has to affect all our other relationships.

You may be reading this book because you've recently found yourself plugged into a relationship with God. As we've said already the theme of this book is growing up within that relationship, but it is important to remember that as our relationship with God deepens and grows, it affects all of the rest of our lives, and particularly our relationships with other people.

How do we grow in our relationships? How do we put things right? The first thing to realise is that many of us are carrying baggage: burdens from the past like bad memories of times when we were rejected, times of bereavement or pain. Whether it was a divorce or whether it was abuse, all sorts of different experiences we have faced still affect us now. Our relationship with God sets us free and brings healing

120

to us so that we may again be able to relate to one another, not on the basis of pain, and not on the basis of brokenness, but as whole people.

Thankfully we have an example for this kind of lifestyle. Jesus was the one person who lived a life of wholeness in the middle of brokenness. He lived a life that was focused on God and others instead of being self-centred like the rest of us. For many of us, self-centredness is a result of pain – I know that for myself there's nothing more likely to get me thinking about my teeth than a decent dose of toothache, and so it is with our emotional states as well. Because we're in pain, we're self-centred. As God heals us of our pain, we become centred outside of ourselves; and that's how we were meant to function, because that's living in the image of God.

TRY THE BIBLE

We all know that any decent friendship between two people can only really exist if they spend time together, communicating and finding out how the other feels and thinks. Not surprisingly this is exactly how it is with us and God; our relationship with him can only really get off the ground once we get down to communication. I would imagine that for many of you communicating with a non-physical supreme life force is not an everyday occurrence, which raises the obvious question of how? We can probably just about get our heads around the idea of prayer, but hearing God? For many that idea is not just weird, it's unnatural.

Hearing God is not weird and unnatural. Unusual – yes, but when it comes down to it, God constantly has something to say; the trick is knowing how to hear it. Want to know where to hear it? Try the Bible. We'll look later at how Jesus constantly quoted the Scripture – not to show off or confuse people, but because it contained the word of God. We need to get into the Bible for ourselves.

The trouble is that many of us are scared of the Bible – it's old, big and short on pictures. With a little work though, it really can come alive and make sense to any of us. There are plenty of excellent guides around that can help you read it every day; some of the best are *Every Day with Jesus*, a series by the United Christian Broadcasters (UCB) called *God's Word For Today* as well as *Disclosure* from Scripture Union. You should be able to find them all in your local Christian bookshop or in your church.

If you're going solo then the best place to start is probably the Gospels (if you're not familiar with the Bible, those are the first four books at the start of the second half of the Bible called the New Testament). These tell the story of Jesus and are guaranteed to amaze. You might like to keep on going once you've finished John and read Acts, the next book which explains what happened after Jesus went back to heaven. This history of the early Church is particularly helpful as it deals with many of the issues that we face today.

There are other ways of reading the Bible too. If you're a methodical kind of person you might want to read two chapters of the Old Testament and one of the New each day, perhaps chucking in a psalm and a few proverbs as well. Sometimes I love reading it as a novel: picking certain books and reading them straight through. The old history books of the Old Testament are good for this, particularly the ones called Kings, Chronicles and Samuel. At times you might like to read a passage as a meditation. You might only want to choose a small chunk or a psalm, but as you read through it slowly and think about it carefully ask God to show you things about it – try it with Psalm 23 first.

You could try studying the Bible – taking a passage and really working through it by finding out what other people have said about it. There are some great books around for this (called commentaries), and you'll have the added bonus of sounding like you've done years of research at the end of it. You might also want to try memorising verses. Find one you like and write it down somewhere that you will look at often. Learning bits of the Bible helps it become part of our lives, just as it ought to. Whatever you decide to do – and I hope you might try all of these in time – don't just think of the Bible as something to be read for entertainment; use it to help you get closer to God.

LIVING THE TRUTH

Jesus knows exactly what we're like – and that includes our weaknesses as well as our strengths. Even though we can read the Bible and find out what he might be saying to us, we need to be able to do more than just mouth the words, but believe them with all our heart. Jesus knew this was the score and at one point said to people, 'Why do you call me "Lord, Lord," and do not do what I say?' He then talked about the man who not only heard the words of Jesus but also put them into practice (see Luke 6:46–9). Jesus said he was like the man who, when building a house, dug down deep and laid the foundations on a rock while his friend only laid foundations on sand. It was not that one built in the desert and the other by a mountain: both were beach houses. The difference lay in how deep the foundations were. The wise man kept digging through the sand until he found rock. When the rain and wind hit the beach his place stood firm while Mr Blag-It found himself sleeping out under the stars. When the storms come to us how deep are our foundations? Are they prepared to withstand the onslaught? So how do we dig deep? By not only hearing the words of our God but also putting them into practice.

Some of us are experience junkies; we leap from one emotionally charged experience to another as if Christianity was just a spiritual rollercoaster and we had a season ticket. Others are teaching junkies and that can be almost as bad.

We desperately want to have listened to *that* tape, gone to *the* seminar or read *this* book. For some of us the need is not for more experiences or more teaching, the need is to begin to live out what we already know. Simply to have input (teaching) with no output (obedience to that teaching) will not result in growing Christians, just fat ones. Believe me – I'm a living advert for the results of a life without much exercise.

John Wimber – an American church leader who died in 1998 – had a classic answer for those in his church who complained that they wanted more meaty teaching. 'The meat's on the streets!' he would say. Jesus said, 'My food is to do the will of him who sent me.' The meat is on the streets. We must find our nourishment from living out the truth of the gospel and not just reading about it.

I am often tempted to call the things that keep me apart from God 'my little weakness' or 'what I do when I'm tired'. These phrases sound quite cute, don't they? The trouble comes when we believe them. It's vital that we Christians perform regular safety checks on ourselves, and I'm convinced that one of the best ones is to have friends in the church to whom we make ourselves accountable. This is something we must choose to do, and it doesn't work if it is forced upon us. There is a guy I hardly know who comes up to me at Christian conferences and asks me how my prayer life is and whether I would like to confess any lustful thoughts to him. So far I have resisted the temptation to punch him. The thing is, he is a stranger. My friends on the other hand know I want them to tell me anything they notice about my attitudes or behaviour which worries them. I know that part of my safety lies in being accountable to them. By having these relationships I am able to be honest instead of cute, calling it by its real name: sin.

I so want to finish the race set before me and not trip myself up on the last lap. So, I resolve to pursue a relationship with Jesus with all that is in me, to read his word and try to live it out, and to stay honest with him and the brothers and sisters he has given me.

God likes that. In the coming chapters we will look at Jesus, whose perfect life illustrates how we can grow into living a life that is marked by an intimate relationship with the Father. Because of that intimacy, we will naturally want to do what God tells us, and by being open to him and the Holy Spirit, by hearing the things that he wants us to do, we will end up getting out and taking God's goodness to the people who don't know him. With that compassion as our lifeblood, we will kick-start relationships with other people which express the very heart of God. And that, my friend, is what it means to grow as a Christian.

2

Getting Intimate

DEVELOPING THE RELATIONSHIP

That classic piece of British cinema *Nuns on the Run* tells the story of two petty criminals who – having stolen a million pounds from their gangland boss – take refuge in a convent, posing as visiting nuns. The crooks happen to be about as convincing as Christians as they are as women and throughout the ninety minutes the laughs keep coming as we see the would-be nuns having a fag, swearing, trying to take confession and getting excited when they end up in the female changing rooms after sport. The highlight for me comes when Sister Amnesia – played by Robbie Coltrane – tries to explain the Trinity (the basic Christian understanding that the Father, Jesus and the Holy Spirit are both one God and three persons – all at the same time!).

'Well,' he/she says to a confused baby Christian, 'it's like a shamrock: three leaves and one plant.' He then delivers a cheerful rhyme that goes 'two in three and three in two; flush them all down the loo.' Hardly Oscar material, I admit, but it made me laugh at the time.

The fact that Sister Amnesia struggled to explain the Trinity will probably come as no surprise to you. After all,

127

how many of us can explain how God can be separate from himself at the same time as being part of himself at the same time as being the Holy Spirit all at the same time as being Jesus? Tricky one, yes? Theologians and people with beards have argued over this point for centuries, and I don't think that I'm in much of a position to be able to help. Perhaps this is one of the eternal mysteries that will only be fully revealed when we meet up with the three of them later. In the meantime though, what you and I can do is try to understand how best to develop a decently full relationship with the Father and the rest of that strange spiritual shamrock.

So where do we look? To Jesus. God made the point of sending him down to earth both as 100 per cent God and 100 per cent human – yeah, I know it's confusing – and consequently we have a fantastically full picture of the best way for us humans to relate to God. After all, if his own perfect and loving Son can't have a good relationship with him then who can? But thinking about father/son relationships as you know them might lead you down the wrong path; there were no tantrums, groundings or teething troubles between these two, just a vibrant, intense and totally mature relationship that was characterised by one special thing: intimacy. Remember how we spent the last chapter banging on about how important it is to have relationships? Well this is phase two: how to get the best, from God.

Jesus' relationship with his Father had intimacy written all over it. From the moment of his birth all the way through to the moment of his death and beyond the two were able to communicate and express love in a way that no other human relationship has ever come close to. The Gospels provide enough information to build up a picture of Jesus that shows exactly how important his intimate relationship with his Father was. Not only did it provide him with support, inspiration and affirmation, but it shows us that through Jesus' death, we too can get close to the Father and enjoy the same degree of intimacy with him.

Looking through the first four books of the New Testament that go to make up the story of Jesus' life, we see a number of times when that life went through major events. Just before he was about to start his final phase, travelling, preaching and healing, Jesus spent a big old chunk of time on his own in the desert. For forty days and nights he ate and drank nothing and resisted the temptations of the devil. This is the first record that we have of him spending time alone, and while the reports of it focus mainly on the temptations of the devil, we do know that he responded to each attack by quoting Scripture. While any conclusion about direct communication between the two of them might have to be left in the air, we know for sure that Jesus concentrated his mind on the truth about God as it was expressed through the Bible.

These passages gave him strength. When Satan first tempted him by offering a solution to his extreme physical hunger, he was playing on the idea that Jesus may have needed to prove himself by firing off a quick miracle. He was also getting to work on any doubts that God would deliver the goods as a provider, but neither sides of the attack worked; Jesus quoted Deuteronomy 8:3, telling Satan that he was 100 per cent dependent on God.

The next temptation probed Jesus for any sense of insecurity about whether God would be able to protect him. Perhaps Satan wondered whether Jesus would give in to a sense of pride that he could test God and win, but, whatever the idea, Jesus again brushed him aside by reminding him that God was not to be tested and that his plan was to be trusted, quoting Deuteronomy 6:16.

Finally Satan probed the Son of God for any psychological need for significance, power or achievement. Jesus told him straight that there would be no compromising when it came to evil, quoting Deuteronomy 6:13. He brought the focus back onto God and the devil was sent packing.

Immediately after this period alone Jesus went straight out and began to preach. He had been fired up by the experience and was sure of who he was and what he was there for. Spending time with God – through his word as well as in prayer – had helped him take a giant step towards fulfilling his destiny.

Going to the other end of his life we see a clear example of how Jesus spent time with his Father. Having finished the last supper, Jesus knew that his arrest and trial were only hours away. He chose to spend his last night of freedom praying in the garden of Gethsemane. Jesus flung himself face down on the ground and cried, 'My Father, if it is possible, may this cup be taken from me. Yet not as I will, but as you will' (Matthew 26:39). This was not rebellion, nor a time when Jesus tried to twist God's arm and get out of doing the dishes. Instead – despite his clear agony – Jesus was submitting to God's rule and authority, saying 'not as I will, but as you will'. This is a key characteristic of Jesus' intimacy with God; he was so close that he was able to make two such extreme statements as 'Get me out of here' and 'I'll do it if you want'. It shows that he was able to be totally honest with God, refusing to gloss over any difficulties with pleasantries or denials. It also shows that he trusted God so much that he was able to walk into terrible torture, head held high telling the world that he trusted his Father. It wasn't just this one night of prayer that meant he was able to go through with the crucifixion – Jesus had been spending time with God for years before that – but it was this night that helped focus his mind and reassure him that what he was about to go through was all part of God's plan.

TALKING WITH GOD

Prayer is our method of communicating with God, just as it was the way Jesus communicated with him too. Through a passage in the book of Matthew we get to sneak up behind Jesus and find out what the exact ingredients are of successful prayer.

This, then, is how you should pray:

> Our Father in heaven,
> hallowed be your name,
> your kingdom come,
> your will be done,
> on earth as it is in heaven.
> Give us today our daily bread.
> Forgive us our debts,
> as we also have forgiven our debtors.
> And lead us not into temptation,
> but deliver us from the evil one.
>
> (Matthew 6:9–13)

Jesus here gives us a model of how to pray to the Father by working through the following stages: beginning by praising God for who he is, what he has done and will do, we should then move on to praying for his work in the world, that it would keep moving on, spreading more of God's love and rule throughout the world. Next comes the time to pray for our own needs, and finally there is room to pray for help in our own daily struggles.

Through this style of prayer we get a picture that God wants a sense of balance to our prayer life. He doesn't just want a shopping list of items we require, nor should we feel that we cannot ask him for anything in the first place. After all, he loves to give good gifts, but if we are constantly begging or refusing to ask, it kind of gets in the way. The Lord's Prayer also shows us that we need to learn to find the balance between actively fighting the work of our enemy and being filled with the positive power of God. Most of all though, Jesus teaches us that we can call God 'Father'. Before he said this, no one would have dreamed of calling God anything other than Almighty, Holy One or a whole host of Hebrew names designed to express the many wonderful and majestic sides of God's character. From this point on, though, things were different: things were personal.

There's another fantastic prayer that we manage to listen in on later in the Bible. In the book of John, Jesus – on the verge of being arrested – prays for his disciples. He tells God about how he has taught them according to God's instruction, how they believed that Jesus was who he said he was. 'All I have is yours, and all you have is mine,' he says in John 17:10. This language reminds us of a wedding ceremony, and the expression of sacrifice is no accident. It is true: everything that Jesus had was God's; he and his Father were one. In that sense we, as his children, can agree with what Jesus said, perhaps even being bold enough to say to God ourselves, 'Everything that we have comes from you, and belongs to you.'

Before we get too carried away and reduce this line to the status of 'nice and cosy verse' (the kind that we repeat only when things are going well or we need cheering up), we must be careful not to miss out on the *huge* implications that lie at the heart of it. By following the first bit with 'and all you have is mine' Jesus turned up the heat and made it much more than a statement of how good God is at providing for us. He held out his hands and said with boldness, 'There is nothing you won't give me.' His Father gave him the key to the cupboard and told him to take his pick.

LISTENING TO GOD

This intimacy was not a one-way thing. There are times in the Bible when it seems as though God is so in love with his Son that he just cannot contain himself. As Jesus was baptised by John, God shouted down from heaven, saying, 'I love you, Son, and I'm totally proud of you.' This picture of God as the ultimate doting dad makes us smile – and so it should. We need to be clear that as well as the responsibility of following God, there is also a fantastic sense of joy and love around. God loves us, and when we get in touch with him and start to get to know him, there are often times when, again, he has trouble containing himself. After all God *is* love – and there's nothing wrong with enjoying the way he shows and shares it.

Luke 9 is interesting, if a little strange. Jesus has taken Peter, John and James with him up a mountain to pray, when suddenly he starts to look a little different. The sleepy disciples are jolted awake to find Jesus – his clothes now looking like a flash of lightning – has been joined by two other men, Moses and Elijah. These two greats of the Old Testament appear 'in glorious splendour', and speak with Jesus about his death (or 'departure' as Luke calls it). As the two visitors are leaving, Peter comments that he is glad he has seen it and then suggests that they put up some sort of memorial to mark the occasion. Just then God does another of his shouting down from heaven tricks, this time telling them that Jesus is his Son and that they should listen to him.

This passage has plenty to tell us about how to have an intimate relationship with God. The first and most obvious point is about the importance of prayer: Jesus and the three disciples took themselves off to pray. They made time for it, and obviously put in a fair old amount of effort to get in the mood by climbing up a mountain. We don't know what they were praying, but I think we can take a wild guess and assume that they weren't all asking for Jesus' face to go all shiny and for two key historical figures to show up for a chat. Because of that, we have to conclude that this amazing experience was all God's idea, which is not too out of keeping for him, especially when you consider many of the ways that he appeared to certain people throughout the Old Testament (burning bushes and all that). God loves two-way communication; he loves whispering to us so quietly that we have to get as close to him as we can, so close that we can almost touch him.

Looking at the story from the disciples' perspective, it's not surprising that they felt a bit drowsy – it happened again in the garden of Gethsemane. We also can get droopy when it comes to relating to God. Sometimes we will literally fall asleep, but more often it's our hearts and minds that need a wake-up. We can too easily have our focus taken away from the things that God is doing, and we sometimes choose to give in to physical needs instead of learning spiritual lessons.

However, I'm not here to have a go at the disciples, especially as they soon realised that what they had seen was a definite treat. Peter was right when he said, 'Master, it is good for us to be here', and without reminding ourselves of the spiritual essence of what is going on around us, we can often get bogged down by issues that are irrelevant. Even though it didn't last long, the disciples were on track when they worked out that God was involved.

Sadly they lost the plot a bit when they suggested setting up a memorial. It may sound ridiculous to us now, but we're all capable of making the same basic error in our Christian lives. What Peter was doing was confusing the need for action with the need for contemplation. Jesus was well into doing things – healing, preaching, casting out demons and feeding huge crowds – but he also knew when the time was right to sit down and enjoy God's presence. This was one of those times, and Peter's idea of calling in the builders was a little too hasty. We all need to find the balance between the doing and the being. We need to learn how to imitate Jesus' perfect harmony in this matter: if we don't, we run the risk of either ending up tired and faithless or fat and useless.

God hadn't finished, and spoke aloud to prove it. There seems to be a dramatic change in the attitudes of the disciples after this – they decide to keep the incident to themselves. What prompted this sudden change from being on the verge of telling the world to telling no one? Obviously it was God's voice that spoke only a few words: 'This is my Son whom I have chosen; listen to him.' I think that they had been taking things for granted. They had forgotten some of the majesty of Jesus and instead had got into the habit of working hard on the business of spreading the word. Sound familiar? Things haven't changed much in 2000 years, and we all struggle with finding the right sense of balance in our lives. Don't get me wrong: spreading the word is a crucial element of our Christian calling, but we do it best when it comes from a place of hanging out with Jesus and just listening to him. What God did was to remind the disciples of the power and majesty of his Son. They realised again just how they should be responding to him, and were reminded of the need for them to listen to what he said.

Pursuing a relationship with God that allows time for soaking up his love as well as doing what he wants means being intimate with him. If we manage to do that we will enter a new phase in our relationship with God – one modelled by Jesus himself. It will take time, prayer and study, but along the way we will be able to love more, to give more, to know about God's own love for us and for others as well as to begin to understand the secrets of his heart. At the end of the day it's all about copying Jesus – after all, nobody did it better.

3

Just Do It

OBEDIENT LIKE JESUS

Like most of us, I never really went in for obedience much
when I was little. In time something must have changed, for
I gradually lost my passion for winding up my parents, but
there was a period when I was the king of 'Just Say No'. My
heyday was when I was eight years old. Every trip out began
with gentle and loving suggestions from my mum and ended
up with me screaming in public places. I can remember
seriously thinking that instead of agreeing to behave myself
in the supermarket, it was much more sensible to sneeze over
the loose vegetables. This thought had been fermenting in
my head for some time, and on one trip when my mother
seemed to have more shopping to do than usual in less time,
I took my opportunity.

I had warmed up with a few failed attempts at trolley
surfing, and when Mum had told me to stop, I quietly moved
on up the aisle. Sneezing had been on my mind so much that
I had even worked out a plan; if I rubbed my face hard and
then stared at a bright light the sneezes would come thick
and fast (which, as any bogied kid knows, is precisely the
best way for sneezes to come). What's more, if I focused my

efforts on the cauliflowers, the results could be truly impressive. With so many crevices into which I could propel my snot, I knew that it was a challenge, but as I calmly prepared the sneezes, I was sure that I was up to the task. I was building up to some spectacular mucus coverage when one of the store workers told me to stop whatever it was I was up to. Now my mum had already told me to behave, and this added instruction just didn't agree with me. I turned towards him, puffed out my chest and made my 3½ foot body look as large and threatening as I could. Throwing back my head I sucked in as much air as possible, but at my furthest point back something went wrong and instead of my lungs filling with air I must have swallowed. As I whipped my head back towards the shop assistant I let out what I hoped would be an all-covering projectile sneeze gross enough to send him home early from work with severe trauma. Instead I viciously assaulted him with a high pitched burp. He laughed and I suddenly felt a lot smaller. Just then my mum came along and scooped me up, taking me off for a quick talking to round the back of the tinned soup section. Humiliated by my failure to follow through, I quietly agreed to do whatever she said.

Thankfully Jesus didn't need a dose of public humiliation or parental dressing down to make him obey. In fact, obedience was one of the great marks of Jesus' life; without it we wouldn't be here today, and we certainly wouldn't have the gift of eternal life in heaven.

We know that God sent Jesus down to earth to be the ultimate sacrifice that would pay for our sins. This was not a last-minute decision or some crazy idea that he regretted later. It was a clear and calculated plan that had been formed hundreds of years before Jesus' birth. How can we know this? The Bible is full of Messianic prophecies – sections that predict the coming of Jesus, the Messiah, and the life he would lead – and together they prove that God had the whole thing worked out in minute detail. They start with his birth, as Micah 5:2 predicts that he would be born in Bethlehem (fulfilled in the events of Matthew 2:1–6 and Luke 2:1–20) and Isaiah 7:14 foretells that he would be born to a virgin (fulfilled in Matthew 1:18–25 and Luke 1:26–38). The prophecies also point to the fact that he would be rejected by his own people (Isaiah 53:1, 3 and Psalm 118:22) which is recorded in Matthew 26:3–4, John 12:37–43 and Acts 4:1–12, tried and condemned (Isaiah 53:8) which is also reported in Luke 23:1–25 and Matthew 27:1–2, and would end up sitting at God's right hand (prophesied in Psalm 110:1 and described in Mark 16:19 and Luke 24:50–1).

But so far these prophecies concentrate on the facts of Jesus' life instead of the decisions he made. Isaiah 53:7 predicts that he would be silent before his accusers, something which happens in Matthew 27:12–14, Mark 15:3–4 and Luke 23:8–10. Psalm 22:14–16 and 17 describe the fact that the Messiah will die by crucifixion, which is fulfilled in Matthew 27:31 and Mark 15:20, 25. The prophets also predicted that the Messiah would die as a sacrifice for sin (Isaiah 53:5–12) which is covered by John 1:29 and 11:49–52 and Acts 10:43 and 13:38–9, as well as the fact that he would be raised from the dead (Psalm 16:10 as fulfilled by Acts 2:22–32 and Matthew 28:1–10).

I'm sorry to shove all these verses at you, but do you see my point? Jesus knew that suffering lay in store for him – he knew he would die and he knew he would be in pain, but he never backed down. Jesus was obedient to the last and he made sure that he went through with the plan, following it in minute detail.

What is even more impressive is the fact that Jesus was not just acting of his own accord, carrying out an idea that he had dreamt up one rainy afternoon. It was God's decision to send him down, and God's idea that he end up on a cross. In this sense, Jesus really was obedient, as he was acting under the instruction of someone else. 'I only do what I see the Father do,' he told people. The fact that the Father had also made a huge sacrifice by sending his own Son to pay someone else's debt meant that this particular game of Simon Says was unlike any other ever played.

Of course, you might be wondering why he did this. Was he a pushover, bored or just keen on trying to please people? None of these suggestions are right, you'll be glad to know. The truth is that Jesus was obedient because he had such an intimate relationship with his Father. He was obedient because he loved. Talking to the disciples, Jesus told them how we Christians are the branches, he is the vine and his Father the gardener. He was happy that his Father loved him, and part of that love had meant trimming off any branches that didn't bear fruit. Jesus applied the same standard of love to his disciples – encouraging them to reach their potential. It involved him trimming some of their branches too, and meant that they had to be obedient to him in the same way that he was obedient to his Father. Later it would cost some of them their lives too, but while Jesus was alive, he made a point of giving them some simple commands: 'Love each other as I have loved you' (John 15:12). This word wasn't just for the disciples of Jesus' day, but for all who claim to follow him at any point in time. If we say that we love him, then we cannot get out of the fact that we have to love others in the same way that he loved us, the same way that God loved him. That means getting down to some serious obedience, sacrifice and radical living. It also means that lives will be changed, saved and turned around, as people are reunited with God.

If we're still in any doubt about the importance of doing what Jesus tells us, there's a final reminder in the form of: 'You are my friends if you do what I command' (John 15:14). Placing these two verses together highlights something interesting; that we don't just obey for the sake of it, but that as friends of Jesus we want to do what makes him happy.

Jesus doesn't just let us off the hook with a simple command to love. OK, so in him love meant dying on a cross and living totally for others, but in us I suspect that there is a danger that we could water it down a little. Perhaps if it was left at 'love' we would be happy just to go around being nice to old ladies and not murdering anyone. The fantastic thing about Jesus was that he knew the way we work and understood that we needed to have things spelt out for us as clearly as possible. That's why he chucked in the bit about *doing* as well as loving, why he made it clear that he wanted something more than just the Pharisees' academic abilities, why he chose people who would put their lives on the line. Christianity is all about finding the balance between adoring him and displaying him, between worship and evangelism. Sadly we often miss out. This time Jesus makes it clear that love without action also misses the point. He wants us to copy his lifestyle – both the things he did and the attitudes that he held. He was in perfect loving harmony with God and was totally obedient to his will.

Even though it might be tough along the way, true obedience as Jesus modelled it will bring about massive transformations. It's important that we understand this and don't just think of being obedient as some pointless exercise that only manages to keep us out of mischief. Done the right way (and that means done the Christ way) obedience can change everything. It is not a passive or wimpy option, it's not the sort of thing that we ought to be slightly embarrassed about. It gives glory to God and brings us all a little bit closer home to him.

THE GREAT COMMISSION

Alongside this Great Commandment to love God and others comes something called the Great Commission. Just before he returned to heaven Jesus gave his disciples a list of jobs to do. We'll look at this in detail later on, but his final speech begins with the words 'go into all the world and make disciples' (Matthew 28:19). This means that we are supposed to get on with the job of evangelism, telling and showing people about Jesus, whose instructions stand side by side with the commandment to get down to some serious worship.

So you see, worship and evangelism are the perfect partnership; they belong together. If we separate them they are both reduced to something less than they ought to be. These are both things that Jesus told us to do. If we are going to try and follow him then we need to take his instructions seriously. We cannot separate worship from evangelism because it goes against everything that Jesus taught. The trouble is that many of us have separated them. Many of us are passionate about the one and try and blag it with the other. We have hidden worship away in the Church and kicked evangelism out into the world.

Acts chapter 2 is a great example of people being obedient to Jesus's twin commands. In fact, it's such a great example that it doesn't just show the jobs getting done efficiently, but it makes it clear to us how the two of them complement (and even depend on) one another. On the day of Pentecost the Holy Spirit fell on the disciples in the upper room. The first response to the coming of the Spirit was worship. The disciples spilled out onto the street 'declaring the wonders of God' in many different languages. As they worshipped a crowd gathered and began to ask questions about what was happening. Peter got up and preached the first evangelistic sermon in the history of the Church. Isn't it interesting that the first evangelistic talk was essentially given to answer the questions raised by the worship of the Church? That is how it should be. Anointed, passionate, intimate worship is one of the best evangelistic tools we have. There is something about the fragrance of such worship that draws non-believers.

At Soul Survivor we have seen this in some of our work

over the years. At the start of last summer, a group of girls started coming to our church, and eight of them became Christians. We asked them what it was about our services that attracted them and helped them on their journey to God. Obviously I was convinced that they'd say it was the teaching. Perhaps they found it not only amusing and informative, but eloquent, captivating and life changing. I was sure that a couple of them would be able to quote their favourite chunks of Pilavachi sermons, and maybe they even had some of my ideas embroidered onto pillows and hand-kerchiefs which they gave away as presents to their family.

I think I got it wrong. Instead of declaring themselves Pilavachists, they described the talks as 'too long' and even 'a bit boring'. I resisted the temptation to tell them that they needed to repent, and swallowed my pride as they carried on. What had impressed them was the devotion expressed in the worship. It wasn't just the atmosphere of the services or the lighting, décor or duration. It wasn't the fact that the guitars were distorted and the bass was fat and funky. What had got them was the content. They seemed to learn more doctrine from the worship than from my sermons. Can you believe it? I was shocked.

> Jesus Christ, I think upon your sacrifice;
> you became nothing, poured out to death.
> Many times I've wondered at your gift of life,
> and I'm in that place once again.

They sing this Matt Redman song to each other at school. My Pilavachi special illustrations have never made it to school. I'm jealous, but kind of pleased too.

Evangelism that does not come from a lifestyle of worship can be very mechanical and dry. Worship that does not result in witness can become a self-indulgent ritual which is boring and repetitive. If there is great rejoicing in heaven over one sinner who repents, then how much more should the salvation of souls affect our worship on earth. These are the basics that we need to obey, just as Jesus did.

REVIVAL THROUGH OBEDIENCE

We humans have a great knack for getting confused. We believed that the world was flat, that draining blood was good for you and that wearing luminous socks was cool. The list of embarrassments is embarrassingly long, and we in the Church have done our bit to add to it. Now I don't want this to come out all wrong, but I think we ought to admit that many of us in the Church were a bit mistaken a few years ago. At times I was right there in the middle of it, loving it and having a ball, but now it's time for the truth.

God is an active God. He loves to roll up his sleeves and get involved with his people. This has happened on many occasions throughout the history of the Church, and I for one pray that it will continue to happen in the future. We tend to call these times revivals, and they often result in people discovering new and astounding things about God's character, falling in love with him even more and going deeper in their relationship with him. One of the most recent of these happened in a city called Toronto on Canada's border with America. This movement within the Church ran throughout the middle and end bits of the 1990s, and started as people rediscovered the joy of being loved by God. For many of us that joy did not result in an ability or great desire to communicate what we had received to others. A lot of good things happened; people got closer to God and rediscovered a fire for him. But something else didn't happen; when we had got closer to God we didn't listen hard enough for his instructions, or if we did hear them, we weren't obedient. Instead of responding to Jesus' command of '*Go*', we preferred the more gentle '*Come*', chilling with God. We fancied the worship a lot more than we fancied the evangelism.

At the time there was a lot of talk about Revival, but I sometimes feel that not all of us have been completely sure what 'Revival' actually means. Revival at its simplest is defined as 'bringing back to life that which was dead or close to death'. In that sense the Church constantly needs reviving. But many of us have been blind to the fact that it had been happening over the years anyway. Festivals like Soul Survivor, Cross Rhythms and Summer Madness in Ireland regularly attracted thousands of young people who were ready to do business with God. That would have been unheard of twenty years ago. In Britain alone, the Alpha courses introduced hundreds of thousands of people to Christ for the first time. This is still going on today, and up and down the country we are still hearing of new initiatives in evangelism springing up which are working. The Church is recovering its passion for Jesus as expressed in worship, its passion for the lost as expressed in evangelism and God's heart for the poor both at home and abroad.

So revival was and is taking place, and yet we need more, much more. It just isn't enough to get a few thousand in here or a few thousand there. If we're going to see big time change, we need to be reaching millions with the news and love of Jesus. At the time it was definitely good that we were hungry for God and desperate to see him do something massive, but we still managed to get confused. We began to feel like revival was a thing which would drop out of the sky at a certain date. This meant that we lost sight of the fact that, actually, Christianity is all about Jesus, not about magic rain or quick fixes. Some of us felt as though if we prayed hard enough, God would one day open a window in heaven and spray revival spray into the atmosphere, like air freshener. As the mist wafted down, people would breathe it in and suddenly fall over at the power of God – instantly transformed into A grade mature Christians. I don't believe this attitude is either biblical or helpful. I know that on the day of Pentecost the disciples waited until the Holy Spirit was poured out before they began to witness, but Pentecost has happened: the Spirit has been outpoured, and we have been called to go.

Revival is Jesus; more of his love, presence, holiness and power. I get quite upset when we still hear more about revival than we do about Jesus. Someone once famously prayed, 'Lord, don't send revival, come yourself' – I like that prayer because it's what Jesus did when he walked the earth. He came down and he spread love, healing, salvation and forgiveness all over through the way he lived his life. It all came through him as a human, weak like the rest of us. The apostle Paul learned that 'God's power is made perfect in weakness' (2 Corinthians 12:9) and found out that the secret of a full life and effective ministry is getting his power in my 'jars of clay' (2 Corinthians 4:7). Back in biblical times they were a little short on high street banks, so anything of value was stored in the home. The clever ones didn't stash their wad in fancy vases that would get stolen straight away, but in the cheapo jars of clay that no respectable thief would have bothered with. Paul uses this picture to show that while we may feel like second-grade jars of clay, God puts the treasure of his life in us. God works through us, not alongside, near or around us. This is a partnership, and we have to see the part that God has given us to play.

There's another lesson to learn from that time in the 1990s. We were in danger of sitting back and waiting for this wonderful thing to happen to us before we got out and did anything ourselves. 'Revival is God's work,' some people thought. 'Best leave it all up to him.' People took trips out to America and Canada – to Pensacola and Toronto – to 'catch the fire' and take it home to their churches. I was one of them and had a great time getting closer to God, but let's not kid ourselves: the idea of going across the ocean to get a blessing, holiness or power and then bring it back with us is kind of bizarre and not at all easy to defend from Scripture.

The lesson that we can learn from all this is that revival will not come when we go across the ocean but when we go across the street. When we go in weakness to our neighbours and try to communicate the love of God to them in a way that is costly and makes us vulnerable. The feeding of the five thousand should be our model: Jesus took the little the disciples had (five loaves and two fish) and blessed and gave thanks for it. He then gave it back to them and told them to feed the people. The miracle happened in the disciples' hands. As they obeyed in faith, God multiplied the food. The disciples did not wait until the bread and fish had become 5000 Big Mac meals before they obeyed. They did it on the spot, putting their obedience before their doubts.

Jesus says, 'Go.' Go now. Instead of looking for yet another blessing, we should look for ways that we can be a blessing. 'Give and it will be given to you, pressed down, shaken together, running over, it will be poured into your lap' (Luke 6:38). It's all part of a simple rule: go and give away what you've been given.

I have learned to my cost that if I have more input (food) than output (exercise) I do not keep growing, I just get fat. Even though a lot of this was going on a few years ago, I am still worried that we in the Church could be in danger of getting fat. We need to exercise by getting on with the business of being obedient to what Jesus told us to do. That means serving the poor as we fight for social justice and as we seek to win the lost. We can learn from this though. We can decide that instead of catching half the message, we will look for the whole story. We know that God isn't just into sitting back and soaking up the easy vibes. He's a God of action as well as relationship – a God of such intense love that he cannot stand to have injustice carry on while his people are around.

He spelled it out for us through Jesus in Matthew 25;

believe me, it doesn't get much clearer than this. In a story to his disciples in which he illustrates the final judgment every one of us must face, Jesus challenges those who are doomed to eternal torment: 'I was hungry and you gave me nothing to eat, I was thirsty and you gave me nothing to drink, I was a stranger and you did not invite me in, I needed clothes and you did not clothe me, I was sick and in prison and you did not look after me.'

The wretched souls protest: 'Lord, when did we see you hungry or thirsty or a stranger or needing clothes or sick or in prison, and did not help you?'

But Jesus' crushing reply is: 'Whatever you did not do for one of the least of these, you did not do for me.'

4

Living in the Real World

As well as having a supremely intimate relationship with the Father and being committed to obey him, Jesus' time on earth teaches us another lesson that should revolutionise the way we live. Wherever he went, whatever he did, Jesus was fuelled by compassion. He saw the sick and he healed them, met the oppressed and set them free, encountered a world living far away from God and showed us the way home. He didn't do it for an ego boost and he didn't do it 'cos he was bored. Jesus did it because it was as much a part of him as his heart and lungs – he wouldn't be Jesus without compassion.

So you won't be surprised when I say that if we want to graduate to wearing spiritual trousers we have to learn how to follow in the footsteps of the most compassionate man who ever lived. Again this isn't a cue for us to hit the panic button, as God is far more concerned about us being on the right tracks rather than at the end of the journey – we never could be a match for Jesus, but we can all have a go as he gives us his power to live.

As ever we hunt for clues in the Bible. Just looking at a list of whom Jesus talked with during his travels throws up some of the lowest and most despised members of society: a tax collector, an apparently insane hermit, a criminal, a poor widow, an adulterous woman, a sick woman, a blind beggar, an outcast with leprosy, a young girl, a traitor, a helpless and paralysed man, a woman from a foreign land, an enemy who hated him and a Samaritan woman. To each of them he preached the same message of love and acceptance, offering hope and salvation through himself.

There's a link that joins each of these people. They were on the edge. (Of course, you could easily argue that there was no Church when Jesus was around, and so everyone was on the edge, how then can we compare the two?) Still, we cannot ignore the fact that Jesus' most astounding and controversial acts – the ones that sent the biggest shock waves throughout society and did the most to turn it upside down – were performed in the midst of sinners. After all, I think it's kind of logical: if imitating Jesus' life is like shining a light, where will it appear brightest, surrounded by other lights or on its own in the darkness? The fact is that we cannot truly copy Jesus' compassionate lifestyle unless we copy it in similar locations, which is why we need to take an honest look at how we relate to the world.

I was in South Africa once when I started to get a little distressed. I wasn't worried about the usual things – too much rain and not enough curry – instead, this time I was getting stressed about the Church. It seemed to me that the white Christian community out there was enjoying a culture all of its own, as if it was happy to be completely separated from the rest of the world. What they had set up was a ghetto, where everything that was going on in the world was being washed down, cleaned up and blandly duplicated ready for consumption by the Christian community.

I heard plenty of teaching out there, too. I heard many people tell young Christians not to drink alcohol, go to nightclubs or listen to any non-Christian music. All these things were the devil's own, and good Christian kids should stay away, choosing instead a diet of Contemporary Christian Music (CCM if you're into the jargon), church events and Fanta.

I saw how all the people had acted on this message, and I was horrified at the result. What was produced was a Christian community that was happy hanging around with itself. They had their own little parties, with their own Christian friends where they listened to their own Christian radio stations which played their own Christian music. They were separated from the world. They were separated from people outside the Church. It reminded me of biblical times, but more of the professional religious men than of Jesus.

One day when I was feeling brave or stupid (depending on how you look at it) I gave a talk. I told people how I thought it was a good thing to listen to non-Christian music. I said that I thought music that wasn't written by Christians was often much better, that I thought it was good to go to nightclubs. I finished up by telling them that I don't think drinking alcohol sends you to hell.

The following Sunday, the pastor of one of the churches in Durban got up and said to the young people, 'I've been told that someone has come into our city and told you that it's OK to listen to non-Christian music and go to nightclubs. I want to tell you, that is trash.' That was quite a shock. I don't know why I was surprised, I suppose I had hoped that by saying what I had said people would see the sense. Instead, it made certain ones out there get kind of agitated.

Back home in England we struggle with many of the same things and face similar issues. Isn't it strange that I had to go to the other side of the world to realise that many of us in the Church think of holiness not first of all as obedience to God but as being separate from the world. We're not really talking about music, clubs or booze here, but instead are examining something at the heart of our beliefs. Now I love South

Africa and all the Christians I've met out there, but I think some had got the wrong end of the stick. What Jesus preached about holy living never prevented him from taking his love out to the people that needed it most. Holiness is a tool, a blueprint for how we should live our lives. As well as knowing what to avoid, true holiness is following God. Our misunderstandings come from the fact that we have signed up for a model of holiness that we see in the Israel of the Old Testament where they were constantly struggling to avoid being contaminated by the other nations and their false gods. Jesus gave us another model. He was the first missionary; he came to contaminate the world with his love and power – that's why we see him spending time with the 'publicans and sinners', the prostitutes, the tax collectors, the Samaritans and all those whom the religious leaders saw as people to avoid.

Here in the UK we have got confused about holiness and compassion, and we still tend to regard holiness as something that keeps us apart from the world, as opposed to something that keeps the world out of us. When he was around in first-century Israel, Jesus encountered the same things I saw in South Africa. The Pharisees and the teachers of the law kept trying to trip him up with the laws about not touching this or that and not healing on the Sabbath. What they were pushing for was for Jesus to say that we shouldn't get involved, not with tax collectors, not with sinners and certainly not with women in the middle of their menstrual cycle. Jesus was touched by a woman who was bleeding. She was healed. Lepers were unclean, not just physically but spiritually as well, but Jesus touched them and they were healed. Respectful Jews regarded prostitutes as untouchables but Jesus cared for them, forgave them and loved them.

Jesus was a man on a mission. In a sense he redefined holiness. Holiness for Jesus was not about the display of knowledge of the law, it was about the passion of the heart, and Jesus' heart beats loud and strong for a certain type of person. He went to the places that respectable religious people wouldn't go, and he managed to go there and still live a holy life. He went to a place where there were drunks and he didn't get drunk. He went to a place where there were sexual sinners and yet he didn't sin sexually. He went with tax collectors and sinners and partied with them, and yet lived a holy life that managed to be so attractive that people responded to him completely. When he went to all these places, he didn't go just to test his willpower, to see if he really could manage to resist temptation. Instead, he went because he was pushed by a deep and violent urge within him. We call it compassion, and Jesus was full of it. It affected his life in every detail – from whom he talked with to how he chose to die. Jesus acted because he loved the people that God had created, and he could not stand idly by and see them suffer without him.

In Luke 19 we read about Jesus travelling to Jericho as the crowd were lining the streets to see him. A very small tax collector called Zacchaeus climbed a tree so that he could get a good look. Now the point about Zac is that he was a social outcast; he worked for the Romans and defrauded his own people. Jesus, seeing him up the tree, says something stunning: 'Zacchaeus, come down immediately. I must stay at your house today.' As a result of those words Zac turned his back on all that he had done wrong. Jesus' words immediately undid a lifetime of self-doubt and shame. Jesus told Zacchaeus that he was worth spending time on, regardless of how bad his business ethics were. We need to learn to be fired by that same compassion – a sort that works outside of church. We can't go on spending our lives retreating from the world into the Church, getting scared at the slightest thing that challenges our faith. We mustn't retreat into our little ghettos, because if we do we may never get out. We've got to get out in the real world and live life to the full as God's people, holy, pleasing to him, fired up by a desire to follow God's lead and spread his love in the midst of a broken and hurting world. 'Get ready,' we need to say to the culture, 'we're coming to your house.'

Sometimes I worry about all our Christian subculture stuff; we've got our own Christian record labels, bookshops, magazines and festivals. We're involved in all of these at Soul Survivor, and I know that each of these can do great things for God, yet the flip side to all that we have built up around the Church is that sometimes these things can create a Christian subculture, a Christian ghetto where we retreat from the world, a place where we don't understand what the world is thinking.

TRUE COMPASSION

Jesus' first miracle was turning water into wine at a wedding feast in Cana (John 2:1–11). He didn't do it as a publicity stunt; he went to the party to enjoy himself. He performed the miracle to make people happy, not only to demonstrate his power and glory. Even more intriguing is the fact that the only people who knew about it were the servants. If you want to see the miracles, be a servant.

There's a Christian lady called Jackie Pullinger. She's written books and has been in the public eye for many years, but neither of them are the reason why she is well known and widely respected. She used to live inside Hong Kong's notorious Walled City – a horrendous slum (thankfully no longer in existence) where society at times seemed to be breaking down in front of her very eyes. She lived surrounded by drug dealers and addicts, prostitutes and gang members, Aids victims and orphans. She worked with anyone who wanted help – offering care and the chance to rebuild a broken life. As a result hundreds of people have become Christians through her work, she has helped to turn a city around and has saved lives, all because of the compassion that she's received from Jesus.

I heard her speak once. She flew over from Hong Kong landing at Heathrow at 6.00 a.m. She spoke at 10.00 a.m. and again at 2.00 p.m. and then caught the 10.00 p.m. flight back to Hong Kong. Not even time for a shop at Harrods. Lots of people came to listen to her talk about the things that were on her mind, and her message was uncompromising. She was clear and straight up in the way that only someone who is actually doing what she says can be. I suppose that was one reason why I found it so shocking. I know this is corny, but she really did remind me of Mother Teresa. I never heard Mother T speak, but I know that she had a knack of cutting through all the complications we make and telling it as it is. This was how Jackie spoke; she was blunt, simple and uncompromising. A little bit like Jesus, I suppose.

Jackie talked about living a life of compassion and service. She talked about sacrifice. She talked about losing your life to find it. She told us how she and the rest of her team had heard about something that was going on back in western churches in 1996. They had heard that Christians in some place had started laughing and falling over. (This seemed kind of strange to them but I don't think they paid it too much attention.) Later she heard that Christians had started flying out to visit this place full of laughter, spending cash on airfares and staying in hotels just to catch the laughter for themselves. It all sounded like a bit of a party, and Jackie and the rest were a bit confused. But they prayed, 'OK, Holy Spirit, your people really need to rediscover the joy of their salvation and it is good that they can take aeroplanes to the laughing. But because this is you, Holy Spirit, after they have taken the aeroplanes to the laughing, some of them will also take aeroplanes to the dying and the crying.'

Jackie stopped telling her story for a while, looking around her.

'And we waited,' she said, 'but you didn't come.' It wasn't as though she was angry – it seemed much more like she was confused by the whole thing.

I was very upset. You see, I've been to Toronto. Twice. On the other hand I've never been much into the Bangladesh blessing. I was cross. How dare someone make a day trip to England to lecture us on how to live our lives? Who does she think she is? She doesn't have any idea about the situation in the British Church. My response was a little bit like that of a Pharisee, I suppose.

The response in others was very interesting. Those who were more mature in years reacted very similarly to me, and it took a while to really understand what she said. The younger ones, however, were in no doubt. They were up the front for ministry, repenting of the fact they had not been giving more of their pocket money to relieve world suffering. They were ready to book their one-way tickets to Hong Kong. As I looked at them and saw how fired up they were, I realised that I am getting old. There was a time when I would have been up there with the best of them, ready to go at a moment's notice for Jesus. Now I have a church and ministry to support. I have responsibilities and commitments. Mortgages have to be paid. Books have to be written. Such is life.

Friends of mine were telling me how the teenagers in their family came back from their youth meeting passionate about how they were going to change the world for Jesus. The change was going to take place in the next few weeks, but they were just wondering whether they should start the international ministry before or after their GCSEs? The parents had just finished their homegroup meeting where one of the members had asked for prayer so he would have the courage to at last tell his work colleagues that he went to church. I've been a bit like that lately – looking for the small things instead of letting my heart beat wildly with God-given compassion.

In becoming worldly wise (cynical) have I lost the passion that results in reckless behaviour, like walking on the water? Have I lost the compassion that leads to a holy boldness, the sort that tears a hole in a roof so that a paralysed friend can be healed (Mark 2:1–12)? We see in the book of Joshua that Caleb was an old man with a young man's heart. He saw with the eyes of faith. He ran the last lap of his life as if it was the first.

I know that this isn't just about physical age – God is not just a God of the young any more than he is just a God of the old. His compassion is compatible with all of us, and all we have to do is keep the fire burning in our hearts and to work it out in our lives. As I have found, to realise that you have lost something is the first step to finding it again. Let us not settle. The first line of a children's song says 'It's an adventure, following Jesus'. Don't lose the sense of adventure. Don't quit. Let us not grow weary. Let's change the world with that same brand of holy compassion that started the whole thing off.

Having compassion means that we need to be a people of our culture, as well as a people who know how to stand counter to the culture in certain areas. We need to be in the middle of it, dishing out love and truth and being genuine and honest with people, but there are certain things that we need to take a stand against. For example, when it comes to greed – something which our culture is full of – our voices need to be heard. That doesn't mean escaping from the culture in order to be generous in our own little clique, but instead being generous right in the middle of the greedy culture: that's where the light shines brightest. Let's be sexually pure in the midst of a culture where there isn't purity. Let's be responsible in a culture where people get off their heads.

That is what compassion is – being like Jesus when he met with the prostitute who poured a year's wages' worth of perfume over his feet (John 12:1–8). He didn't slip or stumble, he remained pure and holy, having mercy on her when no one else would even give her any respect. His compassionate heart was big enough to forgive her for her sinful lifestyle.

Many of us are afraid to really engage with our culture because of a fear of contamination. We are afraid to get out there and put our faith on the line, showing love in the darkest places. Perhaps we are worried that our faith won't hold out, perhaps we worry that we haven't got what it takes and that the radical obedience to Jesus' command of spreading the news is best left to the brave ones like Jackie Pullinger. Perhaps we are right to be scared and aware of the danger that faces us; moving out takes us away from all the religious comforts that we have built up around us. But it simply isn't an option to stay in the cosy warmth of the Church, for how can we show the full outrageous and powerful extent of God's compassion in there? We need to wake up to the fact that we have a spirituality that only works in the Church. That cannot be right, we need to relearn and to find a spirituality that works in the world. For it is God's world, and he loves it. We need to be committed to his world, to be part of his world. It's called incarnation, and it's what God did when he became a human being and lived among us as Jesus. A Jesus spirituality works in the world. Do we believe the Scripture that says, 'he that is in us is greater than he that is in the world' (1 John 4:4)? John 1:14 says, 'The word became flesh and made his dwelling among us.' In *The Message* version of the Bible that particular passage is paraphrased 'and Jesus moved into the neighbourhood'. I love that. We need to be like Jesus: God's representatives in the midst of his broken and hurting world.

5

The Desert

WHY ME?

To be brutally honest, I'd much rather spend the next few pages talking about luxury desserts than spiritual deserts – given the choice, a Triple Chocolate Fudge Walnut Cream Surprise beats intense loneliness and testing any day – but somehow I don't think it would be that useful a chapter. You see we all go through times when Christianity is tough. Instead of being vibrant and full of life, it seems grey, God seems distant and the faith that once had you feeling on top of the world suddenly seems to have run dry. As Christians we call them Desert Times (more on why we call them that later), and they are no more a sign that your faith is weak than the 'Virtually Fat Free' label on the Triple Chocolate Fudge Walnut Cream Surprise means that what lies inside is good for you.

Comforting as that news might be, it can sometimes seem like small consolation when we are actually in the middle of one of these difficult times. When God seems a million miles away, when we're convinced that he's about as interested in us as we are in prayer, it can be hard not to start getting on a bit of a downer about things. After all, when we feel as though we've either been conned, stood up or simply rejected outright, getting ourselves motivated again can seem like an impossible task.

The reason why I can be so presumptuous by including a chapter like this is because difficult times are a natural part of the Christian life. As I said, we *all* go through it, and not only when we are in our early days of getting to know God. These experiences crop up all the way throughout even the longest Christian life; in fact they are actually a vitally important part of the Christian life: not only do they help us put into perspective the mind-numbingly great times that we all enjoy every now and then, but they also teach us one of the most valuable lessons that Christianity ever has to offer: perseverance.

I know that dropping a word like perseverance into a book like this is dumb, but the point is that it's true. Persevering, deciding to stick with it despite the fact that you feel as though you're stumbling about like a zombie is the key to growing up in your relationship with God.

There's a famous story in the Bible that Jesus told. It concerns a rich master who, just before a lengthy trip away, calls three of his servants together and hands them different amounts of cash. He tells each of them to get on with the business of making more cash out of what's in their hands, and goes away. When he returns he calls each of them in and asks to see what they've done with his wad. It turns out that the two who had been given the larger sums had managed to double their purses. The master is happy, but the smile goes when the third servant arrives and tells him that because he thought the master was such a hard man, he stuck the cash in a hole in the ground and had managed to increase its value by absolutely nothing at all.

This story – you can read it for yourself in Matthew 25 – is normally used to illustrate the fact that we all have talents from God that we ought to be using for him. I happen to think that it also can take a slightly different spin: the need for perseverance. Think about the servant – the one who made no profit and did nothing while his master was away. He buried the coin and, presumably, forgot all about it. The clever servants, however, had a different story to tell. Instead of forgetting about things, they carried on, working hard at increasing their return, despite the fact that their master was nowhere to be found. He was unavailable for either advice or reassurance. There must have been times when it looked as though they were about to lose everything – such is the nature of money – and at those times I am sure that they would have been tempted to give up on the whole idea. Instead, though, they carried on, receiving their master's pleasure when he returned.

This is how it should be with us. When God seems far away we too have a choice; either we bury our faith and forget about the Master, or we continue in his absence, carrying out the orders that he has given us until we feel close to him again.

But, you may just be about to ask, how can we be sure that we *will* feel close to him again? In the dark night of the soul, daylight seems a long way off, and nothing can seem certain. Remember how I said that you weren't alone? It's not just Christians today who have been through it, but believers and followers of God throughout history. The Bible is generously seasoned with stories of people who feel as though God is playing an elaborate game of hide and seek with them. In a sense he is; he takes away his presence, his nearness, from them and asks them a simple question: will you search for me?

This is exactly what happened to Moses. Having left the comfort of the palace he found himself in the wilderness for quite some time before his run-in with God in the shape of the burning bush. The same thing happened to the rest of his countrymen a few years later as they spent forty years wandering around the desert trying to find the promised land. This was not necessarily due to the fact that the promised land was a particularly long way away, but more due to their desperate need to rediscover their relationship with God before they rebuilt their society.

Later on in the Bible we hook up with Elijah (1 Kings 17) – surely one of the nuttiest prophets in the whole book. Reading the story it can seem as though his life is a string of easy miracles, joined together by fireproof faith and an almost constant hotline to God. But look closer and it's possible to see the difficult times in there too. When Elijah called a drought, the Lord told him to go and hide at a place called the Kerith ravine and later to another place called Zarephath, both of which were in the desert. Elijah spent three years there, with only a widow and her son for company. Think about that for a while, and it becomes clear that those years were no picnic. In those days, being in the desert or the wilderness meant constant danger and a daily struggle for food. Add to that the absence of any miracles, and we can be sure that Elijah would have had to work hard to keep on track with God. What happens next leads us to the inevitable conclusion that he must have done OK, as he kicked butt on the hugest scale by defeating the prophets of Baal on top of Mount Carmel.

These stories are not confined to the Old Testament either, as Jesus' coming changed little about this natural rhythm of relationship with God Almighty. We'll go into this even more later on, but briefly we know that John the Baptist did his proclaiming about Jesus from the literal desert, and that Jesus too spent forty days on his own.

As we're in the mood for metaphor, let's think about the physical characteristics of these desert and wilderness places. Essentially, they are barren – free from virtually all signs of life – as well as being dry. It is a fight just to find water and survive. Third, they are always inhospitable places, being low on the natural resources that we rely on for comfort. If this is equally true of the spiritual deserts and wildernesses that we all visit from time to time, then the obvious question that springs to mind is why? Why, when God is loving and kind, would he ever want us to go through experiences that seem so destructive?

The book of Deuteronomy answers exactly that question. Having been asked it by the Israelites, the Lord answers.

> Remember how the Lord your God led you in the desert these forty years, to humble you and to test you in order to know what was in your heart, whether or not you would keep his command.
>
> (Deuteronomy 8:2)

BEING HUMBLED

The first thing that is on God's agenda for our difficult times is the process of our being humbled. I know that this works for me because whenever I am not struggling with a desert experience, when life is cushy and everything seems to be working out well, I can start to think that I've got something to do with it. Then I can get around to thinking that I'm self-sufficient, that I can handle life, I can handle ministry, I can handle just about anything that gets thrown at me. I'm not alone in this, and whenever we prosper, there are many of us who start to self-inflate our own sense of importance. By sending us into the desert places, by showing us that we certainly do not have the Midas touch, God offers us the chance of realising the truth: that apart from him we can do nothing of any value.

It wasn't that long ago that I went through my latest – and possibly 'greatest' – rough time. When I first realised that God no longer seemed so close I started to panic. Was this the end of everything, I thought. Was I losing my faith?

Which of my secret sins was it because of? Had God taken his anointing away? Was it ever there in the first place? I went through this usual list of doubts and panics, each of which felt intensely real at the time.

It came to a bit of a climax on Easter Day. I was standing at the front of church trying to lead the meeting, but inside my head was nothing but a panic about what to do next. I had no idea what to do, and absolutely no idea of what God wanted. This was serious, and the feelings of nervousness and panic made the experience far more intense than anything I had gone through in a long while. Of course I tried not to show it, and acted in a most professional manner, but inside was the cry of 'Lord, I don't hear a thing. Help.' I left the meeting with a very real sense of sorrow and pain inside – it had been the culmination of weeks of feeling spiritually alone, and I felt terrible.

Looking back now I can see that before things had started to seem a little stale I had got used to having God's voice on tap, so much so that I had begun to cut corners. Where previously I might have prayed long and hard about a certain decision, I had started to wing it, trusting in God's abilities as a quick fix supplier. I'd been neglecting the relationship and seemed to be suffering the consequences. The thing about going through a desert experience is that you cannot cut corners – they simply are not there to cut. The only options open are either to ignore God or to pursue him – and even then, pursuing him can for a while feel like a wild goose chase.

Despite this – in fact because of this – God humbles us in the desert, stripping us of all our supports. He allows us to stand there and to say, 'Unless you send the rain, I'm going to die of thirst, unless you send manna, I've got nothing to eat.'

LEARNING ABOUT OURSELVES

The second result to force its way out of the whole deal is a rigorous testing of what is in our hearts. Through the revelation of brutal truth about our attitudes and feelings each of us finds out what we are really like. While it may be quicker for God to hand the information to us in the form of a nicely typed and bound personality profile, somehow I don't think we would take things to heart. Instead God uses real life to get our attention and teach the lessons. I'm glad of this because sometimes I can kid myself that emotionally and spiritually things are a lot better than they actually are. Things on the outside can be going well enough that admitting difficulties or even looking at yourself becomes a bit of a non-starter. But of course, as soon as you're in the desert, when the distractions of things going well are a distant memory, looking in at yourself is one of the few things you *can* do. Poor old Moses had to put up with forty years of building sandcastles in the desert with the whingeing Israelites. The dramatic change that needed to take place – the acceptance of the Israelites of God as the one true God – meant that the whole thing took so long. There's no point expecting a desert experience to last half an hour, you may as well be at the seaside for all the good it will do you.

Numbers are significant in the Bible. Seven represents God's perfection, three represents God (as Trinity) and forty seems to get used whenever the writer wants to imply that a large period of time has passed. For example, the point isn't that Jesus spent exactly forty days in the wilderness, but that he was out there for a long time. The same goes for the amount of time it rained during the great flood and the length of time that the Israelites spent wandering and whingeing on their way to the promised land. God understands the value of time, and knows that through the passing of large chunks of it, he can test our hearts.

As well as testing us by making us face up to the truth about ourselves, God also uses desert experiences to refine us, to show up our faults and encourage us to put them behind us. In the early 1990s a bunch of people from Kansas City started coming over and travelling around churches in the UK. These people were all incredibly gifted in the prophetic side of things, and at some point I got it into my head that as soon as they saw people they knew everything they were thinking. When I heard they were coming to my church I was a tad confused. On the one hand I was desperate to see some spot-on prophesying get done, but on the other I was scared that the minute I walked in the door they were going to reveal my most secret of sins to the whole congregation. Having decided to go I made sure that I was ready. For three and a half hours I crawled around my flat on my knees, desperately repenting for any sin I had committed as well as any sin that I might have contemplated committing.

I came out of the meeting with my reputation intact as well as having seen some amazing things, but it was only a few weeks later that I understood how God had spoken to me directly too. I realised that we don't need to wait for the prophet to reveal the things that are wrong in us, in the same way that we don't need to wait for the big meeting before we get down to some honest confession. Instead the good old desert time offers each of us a chance to face up to the truth about ourselves. Deserts offer a quiet alternative to the noise and bustle that we create around us when everything is going according to plan.

The Bible draws out this theme in Deuteronomy 8:

When you have eaten and are satisfied [when I give you manna in the desert], praise the Lord your God for the good land he has given you. Be careful that you do not forget the Lord your God, failing to observe his commands, his laws and his decrees that I am giving you this day.

> Otherwise, when you eat and are satisfied, when you build fine houses and settle down, and when your herds and flocks grow large and your silver and gold increase and all you have is multiplied, then your heart will become proud, and you will forget the Lord your God, who brought you out of Egypt, out of the land of slavery.
>
> (Deuteronomy 8:10–14)

I tell you what, the Bible beats Freud for human psychology any day of the week. Isn't what this describes exactly what happens? When God prospers us and seems to make everything go well, we must remember to praise him. If we don't adopt the habit of worship, that habit of giving thanks even when there doesn't appear to be a lot to be thankful for, then when we eventually do come to the place of prosperity we lose the plot entirely and forget the Lord our God. The practice phase always starts in the desert, when there is less at stake. Once we have shown that we can keep going with God, then he trusts us with more.

THE DESERT FOR OUR OWN GOOD

In Luke chapter 4 the writer covers the phase of Jesus's life soon after he has been filled with the Holy Spirit in the River Jordan. Having been filled he gets led by the Spirit into the desert, where for forty days he is tempted by the devil. I find it interesting that Luke makes a point of telling us that the first thing the Holy Spirit did once he was hooked up with Jesus was to lead him into the desert. I don't know about you, but when I think there's a danger of me being led into the desert, I generally run the other way and do anything possible to avoid it.

But thankfully Jesus was not like me, and he allowed himself out of obedience to be led there. I don't think he went kicking and screaming either; I imagine that he was a willing son, prepared to do whatever it took to bring on the revelation of the goodness and faithfulness of the Creator God. Despite the devil's varied attempts at getting Jesus to give in to temptation, Jesus saw straight through him and answered him by quoting God's word from Scripture.

We too can learn to hear God's word more clearly when things in life are not going so well. It is important to remember that all is not lost forever – desert experiences only ever last for a specific season. If you can use them as a chance to stick your teeth into your faith, then the staleness will always give way to something much better. When Jesus returned from the desert – after God had allowed him to go through all that he needed him to go through – Luke makes it clear to us that he returned on top form: 'He returned to Galilee in the power of the Spirit.' Some of us love being filled by the Spirit, but if we're honest, we lack the sense of direction and purpose that accompanied Jesus' Spirit-filled return. Perhaps we get ourselves in these ruts because we gladly accept the Spirit's first introduction but resist the lead to follow him into the desert.

The main reason behind these difficult experiences can be found tucked away in the book of Hosea. Through the prophet God says, 'Therefore I am now going to allure her; I will lead her into the desert and speak tenderly to her' (Hosea 2:14). He leads us into the desert places too so that we will fall in love with him again.

The Song of Songs is one of the most unusual books in the whole Bible. If the censor had to put a classification on it, it would definitely be an 18. It's the story of a love affair between a king and a young lady, and traditionally Christians have taken it as a picture of Jesus' relationship as the King with us, his Church, as the young lady. In chapters 1 and 2 we see the lover wooing the young lady, which is followed by this in chapter 3:

All night long on my bed
I looked for the one my heart loves;
I looked for him but did not find him.
I will get up now and go about the city,
through its streets and its squares;
I will search for the one my heart loves.
So I looked for him but did not find him.
The watchmen found me
as they made their rounds in the city.
'Have you seen the one my heart loves?'
Scarcely had I passed them
when I found the one my heart loves.
I held him and would not let him go
till I had brought him to my mother's house,
to the room of the one who had conceived me.

(Song of Songs 1–4)

This is a desert experience. They had been close, spending
part of the evening together tenderly exchanging expressions
of love, but then he disappears, playing hide and seek. She
realises what she's missing and is unable to sleep at night, so
she gives up the comfort of her bed and wanders around the
deserted city searching for him. Eventually when she finds
him, in her joy she holds him and does not let him go. She
takes him to the most intimate place of all: the bedroom of
the one who conceived her. The desert is a place where the
Lord plays hide and seek for a while. He asks us – will we
forsake our comforts and search for him? The desert's the
place where we find out how much we love him.

It worked for the people who followed Moses, and it still
works for us today. When we are stripped of everything else
that would give us comfort, everything else that would meet
our emotional and sometimes physical needs, we come back
and fall in love with Jesus all over again.

6

Heart for the Lost

LOVING AS GOD LOVES

It took me a long time to realise that Christianity was more than a collection of rules and regulations. When I was fifteen I decided never to sin again. It didn't work. When I was seventeen I worked out that if I stuck enough 'Jesus – He's the real thing' stickers on immovable objects around Harrow, the second coming would be just around the corner. It wasn't. At the age of twenty-seven I was convinced that all I had to do to win God's love was set up and run a successful open youth group on my own, converting hundreds of ex-offenders along the way. I was wrong.

Thankfully in the middle of all my mess-ups, wrong turns and false starts I've discovered that God is no way near as obvious as we think he is. Instead of wanting to create an army of immaculate soldiers, I suspect that he would be a lot happier with a bunch of passionate and wild warriors. Put another way, God looks for the hidden treasure instead of the printed map. He's not solely after our doing great things for him (even though that is a wonderful aim), because all the spectacular deeds in the world count for little if we don't have the relationship with the Father.

Now that word 'relationship' might cause us a few problems. Are we to assume that we need to 'pull' God? (Not quite.) Do we just dump him when things get a little bit heavy? (Ideally not.) Does God want us to get to know him? (A definite yes.) You see, while it's not a carbon copy of them, relationship with God does have more to do with human relationships than we think. In fact, we've done ourselves and God no favours by separating in our minds the spiritual from the physical. We've put God in a box along with Sunday services, giving to charity and feeling bad. All the rest of our lives – the work, the romance, the pain and the bodily functions – we've stored well away from him. That's a shame, especially as God created us to experience and enjoy those things in the first place.

Any relationship is only as good as the communication that exists between two people. Sadly there are too many marriages around where both sides are so caught up with the minute details, the daily jobs and chores that sit at the front of their minds that they never really *talk*. The image of the tired dad coming home and slouching down in front of the TV for the duration of the evening has become so common that it hardly raises a smile. Talking, expressing ideas, hope, pain and sadness is the key to building strength in any relationship. Without it, not only do we miss out on getting to the heart of someone, but we are kept up on the surface where things soon get stale and dry.

This can happen with God. OK, so he may not be the TV dinner type, but if we don't commit ourselves to spending decent time with him, then we too can miss out on the prize of getting close to him, hearing what he has to say. Having a relationship with God means hooking up with him, down-loading data straight from his heart. It means spending time with him and sussing out exactly what it is that gets him excited and sad. It means being real, being honest with him about the good and the bad. Developing our relationship

172

with God is always on the agenda for us Christians, and in a way this whole series of books is designed to help us go further on and further in.

But hold on: as soon as you start moving in towards God you discover something strange. Just as you think you're going to cosy down with him, enjoying some one-on-one chat and niceness, God turns you around and sends you straight back out again. This is not due to a sudden fit of bad temper from God or bad breath from you, but due to the plain and simple truth that belongs at the heart of Christianity: God's heart is for the lost. Put in English, that means that God loves the poor, the oppressed and the lonely. He loves the underdog and is mighty keen that we step in line and follow his lead. He wants us to get out there just like he did, finding the people who don't know him and bringing them back on home where they belong. God's heart is for the lost.

PASSION FOR THE POOR

But how, you may ask, do we know what to do? Simple, comes the answer: just look at how God has got involved in the lives of his people. When the time came for God to make camp on earth by specifically choosing a nation to be known as *his* people, he made an interesting selection. If I were doing the picking I would have gone out and found the most talented, ferocious, cultured and intelligent people around. I would have picked the Greeks. They would have been brilliant, reflecting all the bits of my even more brilliant character.

Thankfully I'm not God. When it came to decision time God had one crew at the top of his list: the Israelites. They were the lowest of the low, slaves to a cruel race (the Egyptians). They were routinely beaten and killed, and were unable to stand up for themselves when Pharaoh decided to kill all the firstborn males. Calling them poor is an understatement, as their lack of cash was probably the last of their worries. They were the victims of oppression on a scale that we cannot imagine, and God wanted them.

Ah yes, you could be about to say, surely it was a case of finding a diamond in the rough – surely they were brilliant and wonderful underneath it all and God had done an *Antiques Roadshow* job, pulling out a gem from a load of old tat. Much as I'd like to go along with you there, I'm forced to disagree. Not only were they victims, but the Israelites were also a bit crap. Not long after they had been set free they started to whinge. They moaned so much that God decided to postpone their arrival in the promised land until they had learnt to trust and obey him. What was in fact a journey that should have taken a matter of months ended up lasting for forty years, simply because of their incessant whining.

But still God stayed with them. They were rightfully his and had been sinned against. That ignited a fiery passion within him that made him step in and intervene, particularly through faithful types like Moses. Over the years that followed he blessed, forgave, corrected and stuck by the people he had chosen over all the others. Why? Because he was committed to them, even when they were poor and lost. In time they wandered so far away from him that he sent his Son to bring not only them back, but also the rest of us.

The co-ordinates of Jesus' birth should come as no surprise; he was to be the most important man in the history of the world, but he was born a refugee. His words are still remembered today, yet he had no great political influence. He changed not only our lives, but also our deaths. He showed us exactly what God was like and he was born poor, oppressed and an outsider. Later, when he went about the business of setting up his team of workers that would change humanity for ever, he picked another bunch of intellectually challenged muppets. Do you see the pattern?

There's even more evidence on the bench when you start

to look at some of the things that Jesus did during the final years of his life. As well as being poor and hanging round with some of the less brilliant people in society, Jesus chose some even more obvious ways to express the nature of God's heart, by showing the full intensity of his emotions.

The killer passage for checking out Jesus' passion is probably when he raises Lazarus from the dead. He knew the family – Lazarus' sister Mary was the woman who poured perfume on his feet and wiped them with her hair – and it was obviously no secret that he and Lazarus were friends. Mary and her sister Martha sent a message out to Jesus telling him, 'Lord, the one you love is sick', but for some reason Jesus took his time getting there. When he eventually did arrive, Lazarus had been in his tomb for four days. Mary was understandably a little upset about this, and when she first saw Jesus she fell at his feet and told him that if he had been there earlier her brother would still be alive.

> When Jesus saw her weeping, and the Jews who had come along with her also weeping, he was deeply moved in spirit and troubled. 'Where have you laid him?' he asked.
> 'Come and see, Lord,' they replied.
> Jesus wept.
> Then the Jews said, 'See how he loved him!'
> But some of them said, 'Could not he who opened the eyes of the blind man have kept this man from dying?'
> Jesus, once more deeply moved, came to the tomb. It was a cave with a stone laid across the entrance. 'Take away the stone,' he said.
> 'But, Lord,' said Martha, the sister of the dead man, 'by this time, there is a bad odour . . .'
>
> (John 11:33–9)

That line about there being a bad odour has most certainly been cleaned up along the way. The Greek word could be better translated as 'stink', which is not surprising considering that the corpse had been festering in the heat for four days. By that time decomposition would have been well under way and the odour would have been a lot worse than a polite, handkerchief-to-the-nose 'bad'.

Then Jesus said, 'Did I not tell you that if you believed, you would see the glory of God?'

So they took away the stone. Then Jesus looked up and said, 'Father, I thank you that you have heard me. I knew that you always hear me but I said this for the benefit of the people standing here that they might believe that you sent me.'

When he had said this he called in a loud voice, 'Lazarus, come out!' The dead man came out, his hands and feet wrapped with strips of linen and a cloth around his face.

Jesus said to them, 'Take off the grave clothes and let him go.'

It's easy to lose some of the emotion in this passage. Jesus' little aside to God about saying thank you for the sake of the crowd makes it seem as though he was a smooth cabaret act. The 'bad odour' takes away from the reality that many of the people would have spontaneously thrown up when the stone was rolled away. The fact that Jesus held back for a couple of days before he left for Lazarus' town could lead us to think that he was pretty unfussed about the whole thing.

All of these interpretations detract from the fact that this is one of the most intense scenes in Jesus' life. His friend had died. He had spent quite a bit of time with Lazarus and his two sisters, but needed Lazarus to be completely kaput in order for his miracle to have maximum impact. Even though he was aware that he had the power to bring him back to life, Jesus must have found it hard to prolong the pain of a family that he knew and loved. Perhaps that is why he did stay away, as to be around them and sense their agony would have made it too difficult to hold out for such a long time.

ANGRY AT INJUSTICE

So even before Jesus arrives on the scene we can be sure that emotions were running high. As soon as he does turn up and meets Mary who is deeply distressed, he too is 'deeply moved in spirit and troubled'. Approaching the tomb he weeps.

Now for ages when I read that bit of Scripture I thought, 'Oh, that's nice; dear old Jesus wept with Mary.' I thought the fact that the Jews commented, 'See how much he loves him,' meant that he was deeply sympathetic to her pain. I have a suspicion now though, that this isn't the reason for the weeping. The word that is translated here as 'deeply moved' comes from the Greek word which could also be translated 'groaned inside'. Another way that the phrase could have been translated which would also have been completely justified would have been 'Jesus was livid'. But our translators, perhaps keen to maintain an image of Jesus as gentle, have deliberately left it ambiguous. I suspect that the harder translation is more accurate.

Jesus was so angry with the situation that, when he saw the people who had no hope weeping, people who had failed to realise that life stood in the midst of them, his emotions came to the surface for all to see.

If you don't believe that Jesus gets angry, then look at the passage again in which he walks into the court of the Gentiles in the temple where they've got a bit of a tuck shop going (see Mark 11:12–19). Seeing that they were selling stuff for profit in a place where they should have been worshipping, he was so angry that he made a kind of whip and beat them up. Whatever way you put it, he was angry.

And Jesus was angry in this situation, just as he is furious today with injustice, pain and oppression. He wept over one man's death, much as he weeps today over the people yet to find him through their spiritual life. Sometimes we like to think that Jesus sits in heaven and wrings his hands, wincing and worrying about things but without actually feeling passionate enough to do anything. That's wrong, for whenever he sees injustice and the lost, whenever he comes across that which conflicts with his nature, he cannot be anything other than 'deeply moved'.

Approaching the tomb and telling the people to open it, there was obviously a certain amount of doubt as to the wisdom of his plan. While people were worried about a hygiene risk, Jesus asked them if they wanted to see the glory of God. He gave the choice over to them, in a sense making them take responsibility for what happened next. Imagine if they'd moved the stone away and Jesus had said, 'Good, lads, I'm off.' They would have been in serious trouble for desecrating something that was, in Jewish culture, a holy thing. You didn't open up a grave, not if you wanted to carry on living.

They took the risk. Once the tomb was open, Jesus started praying. We're not sure how long it took, but you can be sure that with every passing moment, with every furtive glance back and forth between the hole and Jesus the tension would have increased. The tension wouldn't have been over once Jesus had shouted to Lazarus to come out either, as seeing a four-day-old corpse come shuffling out of a graveyard was hardly an everyday sight. I'm sure there would have been screams and tears of both delight and fear. Finally he told the people to take off Lazarus' grave clothes. Far from being a dry and clinical show of God's power, the raising of Lazarus was about as emotionally charged as you could possibly imagine.

Only Jesus can speak to the physically dead and bring them back to life. Only Jesus can speak to the spiritually dead and bring them back to life. He gets angry when he sees injustice and weeps when he sees the lost.

The old saying, 'If a job's worth doing it's worth doing yourself', probably means nothing to God. Sure he is infinitely more capable than any of us, but life for God is not just about efficiency: it's about relationship. Whenever God sees something to be done he looks around for his people to get stuck in. When he freed the Israelites he first called Moses. When he set up the Church, he first called the disciples. When he raised Lazarus from the dead he first got the mourners to pull back the stone. When Lazarus was out in the open Jesus told the people to remove his grave clothes, giving him a fresh start.

Don't get me wrong though: I'm not saying that we could accomplish all this on our own. Have you tried raising the dead recently? It's not the easiest of jobs to tackle. God created us so that he could share his love with us. We're still signed up for the partnership, and we're still in line for some jobs.

Just as he has done throughout history, God even today wants us to get closer to him in order to take his love out. He wants us to roll away the stones that separate others from him, whether that means releasing them from poverty or oppression or bringing light into their spiritual darkness. He wants us to take off the grave clothes, to disciple and rebuild the lives decomposed by the effects of long-term sin.

Jesus told us plain and simple that he only did what he saw the Father do. He also told us to go – to make disciples, to baptise, to teach and to love – in the same way that he did. We just cannot get out of the fact that God's heart beats wildly for his people, and that he is desperate to heal – using our hands.

This isn't the time to wait: this is the time to soak up some of the passion of our almighty God and see where we end up.

United We Stand

GLORY, GLORY . . .

Long before I was given my first trousers, I was given my first football pyjamas. And my first football comb. And my first football zip-up raincoat. In fact, as far as I was concerned, while there was still football merchandise being sold long trousers could go hang. I had so much football stuff that for over a year I had a recurring dream that my bedroom floor would give in under the weight of it all, sending me hurtling down towards the ground only to have my fall broken by the mid-field section of the 1967 Brighton and Hove Albion team. I don't know why it was Brighton and Hove Albion in the dream, since for as long as I can remember I have had eyes for one team and one team only: Manchester United. As a child I was obsessed with them, and everything I owned was red and white with their logo taking pride of place. By the time my knees were no longer seeing regular sunlight and my parents had got me into long trousers I had collected enough Man U merchandise to write to *The Guinness Book of Records* and ask if I was the biggest football fan in the world. I wasn't. Depressed by their cold-hearted reply I decided to get myself a life and reduce my level of support from visibly fanatical to quietly obsessive.

I'm proud to say that Man U and I are still going strong, and that like any true supporter I've never actually seen them play at Old Trafford. Being a Man U fan these days isn't easy though, especially with the people who've just climbed aboard since they've been winning everything. I was there when things were tough, when we won nothing, when the rain beat down hard upon the cold streets . . .

Sorry about that, it's just that those dark days still make me feel slightly emotional. Anyway, back to business. You see, the thing about supporting them is that in all the years that have passed I've never been so impressed as I was in the 1998–9 season. No other time can compare to the roller-coaster ride that took place from August to May, and it wasn't just the fact of winning the treble – a feat never before achieved in the history of English football – but it was the way we won that left me speechless. It is no exaggeration to say that United are now the English national team. But don't worry, I'm not writing this just to gloat – although that is a very pleasant by-product – I believe that there are some fundamental lessons that we Christians can learn from Manchester United's glory season.

BE PREPARED

Without doubt David Beckham is one of the best players in the world. In fact, when it comes to free kicks and corners, he's probably the best dead-ball specialist there has ever been. (In case you're wondering this means he's good at kicking the ball from a fixed position, not that he's good when there's no air left inside it, although I wouldn't put it past him.) The Adidas TV advert that accompanied the 1998 World Cup showed him curling a ball round a huge stone structure and into a less than huge gap. Obviously the lad's got talent, but if you think he got where he is today

182

simply because of his gifting, you would be wrong.

I've got an interview with Beckham on video in which he's asked what the secret is of his goal scoring abilities. 'I practised, that's what I done,' he replies. 'When I was a kid I used to kick a ball against the wall for hours. I'd kick it with my right foot, and then I'd kick it with my left foot. I'd kick it with my dad and I'd kick it on my own. I practised, that's all I done.'

He's not alone, as his best mate Gary Neville, the United and England defender, will admit. Neville's not the most naturally talented footballer in the world, and as a schoolboy he was the one watching from the side while his brother played for England. United boss Alex Ferguson has said that what impressed him about Gary Neville was his dedication. When the training session is over and all the others are climbing into their Italian suits, little Gary will be on his own going back out onto the pitch to practise some more. His skill and talent have been developed by sheer hard work, making him now one of the best defenders in England.

So what's my point? Well, as Christians we are often exceptionally talented at waiting for God to wave his magic wand and make our lives wonderful. We hang around with folded arms waiting for a chance to do something in public – whether it's playing in a band, preaching or leading a project – unwilling to put any serious hard graft in. Sometimes we'll sit back and declare to God that it's up to him to land us a top job in a prestigious company without even considering that we might have to play a part in the delivery.

This is partly because we have made things too spiritual and partly because we're lazy. The spiritual thing is a result of our believing that if we just pray hard enough then God will sort everything out. Unfortunately that's not the way it works. Think about Jesus – wouldn't it have been easier for God to get involved with some hefty spiritual warfare up there in the spiritual realm than send his own Son down to spend over three decades working hard as a human? No, God knows the value of hard work and we need to do a little revision.

Because we rule out the option of taking some of the responsibility for things ourselves, we seem to spend a fair amount of time staring at closed or only slightly open doors. Too many Christians are lazy with their gifts and then wonder why God doesn't use them more. When David (the king, that is) was anointed by Samuel to be king over Israel you might have expected him to hang around the palace until the coronation, soaking up the vibes and getting accustomed to a life of luxury. After all, being king was an important position, and surely it would have made sense to get acquainted with things. Instead young King David went back to being a shepherd and worked hard at being the best shepherd that he could. While he was busy doing that, God made sure that nothing was wasted, and with the sheep he learned many skills which were to come in useful later on. He learned the lessons of battle as he fought with the lions and bears which tried to attack his sheep. They were particularly useful when it came to sorting out fat-boy Goliath, but were also helpful when he took on the role of commander of his army later on. Caring for his flock taught him how to care for his people, pastoring and leading them through treacherous circumstances. He also wrote his best worship song (Psalm 23) out on the hills as the little bleaters were grazing. Like Moses – who received his preparation for the task of leading Israel out of slavery by spending forty years in the desert – David's teaching ground was unglamorous, private and dangerous.

Even the Lord Jesus had thirty years of preparation for three years of ministry. If David Beckham and Gary Neville were willing to prepare themselves so thoroughly in order to be the best footballers they could be, why aren't we training ourselves and preparing for the highest calling we could have: to serve the living God. If your passion is to lead worship, don't wait until you are asked to play at Soul Survivor or Spring Harvest; prepare now, practise on your musical instrument now, wait on the Lord now. If you think your calling is to be an evangelist, learn all you can about communication skills now, read all the evangelistic books you can now. Whatever your dream, kick the ball against the wall now, and then when the opportunity comes you will be ready.

BE FAMILY

Footballers aren't known for being the most self-sacrificing and humble of people. They earn vast sums of money and work in an industry that constantly compares them against each other. When it comes to most teams, it doesn't take much to see the cracks and work out where the divisions and disharmony lie. One of the unusual and extraordinary things about Manchester United is the way the team seem to get on so well. When Dwight Yorke arrived at the beginning of the season the press was having a field day speculating about whether he would replace their other main striker Andy Cole. For weeks the contest was talked up and the two players were portrayed as rivals for the same position. What happened behind the scenes was that they quickly became best friends off the pitch and established an inspiring rapport on it as a result. After a couple of months most people agreed that Andy Cole had become a better player since Dwight Yorke arrived.

When Beckham was sent off in that fateful World Cup game against Argentina he became one of the most hated men in England. There were death threats, burning effigies, rumours that the only way he could ever survive in the game would be to move to an Italian club for a couple of years. Back home where he belonged though, his manager and teammates rallied round in his time of need and supported him in many ways. He stayed, worked through it, and within months had fought his way back to the top and regained the respect he had lost. Beckham has even been quoted as saying that as a result of all the support he received he wants to play for Manchester United for the rest of his career.

If there can be such a sense of team spirit in a football club, how much more should that be evident in the Church of Jesus Christ? We are commanded by our Lord to love one another as he has loved us. Try reading that line again . . . love each other as he loved us. Considering that Jesus' love took him all the way to the cross, I would say that loving each other in the same manner is a pretty radical thing. One of the images of the Church in the Bible is that of family. Instead, all too often there is backbiting, competitiveness and gossip. We sometimes seem to forget that we are all playing on the same side, and get weighed down with concepts of right and wrong. You don't even have to go so far as to look at the wars that have been fought in the name of Christianity, as you talk to many churchgoers, sadly most local churches will be defined more by the things that people are unhappy with rather than the things that they like.

We are often uncomfortable at church. We tell other people what we think they want to hear – spiritual whitewash that has about as much to do with the reality of how we are actually feeling as drinking a sports drink makes you fit. Instead of being honest we tell people that everything is just fine, that 'me and the Lord are doing well'. What we really want to say is, 'I don't like church and I don't even know if God exists any more.' We've all been there but few of us have actually admitted it at the time. But if we cannot be honest, how then can we be close? If we cannot be real, how can we be family? Do you think that Beckham would have been so touched by the reception that his team-mates gave him if it had gone along the lines of 'Never mind old chap, so what if you are hated by every football supporter in England? Isn't the pitch looking lovely today?'

No, real families are made up of real people, ones that call difficulties exactly what they are, and don't skirt round them with 'Oh yes, but isn't the Lord good'. Jesus never shied away from expressing his stronger emotions: he wept at Lazarus' tomb, was in torment in the garden of Gethsemane, got livid in the temple (twice) and preached with all the passion of someone who knows he is right. If we are going to follow him, church should be a place where we are free to express exactly how we feel, safe in the knowledge that it will provide love and support without strings or condemnation.

PLAY FOR THE TEAM

One of the players I most admired at United during the 1998/9 season was the Norwegian international Ole Gunner Solskjaer. He started out most matches as a substitute, but in the relatively short time that he spent on the pitch, he managed to notch up for himself more goals than the scorers at fourteen out of the twenty-one other clubs in the premiership. When it came to the F.A. Cup final, Solskjaer found himself in the starting line-up in his favourite forward position. After five minutes of the game the United skipper Roy Keane went off injured and Teddy Sheringham was brought on to replace him. Solskjaer had to switch positions to the right wing where, playing out of position, he frankly did not excel. A reason to be unhappy, you may think, but that's not true. As one match commentator said at the time, Solskjaer had 'sacrificed himself for the sake of the team'. He played where he was least comfortable and least likely to shine simply because it was exactly what the team needed at that moment.

Many Christians could learn a valuable lesson from

Solskjaer. Instead of always wanting to be the one scoring the spiritual goals, we need to ask ourselves if we are willing to sometimes serve in an area which is not our favourite. For the sake of the team, for the sake of the Kingdom, are we prepared to do something that goes unnoticed, something that could easily be ignored, let alone forgotten? Are you a team player or are you a lone ranger Christian, striding on ahead of the rest, pursuing your own spiritual ambitions while the rest of the team are wondering where you've got to? In the Kingdom there is only one hero, Jesus, and if we are ever going to achieve our goal of making disciples of all nations we have to learn to play as a team under his captaincy.

NEVER GIVE UP

There is so much teaching in the Bible about persistence, and of all their many attributes, the one for which Manchester United will be remembered the most is that they refused to give up. In the F.A. Cup quarter-final against Liverpool, United were one–nil down with two minutes to go. When the final whistle blew after two minutes of injury time they had won two–one. In the Champions' League semi-final against Juventus they were two–nil down going into the second half. They won three–two. Most famously of all, they were losing to Bayern Munich in that great final with ninety minutes gone. Those two goals, first by Sheringham and then by Solskjaer with virtually the last kick of the match, are moments no United fan will ever forget. Sir Alex Ferguson said after the match, 'These players just don't know how to give in.' You could say there was an element of luck in the way they scored last-minute goals so many times, but they made their own luck by perseverance and persistence.

Winston Churchill was once asked what he thought the secret of leadership was. His reply was, 'Never give in, never give in, never give in.' Surely as the children of the Almighty who know we are on the winning side, we ought to never grow weary but persist in doing good. That means refusing to ditch the faith whenever we get knocked back. It means carrying on with God despite the fact that church may be frustrating or our leaders might be sad. Sticking with Jesus in the face of ridicule and pressure is something we will all have to do if we want to grow up in our relationship with God. Like any marriage, sacking the whole thing at the slightest disagreement is a foolish waste, and God has so much in store for us that to drop him whenever we feel like it is a choice I hope you and I never make. Steve Chalke, a TV presenter and the director of Oasis Trust, was once asked what he considered to be his greatest strength. His reply surprised me. He said, 'I'm a plodder. I keep going. Whether it's a good day or a bad day, I put my head down and keep going.'

Let us be ready for all that God has for us. Let us encourage and support one another. Let us serve one another and put each other first. And then let us play the match with all we have until we hear the final whistle. That's what Man United do – just think how much more we could achieve if we set our minds to it.

8

The Next Step

FEELING USELESS

Ever get that feeling that you're on your own? You know how it goes – a holiday draws to a close and you find yourself back at home, dealing with a come-down that makes everything seem grey and pointless. I get it a lot – coming back from trips abroad or festivals where I've seen the most amazing things happen and have felt 100 per cent on fire for God. Often, the journey back will be my time to think about things and get excited about what I might be in line for seeing God do next. Something happens on the way through the front door though, as usually by the time I've picked up the post and put my bags down, I've forgotten everything that had me feeling so great just moments before. I feel dull and hopeless, and in desperate need of some Chinese therapy. Usually a bag full of beef in black bean sauce with a double helping of banana fritters helps to pull me through the next few hours, but I'm still a mere shadow of my former turbo-charged self.

Knowing that it's going to hit me doesn't help much either, as everything I've tried in an effort to avoid the homecoming blues has more or less failed to keep me from feeling down.

I've tried having friends over, walking through the door backwards and not returning home at all. All that these left me with was a sense of extreme embarrassment that I left the flat in such a state before the trip, a severe bruise on the back of my head and a warning from the chairwoman of my local neighbourhood watch scheme that if I spent one more night sleeping in my car she would be forced to have me arrested on suspicion of being an illegal immigrant.

In short, when I'm at the end of a trip, I'm useless. I might have been preaching as well as I possibly can, maybe even using some of my own material instead of stealing it from other people, but as soon as the environment changes I feel like I'm about as wise as a cardboard monkey.

I was whining about this to a friend of mine recently when he told me to shut up and use my brain. I tried, but nothing happened. He told me to think about the disciples, about how they felt at the end of their trip with Jesus. Again, no result. Eventually, after a lot of work, it became clear. If ever there was a trip to have a come-down from, it was immediately after the death of Jesus. Imagine how close they must have grown – living together for three years, seeing things that no one else had ever seen before. In time they realised that they were hanging around with the Messiah, the man who had been prophesied about and who every fellow Jew was waiting for. To talk about their time together in terms of a buzz doesn't do it justice, but it does explain that they had every reason to feel low afterwards.

Guess what? There's a *but* coming. You see, Jesus knew this – being fully man he knew how they would feel – and so he put them through an intense course during their final days together, preparing them for the future. Jesus' life was too important to be confined to the photo album; it had to carry on, and Jesus made sure that the people he had chosen to train were well equipped to carry things on after he had gone. More importantly, though, Jesus knew that in speaking to the disciples, he was speaking to all Christians that would sign up with him in the years to come. Jesus was speaking to us, telling us how to carry on, how to live our lives in a way that would keep us going forward instead of slouching in a corner complaining about how things aren't so much fun when Jesus isn't around to give a spectacular display of spiritual fireworks.

First of all he left us with a great commandment. Matthew 22:37–40 is our own personal mission statement, pre-packed and sealed for guaranteed satisfaction any place, any time. 'What is the greatest commandment?' asked one of the religious big boys.

> Jesus replied: ' "Love the Lord your God with all your heart and with all your soul and with all your mind." This is the first and greatest commandment. And the second is like it: "Love your neighbour as yourself." All the Law and the Prophets hang on these two commandments.'

This summary that Jesus left us with really couldn't put things any clearer. Into our life-stew should go just two basic ingredients: a full-on love for God and a sacrificial love for those around us.

He also left us with cooking instructions. Later on in the book of Matthew we find Jesus' final words, generally referred to as the Great Commission.

> Then Jesus came to them and said, 'All authority in heaven and on earth has been given to me. Therefore go and make disciples of all nations, baptising them in the name of the Father and of the Son and of the Holy Spirit, and teaching them to obey everything I have commanded you. And surely I am with you always, to the very end of the age.'
>
> (Matthew 28:18–20)

So there we have it – the ingredients and the method. The Great Commandment tells us how we are to live and the Great Commission tells us why we've been left on planet earth. Jesus made it so clear, breaking it down into such bite-sized portions that even the most awkward among us can be clear about what we Christians should be doing.

POWER TO LIVE

Obviously now that I've reached the age of forty-one I've started to entertain the possibility that at some point in the future I might not be on the cutting-edge of contemporary fashion. It's understandable, I suppose, but still, after so long spent being so cool, it does feel funny to think about one day sitting back and letting new things take over. I decided to get in some practice on this recently. Midway through one summer I started to notice that not everyone was following my fashion lead by wearing nylon smocks covered with African art. It seemed that someone was convincing them to opt for a different trend, namely bracelets. Now, I've never really been into jewellery, but I had to admit that this particular fashion had gone big time.

These fabric bracelets were everywhere – assuming you were at a Christian festival, that is – and on them were embroidered the letters WWJD. Standing for What Would Jesus Do?, some clever American businessperson with a flair for marketing had developed a whole lifestyle around a simple product. The idea with them was that the wearer would have a constant reminder to think about what Jesus would do at any given time. This all kind of ties in with the Great Stew mentioned above, especially as loving God and your neighbours as well as making disciples are things that can apply to any situation we find ourselves in.

I don't think that it was because I was jealous or feeling left out, but as I thought about them, something didn't quite fit. Let me explain. In case you've picked up and have only started reading the book at this late stage, I am a Manchester United supporter. It stands to reason, therefore, that one of my main heroes is Mr Beckham. He's an inspirational player, and definitely a good on-the-pitch role-model for any fan (assuming that we have forgiven him for responding to a provoked attack from Simeone in the World Cup game against Argentina in 1998). If I played football – and I don't – I would definitely consider wearing a WWBD? bracelet. Lining up for a free kick I would glance down and ask myself, what would Beckham do? The answer would come back in the form of one of those *Match of the Day* highlights, with our David curling the ball around the wall, past the scrambling goalie and into the top right-hand corner of the net. Simple. Or maybe we're in the park, right in the middle of some free-flowing play. Spoddy Harris has made a darting run down the left wing and I'm faced with a couple of midfield thugs bearing down on me with the intention of doing some serious bodily harm to my fragile frame. What would Beckham do? He'd take the ball to them, move it over to one side and deliver a perfectly placed pass onto the Spodster, leaving him with an open goal and no pressure from the thugs. Again, beautifully simple. But, back to reality, what would I do? In the case of a free kick I'd probably mistime my approach, drive my foot into the ground, spraining my ankle and leaving the ball untouched. When it comes to thugs the chances are that I'd leave the ball where it was, forget about Spoddy Harris and make a run for the safety of the touchline. It's all very well *knowing* what he would do, the trick is being *able* to carry it off.

David Beckham can do a whole load of things that I can't do: he can play football, pull a Spice Girl and wear his clothes with style and panache. Even though some have said that I do remind them of him, having a WWBD? thing on my arm would be worse than useless, it would actually be incredibly frustrating. And so we come back to the Bible. Just to have the Great Commandment and the Great Commission is not enough. To have a constant reminder of what we ought to be doing is helpful, it certainly gives us something to aim at, but if we have trouble trying to copy Becks, how the heck can we hope to pull off a decent imitation of the Son of God?

Thankfully, Jesus saw this problem before it happened, and prepared for us the ultimate antidote to the frustration that comes from not being able to reach our goals. He gave us power. We're not just talking about the power to blag it or the power to fool others, but the raw power to do what he did, and then some.

The book of Acts kicks off with a description of the time Jesus spent with his disciples after he had risen from the dead. At one meal time he told them not to leave Jerusalem until they had received the gift that had been promised. When they pressed him for some more info on this, asking whether it meant the end of time, he replied:

> He said to them: 'It is not for you to know the times or dates the Father has set by his own authority. But you will receive power when the Holy Spirit comes on you; and you will be my witnesses in Jerusalem, and in all Judea and Samaria, and to the ends of the earth.'
>
> (Acts 1:7–8)

When Jesus gave the Great Commission he didn't leave us powerless or unable to follow through. Instead he packaged it up as part of the ultimate Two-for-One deal: If you sign up for the vision, you get the power. But, unlike most Two-for-One deals, this is a darn sight more useful than 1.5 litres of extra non-biological colour-fast washing liquid. This power is dynamite, and with it, the early Church changed the shape of things to come. If you don't believe me all you have to do is read through the book of Acts and check out for yourself the intense relationship that existed between the way they relied on the power that Jesus had given them through the Holy Spirit and the mind-blowing rate of growth that the Church experienced.

They were effective in ways that we as a Church today long to be effective – they reached all sectors of society, exploded with a force never before seen and took beatings and persecution without dropping their belief that Jesus was their ultimate Saviour. In short, the early Church were riding high on a cocktail of obedience and power. Guess what, it's still on the menu.

Some of us need to be reminded of the fact that Jesus gave us the power to carry out the 'To Do' list that he left us with. Some of us need to be reminded that Jesus' offer still stands, and that all we have to do is step up and take it. Of course, doing this means that we have to acknowledge the fact that we *can't* do things in our own strength. It means humbling ourselves and admitting that without God's help, we are unable to achieve all that is expected of us. No matter how intelligent, charming, good-looking or threatening we are, winning the lost for God is totally dependent on our using God's power. What Acts shows us is a practical outworking of the power of God in run-of-the-mill daily situations; it was there to give them boldness when they preached, to give them a love for one another as well as the poor so that they could carry out the works of the Kingdom. But it also meant that they could perform signs and wonders that accompanied their preaching, it meant that they had the power to set people free.

I am convinced that God wants to release that power on us again so that our words and actions would have that extra bite that transforms them into building blocks for the Kingdom of God. I'm not saying that God ever withdrew his gifts, I'm just convinced that we have spent far too long ignoring the fact that Jesus gave us a helping hand. Just like me when I get back from a trip and feel miserable, we've been doing things in our own strength, forgetting that Jesus offers us the power to see things through, the power to rise above our own strength and onto another level.

There's another treat at the bottom of our stocking though: Jesus didn't just give us the power to follow the rules, he also gave us the power to change and become more like him. In John 15 we get a wonderful picture of Jesus as the vine with us as the branches. 'If you remain in me and my words remain in you,' Jesus tells us, 'you will bear fruit.' That means that we don't just have the opportunity to produce more signs of being like Christ, but that we actually can *become* more like Christ, as the fruit is the character of Jesus in our lives.

I don't know about you, but I certainly could do with a helping dose of change. I need to be more like the kind of Mike Pilavachi that God had in mind when he made me and less of the kind of Mike Pilavachi that has since been moulded by the world around me. I've tried changing in my own strength; I've tried concentrating, dieting and shouting my way towards perfection, but nothing has worked. I need the power of Jesus to complete the job – and just in the same way that I need him for salvation, I also need him for the power to change.

Sitting in my car outside my flat, a delicate hum coming from my bag stuffed full of unclean pants and industrially toxic socks, I have sometimes wondered whether it would be possible to pull myself out of the grouchy mood I'm in and put a brave face on it. Possibly, but unlikely. The trouble is that emotions are strong things, and the chances of me being able to override them are a little on the slim side.

GOD'S AUTHORITY

The thing about Jesus is that he not only talked about power, he talked about authority. He didn't just give us the ability to follow his lead, he also had the authority that sent him straight to the head of the queue. His Father had given him authority to act with the full weight of heaven behind him, and that weight meant that he could go right to the heart of things. Think of it as if you were an amazing dancer, able to outgroove any person in any club. The trouble comes when you try to get in – the bouncers don't like you and stop you from entering the clubs. Imagine having a pass that allowed you to swan past even the most grumpy of doormen. You can get in and shake your booty wherever you want and everything's lovely. The power is the moves and the authority is the pass.

For an example of this just think about the story of Jesus healing the paralytic man (Mark 2:1–12). Midway through a seminar in someone's house, a hole appears in the roof and down comes a guy on a mat. His mates were lowering him down, and amidst the chaos and confusion, Jesus performed one of his most significant miracles. He looked at him and said, 'Your sins are forgiven.' This was like going from the frying pan into the fire, and the place erupted. The top-dog religious people simply couldn't understand what made Jesus think that he had the authority to forgive someone's sin. More or less Jesus replied that he forgave sins by the same authority that he told people to walk; in other words, his was a direct power-feed from heaven, and he had the ability to act as God, forgiving sins and restoring life.

There was another incident with a high-ranking Roman soldier (Matthew 8:5–13). His servant was ill and he needed Jesus' help. Unusually, though, he didn't ask Jesus to come and visit the boy. This centurion recognised something in Jesus that others missed; he recognised that Jesus was far and away more in control of the situation than many suspected. People knew he could perform miracles, but remote miracles? Ones where he was a long way off and unable to lay hands on the patient?

The centurion gave away his thoughts by opening up his conversation with Jesus with a chat about authority. He told Jesus that he didn't need to visit, but just to say the word and his servant would be healed. The soldier told Jesus that he understood the nature of authority, especially as he was the kind of guy who was used to giving orders and seeing them carried out. His faith impressed Jesus, so much so that he commented how he had not seen faith as strong in the whole of Israel. He did as he was asked and healed the lad. The centurion understood that it wasn't only about power, but that the ability to harness the influence of heaven made all the difference.

This relates to us in the Church today. We've got kind of used to the idea of power being around – we've seen people healed and lives changed – but we've forgotten that we do actually have authority over all things. Now authority might not be the coolest of words to use – after all, these days we're into each person being right and no one being wrong – but it's true; when it comes to the crunch, God has allowed us to hitch a ride on the back of his power and claim some of it for ourselves.

Read how Jesus sent the disciples out to do his work:

When Jesus had called the Twelve together, he gave them power and authority to drive out all demons and to cure diseases, and he sent them out to preach the kingdom of God and to heal the sick.

(Luke 9:1–2)

That was the twelve. Later he does it with a group of seventy-two. Throughout the book of Acts we can see how even more of the first followers respond to this sending out from Jesus. They were persecuted and they were weak. They had martyrs and they went without any of the legal protection that we have today, but they had *real* power and *real* authority because it came from heaven above.

Not long ago I spent ten days in California speaking at a festival. Three of us went out there to do what we thought was a 'normal' trip, giving out to other people, praying and all that stuff. I tell you, we returned in a complete state. We were exhausted but on the biggest spiritual high we had ever been on. We had stayed with a family who were 100 per cent committed to praying for people and hearing from God 100 per cent of the time. It didn't matter where we were – having a meal, getting ready to go out or driving in the car – they were always on the look out for actively getting Jesus involved in the situation. Not only did we get some physical healing, but we also had some amazingly profound things told us that just had to be from God. It was astounding how accurate they were, and coming back, I almost got tempted to feel a bit down and to start to miss it. Somehow my mood didn't go any further, and I started thinking about what Jesus had done for us. The only difference between the Californian family and me was that they knew that they had the power and authority that came direct from heaven. Knowing that, their lives were a rollercoaster of faith in action.

God's power and authority are continually on offer to us. There is no need for us to beg for them; they've already been given. All that remains is for us to reach out and take them. Finally, let's not get sold the lie of thinking that power and authority are optional extras, put up on offer just to make the ride a little smoother, should we need them. Let's not get it into our heads that we're too cool or too cynical to grab hold of Jesus-style acts of power and authority. This is important, so much so it could be what makes the difference between sitting grumpily on the sidelines, complaining that

God never uses us and being in the thick of it, enjoying the full extent of the essence of God. If we are to reach the lost we need to preach the gospel with wise and persuasive words and all the tools and gifts that he has given us. But more than that, we need to obey the Great Commandment – loving the Lord with all that we have as well as loving our neighbour as we love ourselves – as when the world sees a Church that's in love with its God and loving towards themselves it will be attracted to that God. We also need to know that the Great Commission is for us. Right here. Right now.

Weeping Before an
Empty Tomb

Struggling with God

Mike Pilavachi with Craig Borlase

Hodder & Stoughton
LONDON SYDNEY AUCKLAND

To Ken and Jeannie Morgan.
Thank you for your faithful 'partnership in the gospel'
for all these years. May there be many more to come.

Contents

1 Weeping Before an Empty Tomb   207
   Mary's Story
2 Wasted Dreams   213
   Joseph's Story
3 Wasted Potential   225
   Samson's Story
4 When Bad Things Happen to Good People   237
   Job's Story
5 When We Mess Up   253
   David's Story
6 When You're Just Not Sure   265
   Thomas's Story
7 Beyond the Tomb   277
   Paul's Story

1

Weeping Before
an Empty Tomb
Mary's Story

Picture me at the age of sixteen; lithe, witty, intelligent and charming, wearing the very latest in three-tone brown tank tops and riddled with all the confusion of a young man who had just discovered that girls were nice but almost impossible to talk to. It was at this age that I wrote painful poetry and tried to work out the meaning of life in Harrow. It was also at this age that my dad made me the best promise ever.

It was 1974 and my dad had, for some reason that I still have trouble working out, gone out one day and bought a brand-new car. Looking out of my bedroom window I was amazed to see him cruise around the corner in a limited edition, black, three-door Fiat Cinquecento. I was amazed, proud and scared witless (my first thought being that my dad had become a member of the local Greek Mafia). I soon calmed down though and allowed my natural boyish fascination with all things mechanical/dangerous to take over. I cooed, wowed and dribbled over it with such intensity that I hardly noticed that my dad was trying to talk to me.

'Mike, this is for you. As soon as you're seventeen and have passed your test you can have it.'

Pretty soon I was hyperventilating with excitement. This was without doubt the best present I had ever been given and the euphoria stayed around for days. I thought about it, dreamt about it and told all my friends, ex-friends and total strangers all about My New Car. I was – to put it mildly – on a buzz.

Not everyone believed me, which was a shame but perhaps not all that surprising. What did surprise me, though, was the fact that a few months after that wonderful day, my dad started using *my car*. He said that it was just because his had broken down, and at first he insisted that his borrowing changed nothing. The months went by, his car went to the scrapheap and my old man settled back into the regular comfort of the Fiat. My Fiat. The Ex-Mike Fiat. By the time I was seventeen and eligible to take my test the car was well and truly the property of Mr P Senior. Little P junior – embarrassed, disappointed and upset – was left to stew.

And stew I did. Instead of carrying out the plan I had hatched a year earlier (which involved taking my test as near to the stroke of midnight on my seventeenth birthday as test centre opening hours would allow), I acted as if learning to drive was the last thing on my mind. To prove that I was not hurt I pushed all driving ambitions to the back of my mind. In fact, I made such a big deal of it not being a big deal that it wasn't until I was twenty-eight that I finally got round to learning how to drive.

But as well as being on foot for most of my late teens and twenties, I had also set up a few new rules about how I would go about things; I vowed that I wouldn't ever believe people when they made promises; I told myself to do whatever was necessary to avoid disappointment.

We've all had disappointments in life. Some of them have been the result of our own failings, while others have been caused by the let-downs of others. Whatever the story, coming face to face with the stark realisation that life isn't quite what we thought is common ground for us all.

Mary Magdalene knew about disappointment.

> Then the disciples went back to their homes, but Mary
> stood outside the tomb crying. As she wept, she bent over
> to look into the tomb and saw two angels in white, seated
> where Jesus' body had been, one at the head and the other
> at the foot. They asked her, 'Woman, why are you crying?'
> 'They have taken my Lord away,' she said, 'and I don't
> know where they have put him.'
>
> (John 20:10–13)

Mary was so upset, so gutted that all she could see was her
own pain. 'They' had taken away *her* master. Perhaps there is
even a note of self-pity creeping in there, but looking
elsewhere in the Gospels it's clear that there is more to her
than meets the eye. It is pretty much accepted that Mary
Magdalene and Mary the sister of Martha were one and the
same. In Luke 7:37 she is described as a 'woman who had
lived a sinful life' – a polite way of calling her a prostitute or
a woman who slept around. Jesus was probably the first man
who had ever shown her true respect and dignity, who had
loved her not for what he could get out of her, but simply to
give to her. Jesus changed her life and gave her hope for the
future. We see this in the retelling of her pouring the alabaster
jar of expensive perfume all over Jesus' feet (John 12). She
was so grateful to him that she would have given everything.
I wonder if she ever thought that it was he who had already
given everything for her.

Once Jesus had been crucified, everything changed for
Mary. All her assumptions about life changed. She had spent
most of her life as an outcast, confined to the fringes by
polite society, but in Jesus she had found acceptance. Perhaps
there had been a thought in the back of her mind that it may
have been too good to be true, and with him now dead her

worst fears had been realised. Kneeling before the empty tomb, peering in to see what had happened, Mary was too consumed by her own grief to notice that what she thought were guards were really angels. At this, she turned around and saw Jesus standing there, but she did not realise that it was Jesus.

'Woman,' he said, 'why are you crying? Who is it you are looking for?'

Thinking he was the gardener, she said, 'Sir, if you have carried him away, tell me where you have put him, and I will get him.'

(John 20:15)

Of course Jesus knew exactly who it was that she was looking for, but for Mary, the empty tomb represented a lifetime of hurt and disappointment; of let-downs, foul-ups and the fast-fading echoes of a promise that might have been but – so she thought – never was. So consumed was she with her own grief that she actually mistook Jesus – whose death acted as the trigger for her anguish – for the gardener. She wasn't having a very good day, yet all it took to turn it around was one word:

Jesus said to her, 'Mary.'

She turned towards him and cried out in Aramaic, 'Rabboni!' (which means Teacher).

Jesus said, 'Do not hold on to me, for I have not yet returned to the Father. Go instead to my brothers and tell them, "I am returning to my Father and your Father, to my God and your God." '

Mary Magdalene went to the disciples with the news: 'I have seen the Lord!' And she told them that he had said these things to her.

(John 20:17–18)

Many of us are kneeling in front of our own empty tombs; the pain of a divorce, a father who left us or a relationship that never worked out right. There may have been an accident or the pain may have been deliberate. It may have been a car that was never given or the realisation of wasted potential. We too can be so consumed with peering into these tombs of ours that we fail to recognise Jesus standing right by us. OK, so we may not actually be constantly hallucinating about gardeners, but you get my point, yes? It's all too easy to miss out on God when things are going wrong for us.

The answer? We need, like Mary, to hear him call our name. Then we need to embrace him, turning our focus from the tomb and placing it on him. Does that mean we should all be Black Belt Stiff Upper Lippers? No way – Jesus didn't take Mary from the cemetery right away, nor did he say, 'Cheer up, love.' No, there's a gap in the story that comes between Mary recognising Jesus and him saying, 'Let·go, Mary.' Why let go? Because she was hugging him, right there and right then. He gave her permission to be genuine about her emotions with him, at the same time as presenting himself as the solution. That's what we need to be able to do too; to avoid the wallowing but not resist the welling-up. We need to be genuine, to allow the pain out, but also to look for the life on the other side of it all.

Of course all this can sound a little too easy, a little too trite and contrived – you know, just add water and all the pain will go away. Let's get it straight; that's not what this one's about. This book is about facing up to the real issues that present themselves to us as Christians and to those who aren't. We need to take a good long practical look at how Jesus – the risen saviour – can set us free from the disappointments, doubts, fears and brokenness of our lives.

'Out of our difficulties
grow miracles.'
Jean de la Bruyère

2

Wasted Dreams
Joseph's Story

Over the years I have met a lot of Christians who have been characterised by one major trait: disappointment. I'm not talking about the wrong-sized socks at Christmas or a badly fitted filling, but real disappointment, the sort that stops you in your tracks, turning life a damp shade of grey. Why so? In almost all the situations that I'm thinking of, the disappointment is linked by a common theme: wasted dreams. To those of my friends who feel this way, nothing it seems is more draining of spiritual zeal than the failing of a dream.

But these people aren't alone, as I'm convinced that most of us go through at least one period where plans and aspirations appear to have come to nothing. We may have been fired up on inspired visions of tremendous works that we could do for the Lord, or perhaps we have been holding on to a promise that we believe came direct from God about how he would use us in the future. It may be that our plans were centred on having the ideal family unit – the cutely gap-toothed kids and the powerful estate on the driveway – or the ideal career combining money and power. This despair can affect us all, regardless of our beliefs. As the thinker Thoreau once said, most of us 'live lives of quiet desperation'.

But why do we go through these feelings? For many of us the reasons aren't so far beneath the surface as we might like to think. As time moves on and our bodies shuffle on from youth towards the inevitable, we are forced to replace the 'live forever' attitude of our younger days with a more measured 'pensions and central heating' orientated view of things. In short, we grow up, and that is the problem; for no one can dream dreams quite as magnificently as they did when they were a child.

Let's not limit ourselves to the middle-aged though. Just because they're called mid-life crises doesn't mean they come along only in the middle of our lives. I read a story about a public schoolboy who went missing from his room one day. His housemaster couldn't find him and, on questioning his friends, all he could find out was that the pupil had sold all his CDs just one week before. Eventually he came across a note. Fearing the worst, he read on. It went something like this:

> I've had enough. I can't take the pressure of knowing that my life is already mapped out in front of me while I have no power to change it. Things are moving too fast and I have no time to think. I need time to think. I'll be back when I'm ready.

The boy – who had just completed his GCSEs the previous summer – had sold his music to buy a one-way ticket to Tobago. The note explained how he was going to fly out and meet up with a fisherman whom he had met while on holiday there a summer or two ago.

The reason why this story struck me as so interesting was because of the language of the note; feeling that time is running out, that life is all mapped out in front of you and that you are powerless to alter course is something that we associate far more often with middle-aged business people, weighed down by the burdens of finance and people. To hear them from a sixteen-year-old is – to say the least – unusual. But I know how he felt. The sensation of being trapped is never nice. Actually that's not entirely true; I once dreamt that I was trapped in a parallel universe where the currency was Sweet and Sour Pork and I was a millionaire. It wasn't so bad. What's so bad about feeling that you are trapped is when it comes double-packed with the belief that the future ahead of you is nothing like the future that you had previously been banking on. The schoolboy who did a bunk had probably spent years dreaming of freedom and good stuff. It's just a guess, but it's not hard to imagine how easy it would have been to get thrown off course by the thought of his future being made up of nothing more than years of never-ending pressures, whether study or work. Wasted dreams; there's nothing quite like them.

Thankfully the Bible has something to say about this. Actually that's a bit of an understatement, for through the story of Joseph we are given a close-up view of one of the most extreme cases of long-term disappointment that I can think of. Joseph not only had it tough; he also had been convinced that God had fantastic things in store for him. Watching the years trickle by from a prison cell in a foreign land, he could be forgiven for thinking that something had gone wrong somewhere. Joseph's story is a textbook example of how to endure the worst but still hang in there with God.

As the story opens we meet Joseph living in the town of Hebron with his eleven brothers and one sister.

Joseph, a young man of seventeen, was tending the flocks with his brothers, the sons of Bilhah and the sons of Zilpah, his father's wives, and he brought their father a bad report about them. Now Israel loved Joseph more than any of his

215

other sons, because he had been born to him in his old age; and he made a richly ornamented robe for him. When his brothers saw that their father loved him more than any of them, they hated him and could not speak a kind word to him.

(Genesis 37:2–4)

And so we get the picture of the Golden Child syndrome. Joseph – favoured by his father Jacob (also called Israel) – obviously gets an easy time of it, staying at home with Dad while his brothers work hard with the flocks. Not only that but his dad (obviously with a good feel for what would and wouldn't work in late twentieth-century musicals) gives him an Amazing Technicoloured Dreamcoat, failing to do the same for the other eleven of his sons.

Understandably all this did very little to give the brothers a good opinion of Joseph, but if ever their affection for him was in question, it went right out of the window when they remembered how he had decided to give his dad 'a bad report about them', grassing them up for some offence or other.

However, these two offences were nothing compared with what came next. Joseph had a dream. Oh dear.

'Listen to this dream I had: We were binding sheaves of corn out in the field when suddenly my sheaf rose and stood upright, while your sheaves gathered around mine and bowed down to it.'

His brothers said to him, 'Do you intend to reign over us? Will you actually rule us?' And they hated him all the more because of his dream and what he had said.

Then he had another dream, and he told it to his brothers. 'Listen,' he said, 'I had another dream, and this time the sun and moon and eleven stars were bowing down to me.'

When he told his father as well as his brothers, his

father rebuked him and said, 'What is this dream you had? Will your mother and I and your brothers actually come and bow down to the ground before you?' His brothers were jealous of him, but his father kept the matter in mind.

(Genesis 37:6–11)

Joseph's arrogance and stupidity are plain to see, yet unfortunately the matter does not just end there. Up to this point in the Bible, it's clear to see that God had been in the habit of speaking to his people through various means about the future of the nation of Israel. He spoke to Abraham in a dream when he made his covenant with him and told him of the future of his new nation (Genesis 15:12–21), as well as to Jacob when he saw his ladder reaching to heaven (Genesis 28:10–15). So it makes sense that at this key point in Israel's formation (Jacob's twelve sons were the beginning of the twelve tribes of Israel) God would have a couple of things to say. Despite his monumental lack of tact and consideration for his brothers' feelings, Joseph was right; his dreams were from heaven. Eventually the contents of the dream were proved right, but not before Joseph's life seemed to take a massive detour.

As you probably know, things started to go wrong when Joseph was sent out by his father to find out how things were going with his brothers and their flocks. He travelled the thirty miles from Hebron to Shechem, only to discover that they had moved on a further twenty miles to the city of Dothan. Spotting him far off as he approached, his brothers plotted to kill him or at least arrange it so that he would be killed by a wild animal. Eventually Joseph ended up being sold as a slave to some travelling Midianite merchants on their way to Egypt.

Once in the foreign country – surrounded by unfamiliar people, language and customs – this good Jewish lad gets bought by Potiphar, a high-ranking official in Pharaoh's council. Due to some exceptionally good work on behalf of the young Israelite, Mr Potiphar takes a shine to Joseph and promotes him to the position of Chief Slave. Unfortunately he is not the only one who reckons that Joseph is worthy of attention, as Mrs Potiphar tries to seduce him. Deciding that a career as a gigolo was not quite what he had in mind, Joseph spurns Mrs P who convinces her husband that Joseph had tried to rape her. Soon Joseph is not only a slave in a foreign land, but an innocent prisoner too. Not quite the upright sheaf surrounded by bowing subjects.

In prison he meets a couple of Pharaoh's servants, the cupbearer and the baker. They tell him about a couple of dreams that they have had and Joseph asks God for the meaning. Delivering the interpretation that the baker will be executed and that the cupbearer will be released, he makes sure that the cupbearer agrees to remember Joseph once he's out and try his best to ensure his release.

On the third anniversary of his reign Pharaoh had a bit of a clear-out, hanging the baker and releasing the cupbearer, just as the dreams had been interpreted. 'The chief cupbearer, however, did not remember Joseph; he forgot him' (Genesis 40:23). Can you imagine Joseph's frustration and disappointment as he realised again that the interpretation of dreams that he thought were from God only ever seemed to lead him into trouble?

It takes a couple more years for the story to move on, when it's Pharaoh's turn to have a confusing dream. None of his sorcerers or magicians can work out the meaning behind the fat cows and the thin cows, but as the cupbearer remembers his old cell-mate, Joseph gets the call once again. Joseph could easily have given up at this point, saying that he didn't 'do dreams', that they just caused too much trouble. Instead he decides to ask God for the interpretation, which he duly receives and communicates to a very grateful

Pharaoh, who busts him out of jail and gives him the job of chancellor of the exchequer. Nice.

Of course Joseph's interpretation of the dream not only made sense at the time, it also outlined the precise way that things were going to happen; true to form there was a seven-year period of economic and agricultural boom which was followed by seven years of killer bust. The famine threatened the lives of Egypt's neighbours, but under the prudent eye of Joseph, Pharaoh's stores had enough grain in them to ride it out.

So Israel's sons were among those who went to buy grain, for the famine was in the land of Canaan also. Now Joseph was the governor of the land, the one who sold grain to all its people. So when Joseph's brothers arrived, they bowed down to him with their faces to the ground. He played with his brothers for a while, who remained unaware of the true identity of the man they were dealing with.

Then Joseph could no longer control himself before all his attendants, and he cried out, 'Make everyone leave my presence!' So there was no-one with Joseph when he made himself known to his brothers. And he wept so loudly that the Egyptians heard him, and Pharaoh's household heard about it.

Joseph said to his brothers, 'I am Joseph! Is my father still living?' But his brothers were not able to answer him, because they were terrified at his presence.

Then Joseph said to his brothers, 'Come close to me.' When they had done so, he said, 'I am your brother Joseph, the one you sold into Egypt! And now, do not be distressed and do not be angry with yourselves for selling me here, because it was to save lives that God sent me ahead of you. For two years now there has been famine in the land, and for the next five years there will not be ploughing and reaping. But God sent me ahead of you to preserve for you

> a remnant on earth and to save your lives by a great deliverance.'
>
> (Genesis 45:1–7)

Joseph's story gets me for many reasons; I love the accuracy of his interpretations, the boldness with which he takes on the challenge of succeeding where Pharaoh's best had failed. But as well as those characteristics I love the fact that in many ways the story is so normal; he was stupid and arrogant when he was younger and then for years his life was not easy, the spiritual fireworks were not going off and Joseph looked every bit the failure. Yet he hung in there, and that gives me hope. Joseph didn't consider his life to be a waste simply because it hadn't progressed at the speed and in the order that he had hoped.

Too many of us get floored by the wasted years, months and even weeks – just one period of time where things don't seem to be heading in the right direction can be enough to send us back to apathetic mediocrity with our tail between our legs. Maybe it was a failed exam or a broken relationship, a change of family circumstance or a force way beyond your control. When things look as though they aren't going to work out quite the way we had thought, the temptation to give in can be great. It can be so much easier to write off an unfulfilled dream as a mistake or a waste than to risk the pain of patiently waiting for it to be fulfilled.

This wasn't on the menu for Joseph. He refused to get bitter, to consider all that had once sparked his hope to be false. He stuck with it and remained true to the dreams that God had given him. Instead of turning away from God he turned towards him, getting closer to him and depending on him. For proof of that just look at what the Scriptures have to say about the children born to Joseph while he was in Egypt:

Joseph named his firstborn Manasseh and said, 'It is because God has made me forget all my trouble and all my father's household.' The second son he named Ephraim and said, 'It is because God has made me fruitful in the land of my suffering.'

(Genesis 41:51–2)

Joseph faced questions and tests and so do we. It may not come down to being sold into slavery, but there will be plenty of chances for us to get the hump with God for not working things out to our precise specifications. Will we get bitter when this happens? Will we decide that God has got it wrong? Are we really that brave?

'For my thoughts are not your thoughts, neither are your ways my ways,' declares the Lord.

(Isaiah 55:8)

Will we live a life in expectation of the fulfilment of God's promises? If so, I think it's a reasonably sound idea to get to grips with this verse from Isaiah – after all, God's ways can seem mighty strange at times. Funnily enough, though, they always seem to work out best.

It comes down to choice between our way and learning God's way. At the end of it all, faced with the sight of his brothers pleading with him for food, Joseph could easily have exacted a little sweet revenge for their treatment of him. It would have been so easy for him to have them taken away and 'dealt with'. But God had taught him a few lessons throughout his stay in the foreign land. He had taught Joseph about his sovereignty; reminding him that God was in charge. He dealt with Joseph's arrogance so that when his family finally did bow in front of him, Joseph didn't make a big deal of it. Joseph's first dream of sheaves bowing down before him finally came true over twenty-two years after he had it.

221

Instead of sticking his tongue out he told them of God's plan, how he had been sent to serve them: 'God sent me ahead of you to preserve for you a remnant on earth and to save your lives by a great deliverance.'

Sometimes God delays fulfilling the dreams so that we might have enough time to learn valuable lessons. It may not just be arrogance that needs to get sorted within us; it may be that we need to recognise God's sovereignty over our own ability. Personally I had plenty of dreams that seemed to have got lost along the way. When I was fifteen I had sermons in me that I was convinced were going to spark huge revival worldwide. I would practise in front of the mirror, alternating between my light-hearted 'rolling in the aisles' delivery and my stern 'on your knees' calls to repentance. At times I was so convincing that I even went forward myself. Working as a second-rate accountant I wondered where it had all gone wrong. Each day I sat there, internally grieving the potential that I had been so convinced would one day be unleashed on a sinful world. I felt embarrassed and let down, worrying that all my zeal had gone to waste.

I had to wait. It was thirteen years before I got round to preaching, and in that time I figured out that there are two modes of waiting on offer. The first – and by far my favourite for most of my twenties – is waiting with your thumb in your mouth. 'Well God,' you say to yourself, 'I don't suppose you're ever going to use me.' The second – and what I found to be by far the most elusive – is to wait as Joseph did; expectantly. In the waiting he lived a faithful and obedient life, taking what opportunities he had to do God's will. Eventually this faithful young man got to see his early dreams fulfilled in ways that he could never have imagined before.

God doesn't want merely to use you for the sake of it – that's not why he gives us dreams and ambitions. God wants more than to just do stuff through you, he wants to do it *in* you. We have a saying in our church: we have to go deeper before we go further. The gap between getting the dreams and seeing them fulfilled is the time when it's up to us whether we go deeper with God. That way, when things are moving along nicely and he's taking us further along with him, fulfilling our dreams, we won't let him down.

'Faith is often strengthened
right at the place of
disappointment.'
Rodney McBride

'Your worst days are
never so bad that you are beyond
the reach of God's grace. And
your best days are never so good
that you are beyond the need
of God's grace.'
Jerry Bridges

3

Wasted Potential
Samson's Story

While the thought of having to deal with a whole load of wasted dreams is not exactly a pleasant one, there is one thing that I find more tragic and disturbing: the worry that one day I may wake up believing that I have wasted my potential. I've seen it happen to some of my friends and my guess is that you will have seen the same; talented people, those with loads going for them who get tripped up by some kind of fatal flaw. Perhaps not quite as extreme as the story of ambitious Mr Macbeth, but these are people who somehow end up sacrificing their ability. Please don't get me wrong, I'm not condemning them or pointing the finger – there are plenty of things I do that get in the way of my relationship with God – I simply find it sad when our taste for the forbidden fruit gets in the way of the good things that God has in store. It might not be a fatal flaw that gets in our way though; sometimes the simple act of making wrong choices can alter our course, leading us towards disappointment instead of satisfaction. Whatever the reason, there's nothing quite as sad as the tombstone that reads 'He Had Potential'. Maybe I feel strongly about this because of all those 'Could

WEEPING BEFORE AN EMPTY TOMB

Do Better' reports I got while at school, but I'm sure that
God feels the same; urging us to put down the things that
threaten to distract and destroy us.

Samson is a classic case of someone who was jam-packed
with potential, but who because of both character flaws and
bad choices ended up far away from a glorious ending. His
story starts in the Old Testament at a time when his people
were in the middle of a long period of occupation by their
enemies.

> Again the Israelites did evil in the eyes of the Lord, so the
> Lord delivered them into the hands of the Philistines for
> forty years.
>
> (Judges 13:1)

This whole thing of Israel's sin being followed by a period of
occupation is part of a pattern that appears throughout the
book of Judges. What happened was that the nation of Israel
would sin and begin to worship idols, so God would place
them under the control of one of their neighbours. These
enemy nations would rule over them for some time until the
Israelites repented of their sin and asked God to set them
free. In stepped God, who would raise up a deliverer who
would lead them out of slavery and back to freedom.
Eventually however, the whole thing would happen again as
the Israelites wandered off and started worshipping their
idols once more. This cycle is repeated throughout the book
of Judges, and the story of Samson appears in the seventh
and last of these cycles.

The opening verse mentions that the Israelites were
'delivered into the hands of the Philistines' – a particularly
savage and warlike people with roots in Egypt.

A certain man of Zorah, named Manoah, from the clan of
the Danites, had a wife who was sterile and remained

childless. The angel of the Lord appeared to her and said, 'You are sterile and childless, but you are going to conceive and have a son. Now see to it that you drink no wine or other fermented drink and that you do not eat anything unclean, because you will conceive and give birth to a son. No razor may be used on his head, because the boy is to be a Nazirite, set apart to God from birth, and he will begin the deliverance of Israel from the hands of the Philistines.'

(Judges 13:2–5)

The deal with Nazirites was that they took a vow that they would separate themselves from much of the world in order to be of service to God. The word comes from the Hebrew verb *nazar*, which means 'to separate, to cut off'. It seems that God had a specific task in mind too – and not a bad one at that – 'he will begin the deliverance of Israel from the hands of the Philistines.' Not bad for a foetus.

So we see that even from before his birth Samson had potential as well as some strict guidelines for him to follow. As a Nazirite he was forbidden to touch a dead body of any kind, drink alcohol or have any contact with grapes or to cut his hair. These rules helped to set him apart as well as to paint a powerful picture of our need for dependence on God. For example, that thing with the hair was actually quite radical; having long hair (and I mean really long – longer than the women of the day) in the Scriptures was a rather shameful thing for a man and was considered to be a sign of weakness. Nazirites openly displayed their weakness in this way, a clear statement that they were totally reliant on God for their strength. Unfortunately, Samson was just a little too good at showing his own weakness.

The early years were promising. We are told that 'he grew and the Lord blessed him, and the Spirit of the Lord began to stir him while he was in Mahaneh Dan, between Zorah and Eshtaol' (Judges 13:25). Having been born with a silver spoon

in his mouth (the angel of the Lord bringing back the results
of the pregnancy tests as well as outlining his CV), to have
the Spirit of God brood over him must have made his parents
believe that his place as firestarter to the delivery of Israel
was in the bag.

Unfortunately things began to go wrong:

> Samson went down to Timnah and saw there a young
> Philistine woman. When he returned, he said to his father
> and mother, 'I have seen a Philistine woman in Timnah;
> now get her for me as my wife.'
>
> His father and mother replied, 'Isn't there an acceptable
> woman among your relatives or among all our people?
> Must you go to the uncircumcised Philistines to get a wife?'
>
> But Samson said to his father, 'Get her for me. She's the
> right one for me.'
>
> (Judges 14:1–3)

Timnah was a small town about four miles away from
Samson's home in Zorah, and it is this first recording of
a Samson away-day that gives us a clear picture of his
weakness, particularly when it came to the *laydeees*.

The first thing to note is that Samson's decision to marry a
Philistine woman was a big no-no. The fact that God would
use this woman to bring down the Philistines does not
condone the fact that Samson broke the rules. Instead it says
far more about God's grace and ultimate sovereignty. Samson
should have known better than to contravene God's explicit
commandments that intermarriage between the Israelites and
those from other nations was strictly off limits. The Old
Testament explains that because of his love, God decreed
that his people should marry within their own nationality. A
member of an idolatrous people would pollute a good Israelite
household, as well as being no fun for the 'foreigner'. It all
feels a tad funny talking about 'racial purity' in this day and

age (normally we leave that up to the bigoted fascists), but we need to take it in context; these were violent enemies and everything was at stake.

Samson, however, thought with his pants, stamping his feet and getting his own way when his parents questioned his decision. Living so close to Timnah and the territory of the Philistines is a useful picture of how Samson lived on the edge spiritually as well as physically. Instead of taking care he blustered his way through, putting self before God.

Before we judge him and put him on the scrapheap, it's vital to remind ourselves that God's ways are not our ways, and that he can still choose to use people despite their failings.

> Samson went down to Timnah together with his father and mother. As they approached the vineyards of Timnah, suddenly a young lion came roaring toward him. The Spirit of the Lord came upon him in power so that he tore the lion apart with his bare hands as he might have torn a young goat. But he told neither his father nor his mother what he had done.
>
> (Judges 14:5–6)

Just check out that power; ripping apart a lion as if it were a goat shows that Samson was seriously anointed.

> Some time later, when he went back to marry her, he turned aside to look at the lion's carcass. In it was a swarm of bees and some honey, which he scooped out with his hands and ate as he went along. When he rejoined his parents, he gave them some, and they too ate it. But he did not tell them that he had taken the honey from the lion's carcass.
>
> (Judges 14:8–9)

Oh dear. Not only did Samson make the mistake of touching a dead animal, he also was a bit sly in not telling his parents where the honey came from, so causing them to defile themselves by eating from an unclean animal. In fact, if you think about it, the whole thing's quite symbolic: he performed a spectacular act that gave glory to God, ripping apart flesh under the power of the Spirit. Later his fleshly appetites outweighed his spiritual resolve and he satisfied his hunger by munching on a parasite that had lived off the by-product of God's glory.

You have to question exactly what Samson was doing there in the first place. After all, his Nazirite vows forbade him touching not only wine, but grapes too. Pretty hard thing to avoid grapes in a vineyard. What's more, it's kind of strange that he would be poking around inside a lion's carcass anyway, especially when you add in the danger element of a swarm of bees being present. Altogether the picture pulls into focus and we conclude that Samson was wilfully and on many different counts trying to break God's laws. It wasn't as if he slipped up in a nano-second; he broke through many barriers – the vineyard, the dead lion, the honey – in order to satisfy his appetite. Playing with fire, a life on the edge, call it what you will, Samson couldn't resist taking chances.

The risk-taking continues at his wedding. Samson provokes the Philistines by setting them a riddle, agreeing with them that – should they work it out within the seven days of the feast – he would give them 'thirty linen garments and thirty festal garments'. These were exceptionally expensive threads (a man might expect to own one in his entire lifetime) and Samson was setting himself up to give them each two. If they didn't get the solution then they were to give him two of the garments each, so there was a reasonable incentive for the Philistines to work it out and for Samson not to tell them. What was the riddle, you ask?

'Out of the eater, something to eat; out of the strong, something sweet.'

(Judges 14:14a)

Again he's walking a tightrope, referring to a secret miracle of God's, using it to line his own pocket.

For three days they could not give the answer.

On the fourth day, they said to Samson's wife, 'Coax your husband into explaining the riddle for us, or we will burn you and your father's household to death. Did you invite us here to rob us?'

Then Samson's wife threw herself on him, sobbing, 'You hate me! You don't really love me. You've given my people a riddle, but you haven't told me the answer.'

'I haven't even explained it to my father or mother,' he replied, 'so why should I explain it to you?'

She cried the whole seven days of the feast. So on the seventh day he finally told her, because she continued to press him. She in turn explained the riddle to her people.

(Judges 14:14b–17)

Once more we see Samson's inability to say no to the flesh. This time, however, instead of defiling his immediate family, he travels to Ashkelon (a coastal town thirty miles away) where he murders, loots and pillages until he has enough cash to pay back the now rather happy Philistines. It's a terrible story, made even more confusing by the fact that God appears to help him, as 'the Spirit of the Lord came mightily upon him' during the killing spree. With thirty men dead it's hard to see how God's hand could be on Samson's Great Escape, but I guess that's just the way things go; God sometimes does give us more than we deserve to help when we're up against a wall. One thing's for sure, I wouldn't like to expect God to do that sort of thing every time I messed up.

There followed a few more mess-ups, but eventually Samson ends up ruling the Israelites in peace for twenty years. That is until he makes a total hash of it all and takes a trip to Gaza, where he sleeps with a prostitute. Doh! What a chief. Twenty years of victory, twenty years of peace and he throws it all away for one night of sex. Remind you of anyone? In our own ways we all do it, I suppose; we all can taste the intimacy of a relationship with Jesus, all know that he really is all that we need to get by, but we chuck it away for a moment's gratification.

> The people of Gaza were told, 'Samson is here!' So they surrounded the place and lay in wait for him all night at the city gate. They made no move during the night, saying, 'At dawn we'll kill him.'
>
> (Judges 16:2)

Yet again the Lord is there for him, saving him miraculously by allowing him to escape through the Philistines at night and rip off the gates at the city wall, which he carries on his back the thirty-eight miles to Hebron. Then we read: 'Some time later, he fell in love with a woman in the Valley of Sorek whose name was Delilah' (Judges 16:4).

It's the same old pattern; he messes up, God helps him out. This time it's another pagan woman who catches his eye, Delilah (whose name in Hebrew means 'weak'). Not surprisingly considering the amount of grief that he has caused them over the years, the Philistines are quite keen on the idea of Samson being six foot under. The Philistine lords ask Delilah to find out the secret of his strength, offering to pay her 1,100 pieces of silver each should she comply, making the total purse 5,500 pieces of silver.

Of course Delilah cannot resist and sets about trying to discover the secret of his might. What follows is pure farce; immature Samson plays along with the gag by telling Delilah a lie about what makes him so powerful. Each time Delilah passes on the lie to the Philistines, who try out the theory on him at night. First they are told that if he is bound with fresh bowstrings he will be helpless. He isn't. Then they take his advice and try tying him up with new ropes, but these fail to hold him. Having been told that if seven locks of his hair were woven into a web he would be helpless, Delilah tries it but he wakes up, rips the loom right off the wall and walks out the door. Finally she tries a new tack:

> 'How can you say, "I love you," when you won't confide in me? This is the third time you have made a fool of me and haven't told me the secret of your great strength.'
>
> (Judges 16:15)

He caves in, telling her:

> 'No razor has ever been used on my head . . . because I have been a Nazirite set apart to God since birth. If my head were shaved, my strength would leave me, and I would become as weak as any other man.'
>
> (Judges 16:17)

Finally Samson has given up the last of his Nazirite vows. Succumbing to Delilah it doesn't take long for him to cave in and for the Philistines to capture him, gouge out his eyes, humiliate him and set him to work pushing a great millstone round and round (a task usually carried out by oxen).

Samson ends up in misery with his enemies laughing at both him and his God. I've known people who have ended up in almost similar situations, and in each situation, like Samson, it all starts with the little sins. Samson chose the wrong girl and had a sweet tooth, yet these were the seeds of his own destruction. Some of us have justified other things; a little greed, lust or selfishness can seem so trivial, so easy to forget about. Once they're done and we find that God still seems to be with us, that he still answers prayers and still seems to care about our lives, then the temptation can come to think that we have got away with it. And so we carry on, taking another bite at sin's apple, dulling our senses to the bitterness of its taste.

When Samson was finally caught by the Philistines and they gouged out his eyes, he lost not only his strength but his vision. We too can fall into that trap, as when our crimes catch us up we can lose that clarity which once made us so sure of where we were going.

> While they were in high spirits, they shouted, 'Bring out Samson to entertain us.' So they called Samson out of the prison, and he performed for them.
>
> When they stood him among the pillars, Samson said to the servant who held his hand, 'Put me where I can feel the pillars that support the temple, so that I may lean against them.' Now the temple was crowded with men and women; all the rulers of the Philistines were there, and on the roof were about three thousand men and women watching Samson perform. Then Samson prayed to the Lord, 'O Sovereign Lord, remember me. O God, please strengthen me just once more, and let me with one blow get revenge on the Philistines for my two eyes.' Then Samson reached toward the two central pillars on which the temple stood. Bracing himself against them, his right hand on the one and his left hand on the other, Samson said, 'Let me die with the Philistines!' Then he pushed with all his might, and down came the temple on the rulers and all the people in it. Thus he killed many more when he died than while he lived.
>
> (Judges 16:25–30)

For the first time in the whole of the record of Samson's life we read of him praying. Up until then he had been taking

God's mercy for granted; there is no record of him spending time with the Lord, no record of him carrying out any of the spiritual disciplines. It was only at the eleventh hour, after he had repeatedly failed to do the right thing, that he finally wised up and cried out to God in his weakness. I think that last line is one of the saddest in the Old Testament; a mighty warrior with God on his side, his greatest battle was his last. In spiritual terms that means that in his death he did more good than he had managed to do in the whole of his life. What a life of wasted potential.

There are many of us who, on looking back over our Christian lives, will decide that the years are marked by wasted potential instead of well-used talents. Let's not do that, let's take every day and live it for Jesus, putting his agenda before our own, trying to go by his values instead of the world's. That's what living life to the max is all about, using your gifts and talents in the very best way. Let's not sit on them, longing to be a preacher when really our talents make us an administrator, or hoping for the break as a worship leader when really we're best at caring for people and giving them time and love. As well as making sure we're making the right choices, we need to get down on our knees before God, making sure we're in the right place, that instead of sin we're marked by holiness.

As Oscar Schindler weeps at the end of *Schindler's List*, mourning all the things he could have done to save even more people, I always feel like shouting, 'but you have done so much'. One of my biggest fears is that I'll end up weeping for the things I never did and that there won't be anything to show for my life. I don't want that, I want to live the life God's given me to the full. I want to enjoy every last drop of life that's in my body, and that means staying close to him, following him, learning to adore him more. Wasted potential may be a terrible thing, but it's not the only thing on the menu; there's plenty more to choose from.

'The ultimate measure of a man is not where he stands in moments of comfort and convenience, but where he stands at times of challenge and controversy.'

Martin Luther King Jr

4

When Bad Things Happen to Good People

Job's Story

I suppose my only real claim to fame is that my brother once sold Lady Diana a pair of tights. (OK, so it might not be much, but it's all I've got.) It happened when both of us little Pilavachi boys worked at Harvey Nichols (pronounced *Harvey Nicks, Darling*) in Knightsbridge; Peter downstairs on Tights For Royalty and me upstairs in the slightly less glamorous Accounts department. For seven years I pushed paper and worked hard towards my eventual accreditation as World's Worst Accountant. Quite an achievement, I think you'll agree, and I'm glad to say in all humility that I fully deserved it.

When I started the job I was introduced to the rest of the department personnel, and quickly worked out the particular dynamics of the office. I say quickly, as working out the personality types on offer in a room full of accountants is not exactly the hardest job in the world. One person that did get my attention though, was Pat. She was the nicest person in the office, and it was clear that everybody else agreed. Not only was she kind, generous and caring, but she always seemed to have a smile on her face and was ready to chat and be interested in whatever anyone told her. Pat was one of those gold-dust characters who enhance the life of a place simply by their presence.

But there was a history that lay behind Pat which was at odds with the smile. I knew, mainly because people avoided talking about it, that she had been through some difficult times in her past. One day my colleagues told me. A few years previously Pat had been diagnosed as having cancer of the lymph gland, and many thought she was going to die. Against the odds she had managed to pull through, although as a result she was left unable to have children. They told me about her husband, Jan – a first generation Hungarian who worked hard in a factory. They were very much in love and, because of the cancer, they knew that all they had in the world was each other. My colleagues told me how traumatic her encounter with cancer had been, but that it was in remission and for the previous few years she and Jan had been rebuilding their lives together.

One day she didn't look so well. The days turned into weeks and the weeks into months, and Pat continued to deteriorate. After one of her regular check-ups she found out that the cancer was back. They tried the same treatment as before, but slowly she seemed to get worse. Eventually she stopped coming to work and the next time that I saw her was when we visited her in hospital. What I saw shocked me; she was in a terrible state, and both she and Jan knew it. They both cried and I couldn't handle it. I didn't visit again. One month later she died. She loved and wanted children, but she left none behind. Jan was left alone in a foreign country. We all asked, 'Why her?' Of all of us in the department Pat was the last person to deserve so early and tragic a death.

The biggest question that we can ask God is: 'Why?' Eventually most of us take our turn to do so, as throughout life we all encounter trauma and tragedy. It is then we find out that somehow the answers that seem so valid when things are going well appear inappropriate and unsatisfactory. The truth was that for us, there was no answer to the question, 'Why Pat?' As a Christian that confusion took on a different twist for me from that of many of my colleagues, and it stayed with me for years to come.

I'm reminded of Pat whenever I hear about the casualties of earthquakes or other 'natural' disasters. When harmless civilians are killed, the weak are exploited or lives are claimed by epidemics, when I'm reminded of how it seems that it is always the innocent that suffer the most, I cannot help but ask, 'Why?'

There have been a few people throughout the ages who have resisted this urge to question the Almighty. Considering it blasphemy or a lack of respect, they have tried to gloss over the issue of suffering by encouraging people to concentrate on the good rather than the bad. While I'm all in favour of a bit of positive thinking, I cannot help but think that this attitude does more harm than good. I believe that we all need to search for answers, in much the same way that I believe we need to grieve at the loss of a loved one. Treating funerals as celebrations of the life passed away can deny our need to mourn and say goodbye. Yes, the person may have gone to a better place, but ours is a sadder place for their passing. It's the same with suffering; yes, God is in charge, he does see the bigger picture, but we do people a disservice when we tell them that asking about suffering is a no-go area.

As Christians we believe that God is all-powerful, as well as being all-good. Take that line of reason and it's not long before you find yourself being asked, 'Well, if God is all-powerful he should be *able* to stop suffering. If he is all-good, he should *want* to stop suffering.' The logical conclusion would be, 'In that case, which one isn't he: all-powerful or all-good?'

When I was at school I had trouble with maths. It made little sense and try as I might, I just couldn't seem to get my head around it. Worse of all, though, was algebra. All that stuff about x+y=2(y-z) had me scratching my head till the page disappeared under a flurry of dry scalp. That kind of mental block is familiar to many of us out of the classroom too, especially when it comes to the million-dollar question: why do bad things happen to good people?

Actually, it's not only good people that bad things happen to, and I feel that now is the time to tell you about Louis and Albert. Some time ago I decided that I needed a pet. I gathered my friends about me and held lengthy discussions about precisely what type of animal would be suitable for a disorganised, travelling young man such as myself. A dog was too much commitment and the fact that my flat is on the third floor ruled out a cat. I've killed more fish by overfeeding than I think is healthy and I don't like hamsters as they give me the creeps. Then I met Louis and Albert. Actually, I first met Sergeant Jenkins, a beautiful macaw parrot, but it all seemed a bit much so the pet shop owner took me to the budgie section where Louis and Albert introduced themselves. I was sold, and so were they, and the three of us returned home to start our new life together.

I fed them every day, talked with them constantly and would even phone up and talk to them over the answerphone while I was away just so that they didn't get too lonely without me. It was a wonderful time for all of us.

One day I returned home to find Louis lying belly-up on the floor of the cage. Wondering whether he was merely sleeping I tried to wake him, but it soon became clear that this was one nap that he would not be waking up from. He was dead, kaput, an ex-budgie – and I was distraught. The funeral was brief but heartfelt, and Albert and I tried our best to piece things together as a twosome. To be honest, he was a real rock at the time, and I suspect the strain of having to be strong for me was a deciding factor in his own death, barely a week later. Again I found him belly-up on the floor of the cage, and this time I knew that this signalled the end of Albert's brief time on this earth. What had they done to deserve it?

There's a book of the Bible that is written to answer that very question (although not specifically about budgies). Like my algebra problems, however, the answer at the end of it is very different from the one that we may have anticipated at the beginning.

Job (along with Psalms, Proverbs, the Song of Songs and Ecclesiastes) is part of the poetry section of the Bible. That means it was written with a purpose but also with a little creative imagination. Some people don't believe that there ever really was a person named Job – or at least if there was, that his story didn't follow quite the same script as we see in the Bible – but whether it is true or metaphorical, I am convinced that God inspired the writing of Job in order to speak to us about this whole question of suffering.

In Job we come face to face with someone whose suffering was grotesque. It was even worse than the suffering endured by my friend Pat, and at times it all can seem too much. We pick it up at the beginning:

> In the land of Uz there lived a man whose name was Job. This man was blameless and upright; he feared God and shunned evil. He had seven sons and three daughters, and he owned seven thousand sheep, three thousand camels, five hundred yoke of oxen and five hundred donkeys, and had a large number of servants. He was the greatest man among all the people of the East.
>
> (Job 1:1–3)

What a beginning; Job had it all. Not only was he wealthy financially, but he had a thriving family and a spot-on relationship with God. David Beckham, after having won the treble in 1999 with Manchester United as well as becoming a father for the first time, said, 'Life doesn't get better than this; I've got everything I want and I couldn't ask for more.' He could have nicked the line from Job, for the Old Testament figure was pretty much about as happy as it was possible to get.

Job was such a top fella in the eyes of the Lord that whenever his sons had a party, Job would make an offering to his God just in case his kids had sinned and cursed God in their hearts. Talk about holy; the guy was even atoning for sins that hadn't happened.

After the scene has been set things turn a little bizarre:

> One day the angels came to present themselves before the Lord, and Satan also came with them. The Lord said to Satan, 'Where have you come from?'
>
> (Job 1:6–7a)

Excuse me! What the heck is all that about? I mean, Satan wandering around heaven, bold as brass, chatting with God. It's just plain weird.

> Satan answered the Lord, 'From roaming through the earth and going to and fro in it.'
>
> Then the Lord said to Satan, 'Have you considered my servant Job? There is no-one on earth like him; he is blameless and upright, a man who fears God and shuns evil.'
>
> (Job 1:7b–8)

The picture we get of this cosy little scene is God bragging to Satan about how much of a good old boy Mr Job is. 'See my boy Job?' you could translate it, 'Well, he's rock 'ard.'

'Does Job fear God for nothing?' Satan replied. 'Have you not put a hedge around him and his household and everything he has? You have blessed the work of his hands, so that his flocks and herds are spread throughout the land. But stretch out your hand and strike everything he has, and he will surely curse you to your face.'

(Job 1:9–11)

According to Satan, Job's only as 'upright and blameless' as he is because God has been on his side. He is accusing God of having a follower who is only loyal as long as the sun is shining and the blessings are flowing. And as you can imagine, this kind of fighting talk cannot go ignored and God agrees to the challenge with the strict proviso that while he can do whatever he wants to his wealth, Satan cannot lay a finger on Job.

One day when Job's sons and daughters were feasting and drinking wine at the oldest brother's house, a messenger came to Job and said, 'The oxen were ploughing and the donkeys were grazing nearby, and the Sabeans attacked and carried them off. They put the servants to the sword, and I am the only one who has escaped to tell you!'

(Job 1:13–15)

Ouch!

While he was still speaking, another messenger came and said, 'The fire of God fell from the sky and burned up the sheep and the servants, and I am the only one who has escaped to tell you!'

(Job 1:16)

That hurts.

> While he was still speaking, another messenger came and said, 'The Chaldeans formed three raiding parties and swept down on your camels and carried them off. They put the servants to the sword, and I am the only one who has escaped to tell you!'
>
> (Job 1:17)

Again, not exactly 'good news'.

> While he was still speaking, yet another messenger came and said, 'Your sons and daughters were feasting and drinking wine at the oldest brother's house, when suddenly a mighty wind swept in from the desert and struck the four corners of the house. It collapsed on them and they are dead, and I am the only one who has escaped to tell you!'
>
> (Job 1:18–19)

Oh dear.

All it took was a few moments and Job's wonderful life was wiped off the board. Not only his wealth, but his family too – that's a pretty hard blow to recover from. I know how I'd react, and I'm sorry to say that it would be nothing like Job's response:

> At this, Job got up and tore his robe and shaved his head. Then he fell to the ground in worship and said: 'Naked I came from my mother's womb, and naked I will depart. The Lord gave and the Lord has taken away; may the name of the Lord be praised.' In all this, Job did not sin by charging God with wrongdoing.
>
> (Job 1:20–2)

That is incredible. To be able to see the Lord so clearly through tragedy, to have such maturity in the midst of so

244

great a tragedy is something I can only dream of achieving. But that's not the end of it, as once again we see Satan taking a stroll around heaven. Bumping into God a bit of the old familiar chat starts up as God teases him for not being able to throw his protégé off balance. 'Ah,' says Satan, 'that's because you wouldn't let me trouble him physically. Now if Job got sick, then he'd turn his back on his God.'

> The Lord said to Satan, 'Very well, then, he is in your hands; but you must spare his life.'
> So Satan went out from the presence of the Lord and afflicted Job with painful sores from the soles of his feet to the top of his head. Then Job took a piece of broken pottery and scraped himself with it as he sat among the ashes.
>
> (Job 2:6–8)

What a horrific picture; the most upright and blameless man in the whole of Egypt and he's cutting himself with broken pottery to get relief from the sores that cover his body. His wife – probably like most of us – questions his sanity: 'His wife said to him, "Are you still holding on to your integrity? Curse God and die!"' (Job 2:9). But for the second time he hits back with a home-run of spiritual maturity: 'He replied, "You are talking like a foolish woman. Shall we accept good from God, and not trouble?" In all this, Job did not sin in what he said' (Job 2:10).

I'm not sure how things work for you, but I feel reasonably confident that my faith in God can stand up to certain testing – bereavement, stress and worry – but as soon as my health goes, I'm in trouble. It can be as insignificant as a mild headache, but it can be enough to have me growling, spitting and generally getting ready to renounce my faith. A cold is not something to be kept to myself, instead I make a point of telling as many people as possible how cursed I am and try to bleed people of every last drop of sympathy they have going. In short, I am a nightmare, and compared to what Job went through, I am a worm. No matter what the devil threw at him, Job remained faithful to God and refused to throw in the towel on a relationship that was beginning to show him the extremes of human experience.

Any similarity between me and Job is limited to the fact that we both had visitors. While mine generally don't stick around for long, Job's three bearers of grapes and advice spent a considerable amount of time at his bedside.

> When they saw him from a distance, they could hardly recognise him; they began to weep aloud, and they tore their robes and sprinkled dust on their heads. Then they sat on the ground with him for seven days and seven nights. No-one said a word to him, because they saw how great his suffering was.
>
> (Job 2:12–13)

Yes, you guessed it; they were just the sort of visitors you don't need when you're ill. For the next thirty-six chapters the three visitors discussed with the patient every aspect of his affliction, trying wherever possible to be helpful. They weren't. As Job bemoans his very existence, Eliphaz the Temanite, Bildad the Shuhite and Zophar the Naamathite try their best to offer explanations for his predicament. They suggest that his suffering is a result of sin, but they are wrong. Suffering does not always indicate wrongdoing; if only it did we wouldn't even be bothering with a chapter like this.

So while the three chaps are busy trying to persuade Job to confess to a crime that he didn't commit, you could be forgiven for wondering what God was up to. In truth God is silent for the vast majority of the book, allowing the visitors to fill it with a whole load of misinformed nonsense. Finally, God speaks in Job 38: 'Then the Lord answered Job out of the storm. He said: "Who is this that darkens my counsel with words without knowledge? Brace yourself like a man; I will question you, and you shall answer me"' (Job 38:1–3).

It's as if the Lord suddenly brings the place down. 'Who are you to question me?' he asks. It's his job to do the asking, not that of foolish men. God didn't come to give Job answers, but to ask things of him ... 'Where were you when I laid the earth's foundation? Tell me, if you understand. Who marked off its dimensions? Surely you know!' (Job 38:4–5).

The hint of sarcasm helps to show us just how ridiculous it is for Job and friends to be questioning their Maker. God reinforces the point: 'Will the one who contends with the Almighty correct him? Let him who accuses God answer him!' (Job 40:2).

Finally Job realises his place: 'I am unworthy – how can I reply to you? I put my hand over my mouth. I spoke once, but I have no answer – twice, but I will say no more' (Job 40:4–5).

God replies with his second questioning of his servant: 'Would you discredit my justice? Would you condemn me to justify yourself?' (Job 40:8).

Do you see what God has done? In asking Job where he was when the earth was being made he is accusing him of discrediting the Lord's power. In asking him whether he would 'discredit his justice', he is accusing Job of not believing in his goodness. Ring any bells? The twin doubts of, 'Is God really powerful enough to help?' and 'Is he really good enough to care?' are heard not only today, but they have been around since the earliest days of humanity.

This part of the story gives us an interesting insight into God's response to these two doubts about his nature. It's clear that in this case God sees them as a little more than just questions – please be clear that the Bible isn't suggesting that asking questions of God is wrong – and that they have become more like condemnation. As God said, was Job trying to condemn him to justify his own self? We can be guilty of exactly this same attitude; we write God off as being too low on power or love to make a difference, and we use the argument to justify all manner of bad deeds. Take wars for example; we allow them to carry on, pulling the trigger ourselves as a nation or people group, and then ask God why he doesn't intervene. Sometimes the buck really does stop with us, and it doesn't take a genius to work out that most suffering on this earth can be traced back to the human race.

Finally Job responds:

'I know that you can do all things; no plan of yours can be thwarted. You asked, "Who is this that obscures my counsel without knowledge?" Surely I spoke of things I did not understand, things too wonderful for me to know. You said, "Listen now, and I will speak; I will question you, and you shall answer me." My ears had heard of you but now my eyes have seen you.'

(Job 42:2–5)

This incredible ending leads us right back to the answer to the question 'Why?' Job at last realises that there is a bigger picture, one that he can neither fully see nor fully comprehend. Too many of us in our enlightened, scientific post-modern age treat God like we would any other lab experiment. We want to shove him under a microscope, prod him, dissect him and pull him apart for explanations. 'Is he worth following?' we ask ourselves. 'Only if he comes up to our high standards and expectations', comes our self-inflated reply. Actually there is a mystery that surrounds suffering, and many of the answers we won't even understand. But more important than our question of 'Why?' is God's question to us: 'Will you hang in there, even though you don't understand?'

Job finally sussed that one out. He knew that we are not

capable of understanding fully the reasons behind suffering and, after all, if God really is God, shouldn't there be a few things up his sleeve that we cannot quite grasp? Will we choose to turn away, angered by the affront to our own ego that God should inflict such pain on us, or will we press on with him? We weren't there when he created the world, and we certainly don't have knowledge on all the mysteries surrounding him, but thankfully it's not about knowledge; it's about trust. The only answer that works for me when things are going badly are Job's words: 'My ears had heard of you but now my eyes have seen you' (Job 42:5).

When I think of Pat I still don't have an answer to the 'Why?' question. This side of heaven I'm sure I will always be perplexed about the reasons why she died. But in the meantime, I do have an answer, one that keeps me in the best place for me; the answer is God. My ears had heard of him, but it wasn't until I saw suffering that my eyes saw him too. Pat's death showed me more of God; his suffering, his determination and, yes, his love and his power.

It is important to remember that while we're trying to take responsibility for our own part in suffering, we must not fall into the trap of thinking that God stands apart from it, aloof and uncaring. This is what I mean about seeing God in Pat's suffering; you see, Jesus suffered on the cross. He went through agony, through hell itself, and there is no pain that he has not felt. God is not oblivious to our pain, he sent his Son to share ours with us. But why, you may ask, if that is so, doesn't God simply take our suffering away? Wouldn't it be better all round if he did?

The story of Job contains our answer; do we wait until we understand the mystery before we bow the knee, or do we choose to be satisfied with God in the present? God makes clear which line of action he endorses.

Of course, there's one problem with Job's story; real or not, he was just a guy who got caught up in some wider and slightly bizarre goings-on. There happens to be another character in the Old Testament who was a prophet and who was actively trying to do God's will. In allowing Jeremiah to suffer, God ran the risk of sabotaging his own plans, yet again we get involved with a story where suffering was no stranger to one of God's people.

Jeremiah was called to be a prophet when he was just a child, and grew up in one of the most difficult times of Judah's history. His career spanned four decades and he prophesied over the last five of Judah's kings. The prophecies kicked off just before the people were about to be exiled from their country after a period of intense sin. Unfortunately they chose to ignore Jeremiah's words and their immediate fate was sealed.

Yet Jeremiah remained faithful to his God. Not that that was easy, you understand, as throughout his life Jeremiah went through some serious suffering: the first two kings who he prophesied over and liked were exiled and put to death (Jeremiah 22:10; 22:15). He was persecuted (15:15–19), plotted against (11:18–23), imprisoned (20:2), slandered (26:11), imprisoned again (37:14–15) and, most humiliating of all, was thrown down a cistern (38:4–6). He ended up in a terrible state as the events took their toll on him both emotionally and physically. They called him the 'weeping prophet' and the other book he wrote was called the Lamentations of Jeremiah. In Jeremiah 8:18 he despairs of comfort and in Jeremiah 13:17 he wants to break into tears for Judah. Jeremiah 9:2 sees him wanting to abandon Judah to her fate, and by Jeremiah 15:10 he wishes he had never been born. God comes in for a bit of stick as Jeremiah accuses him of wronging him (20:7) as do other people when he wants to get even with his 'tormentors' (18:19–23). Not only does he have to contend with this level of suffering, but he also has to deal with the anger and frustration welling up within. Yet he hung in there with God. Jeremiah poured out his heart and his pain before God, which is precisely what kept him going.

He may have been slightly short on answers, but Jeremiah the broken man carried on doing God's will because he never allowed his pain to get in the way of his relationship with his Lord and Saviour. Sadly, I've met Christians who haven't done the same; their pain has got in the way and instead of feeding off God, they have followed a path that has taken them further from him, the only true source of comfort for all of us.

What are we feeding off? There really only is a choice of two; either we feed off our problems or we turn to God. Choosing to focus purely on our pain and resentment will only ever lead to bitterness. Choosing to turn to God does not mean ignoring the pain, but it does mean putting him before it. As Job and Jeremiah discovered, our God is bigger than our suffering. Following God does not mean a free pass around suffering, it's actually far more likely to lead us towards it. For God, you see, is mysterious. But he is good, and he is powerful. It all comes down to where you draw the line; is there a heaven and eternal life? If this earth is all we believe that we've got, then of course suffering can seem like such a waste. If there is a God-given life after death, the suffering we encounter here on earth gets put in a distinctly different perspective. Where's your line in the sand?

'When the storms of life strike, it's what happens in you that determines what happens to you.'

Jerry Saville

'Trials are medicines which our gracious and wise Physician prescribes because we need them; and he proportions the frequency and weight of them to what the case requires. Let us trust his skills and thank him for his prescription.'

Sir Isaac Newton

5

When We Mess Up
David's Story

Over the years, I'm sure I've noticed a change in what newspapers choose to cover. Every time I turn a page now it seems as though I'm confronted by another revelation about the slip-ups and let-downs of some high-profile personality. From politicians to clergy, media stars to family doctors, it looks like there's an army of skeletons waiting to fight their way out of the closet and onto the front page. Not so when I was young; all I ever seemed to notice were pictures of Olivia Newton-John.

Even as I'm writing this the papers are full of stories about libel trials and the fall from grace of one of politics' more flamboyant stars. It was all this kind of sleaze that helped bring down the Tory government in the 1997 election, and much the same kind of muck that ruined the careers of numerous American TV evangelists and dodgy politicians. People ask whether this will ever end, whether truth and honesty will ever be the norm again.

I'm afraid I've got news for those people yearning for the glory days of the distant past; it's always been this way. People have always sinned, slipped up and made an almighty hash of this thing called life. Want proof? Just look at the Bible.

Before we do though, let's get a few things straight. People say that there are three categories into which our common failings fall. First is money; the desire to acquire. When things are put above people in terms of importance, this can have serious side effects for those we have trampled on to get to our treasure. Second is sex; the appetites of the flesh. History has been littered with the exploits of Valentinos who have stopped at nothing to satisfy their selfish urges. Finally there's power; the desire to dominate. Whether it's in a relationship or over a whole population, the lust that some have for power has been the driving force behind oppression the world over. But let's not get too smug; if we're honest, we're all capable of falling. If we're really honest, we've all slipped up already. Is there a way back from these mistakes? How can we avoid them in the first place?

If there's one character in the Bible who understood the twin tastes of success and failure, it's David: from humble shepherd boy then anointed to be king of Israel, back to humble shepherd boy and then to slayer of Goliath and saviour of the nation. Then there's all that stuff when he's on the run from Saul, the wars and the torment. Finally we catch up with him in middle age, nicely settled as king over the nation he has defended for so long.

> In the spring, at the time when kings go off to war, David sent Joab out with the king's men and the whole Israelite army. They destroyed the Ammonites and besieged Rabbah. But David remained in Jerusalem.
>
> (2 Samuel 11:1)

And this is where it all goes wrong. David's mistake is clear to see. Instead of going off to fight as was the custom, David decides to take it easy and sit this particular battle out at home. He stopped doing what he was supposed to be doing as a king and left himself wide open to attack.

I remember the leader of the Vineyard church, John Wimber, once said that he didn't have time to sin as he was too busy serving the Lord. Hearing that sort of thing is enough to cause me to have a seizure. Does this mean we're all supposed to fill every spare moment of the day with 'Christian' work, look knackered and have no social lives? Having thought about it, I feel better. I don't think that's quite what he was getting at, but I do believe he had hit on a truth; you see, the more time I have doing absolutely nothing, the more I seem to sin. Once I forget about what I'm supposed to be doing (keeping my mind focused on Jesus), it's easy to get down to all that other stuff. Obviously we all need rest, relaxation and plenty of time to enjoy ourselves – without those good things we miss out on much that God has given us – but if, like David, we forget about what we've been called to do, things could easily turn sour.

> One evening David got up from his bed and walked around on the roof of the palace.
>
> (2 Samuel 11:2a)

So we see David taking it easy, having a quick snooze before dinner perhaps. There he is, just mooching around the place trying to soak up the time.

> From the roof he saw a woman bathing. The woman was very beautiful, and David sent someone to find out about her.
>
> (2 Samuel 11:2b–3a)

A mere coincidence that he should see a woman bathing? Rubbish! He was in a prime position for perving and he knew exactly what he wanted to get in his sights. He was gagging for it and what's more, he obviously didn't just turn away after his first glance, he made sure he had a good look at her. Then he took it further, sending someone to find out about her.

> The man said, 'Isn't this Bathsheba, the daughter of Eliam and the wife of Uriah the Hittite?' Then David sent messengers to get her.
>
> (2 Samuel 11:3b–4a)

Even when he found out that she was married – and to one of his soldiers – he still pursued his urges and had her delivered to his room where he slept with her.

> Then she went back home. The woman conceived and sent word to David, saying, 'I am pregnant.'
>
> (2 Samuel 11:4b–5)

Not good, huh? David had landed himself in it big time, and was surely about to run the risk of facing a serious drop in his approval rating. But it gets worse. Instead of owning up, confessing and opting for a clean start, David wades even further out into the sewage of his own mistakes. He abused the power of his kingship, called Uriah to come and see him and eventually sent him out to the front line, having given the order to all the other troops to withdraw. Stranded, Uriah was defenceless and was killed in battle. In order to make space for his sin, David compounded his adultery with murder, ending up a wretched and miserable man.

Yet God had mercy on him. He sent David a prophet by the name of Nathan, who told him this story.

> There were two men in a certain town, one rich and the other poor. The rich man had a very large number of sheep and cattle, but the poor man had nothing except one little

ewe lamb that he had bought. He raised it, and it grew up with him and his children. It shared his food, drank from his cup and even slept in his arms. It was like a daughter to him.

Now a traveller came to the rich man, but the rich man refrained from taking one of his own sheep or cattle to prepare a meal for the traveller who had come to him. Instead, he took the ewe lamb that belonged to the poor man and prepared it for the one who had come to him.

(2 Samuel 12:1b–4)

David was furious. Any man who would do such a thing should be punished by death. He must have been a bit sleepy as he didn't quite get the point of the story. Thankfully Nathan spelled it out for him:

You are the man! This is what the Lord, the God of Israel, says: 'I anointed you king over Israel, and I delivered you from the hand of Saul. I gave your master's house to you, and your master's wives into your arms. I gave you the house of Israel and Judah. And if all this had been too little, I would have given you even more. Why did you despise the word of the Lord by doing what is evil in his eyes? You struck down Uriah the Hittite with the sword and took his wife to be your own. You killed him with the sword of the Ammonites. Now, therefore, the sword will never depart from your house, because you despised me and took the wife of Uriah the Hittite to be your own.'

(2 Samuel 12:7–10)

What an amazing passage. That line about how much God had given him and how he would have given him even more does me in. They are the words of a father to a son, tender, generous and kind. Yet David took something that wasn't his; the world was not enough.

257

This is a familiar scenario for many of us. We too can seem to have it all – the giftings, the friendships, the opportunities to be satisfied and fulfilled – yet we can't keep our fingers away from the things that do not belong to us. Somehow things are never enough and we are left wanting whatever we think shines brighter than the treasure in our own possession. We can be like magpies, just in the same way that David was. Something catches our attention and that's the end of the story: we simply have to have it. The 'it' in question can be anything at all, from material possessions to satisfaction to influence, the three sides of the money–sex–power triangle.

When he was the richest man in the world, John Paul Getty was asked how much money he needed to be happy. 'Just a little bit more,' he replied. It's true, we cannot resist the urge within us to chase after the things that do not belong to us.

When David was told by Nathan that God knew about his sin, he repented. It wasn't just a quick 'Sorry, God' either, but one of the most heartfelt pleas in the Bible. What caused this change of heart? It could only have been one thing: the word of God. It wasn't down to clever arguments or a cunning trap to bring David back to his knees before his Creator, but the perspective of divine truth. For me too, I know that when I come into contact with God's word – whether through the Bible or a prophecy – it can often cause the most radical turn around in my life. Knowing that God knows about us, that he cares and wants to guide us is reason enough to follow his lead.

We need to keep listening out for God's voice. If we're not there's a real danger that we, like David, will become blind to the sins and potential pitfalls that lie in our path. I'm sure that's what happened, that David rationalised his fall bit by bit without ever really seeing the whole picture. After all, he had probably been going off to war every spring for years and felt like he deserved a rest. Perhaps we might feel similarly if we'd been reading our Bibles and praying every day for months. Maybe a big chunk of regular attendance at church might be traded for 'Well, I'll just take a few weeks off'. It might be that we've been doing well with giving money to the poor – 'Just a little bit spent on myself instead won't hurt.' At the beginning none of these seem like a big deal; of course it was OK for David to take it easy at home one season, of course God isn't going to burn you up for missing a few days' quiet times or church visits. And after all, you did work hard for that cash. Of course none of these are so wrong but, like David, the stopping of doing good things can so easily become the starting point for doing bad things.

While one thing was leading to another, David was busy making excuses every step of the way. Standing on the roof checking out a fine-looking lady, well, why couldn't he find out her name? After all, he was the king. So what if she's Uriah's wife? A little fun won't hurt. Once Bathsheba is pregnant David even manages to excuse murder in an attempt to cover his back. Little lies can lead to bigger lies, and without something stopping them, their momentum can increase at an alarming rate.

We know that God forgave David, but it is also clear that he had to live with the consequences of his actions for the rest of his life. The son born to Bathsheba was ill and David pleaded with God for his child's life, yet the boy died. David was forced to live with this grief from that point on, much in the same way that there are consequences to be paid whenever we mess up too. It's not all gloom though, for when David turned and said sorry to God, the Almighty had mercy on him, not only forgiving him but restoring his relationship with him.

We Christians can get very confused, particularly when it comes down to this whole issue of sin and consequences. Because we know that Jesus died to pay for our sins, we assume that somehow wiping out the consequences of our actions gets thrown in with the bargain. Unfortunately this wasn't the case for David and it certainly isn't the case for us. The scars may stay with us, but like David we won't be kept at arm's length by a cold and uncompassionate God. Look back at Psalm 51:1–3:

> Have mercy on me, O God, according to your unfailing love; according to your great compassion blot out my transgressions. Wash away all my iniquity and cleanse me from my sin. For I know my transgressions, and my sin is always before me.

David knows the truth about his deeds – that his sin has placed a barrier between him and God. Only his Creator has the power to tear it down and the mercy to welcome David back into his presence. He's right, too, about his sins being always before him, about it always being around to remind him. He was surrounded by the litter of his mistakes – Bathsheba, mourning for the death of both her husband and son; the graves of both Uriah and the son born out of David's night with the dead man's wife.

You could be forgiven for thinking that it was against this husband and wife that David had sinned, but he has realised something profound: 'Against you, you only, have I sinned and done what is evil in your sight, so that you are proved right when you speak and justified when you judge' (Psalm 51:4).

He's right too; it was when he turned his back on God, when he stopped doing what was right in his anointed and appointed role that he started doing evil against other people. 'Surely I was sinful at birth, sinful from the time my mother conceived me' (Psalm 51:5). This is a controversial point, as some scholars have suggested that David was an illegitimate child, the product of his father Jesse's relationship outside of marriage, with another woman. It is suggested that these facts about his conception made David far more likely to sin sexually. I find that a hard line of argument to follow, leading on to the rocky ground of superstition and a denial of responsibility. What I do agree with, though, is that David probably had a weakness for the ladies, regardless of his birth. Perhaps his life was a constant battle between his urge for sexual adventure and his desire to serve his God. Let's face it, he wouldn't be alone in that, would he?

We all have particular areas of weakness, sins that we are more likely to turn towards than others. These may well be as a result of our childhood; if we were raised against a backdrop of an abusive and destructive relationship it stands to reason that our own approach to relationships might be slightly off-centre. If we are told every day that responsibility is a bad thing, that we need to look out for number one regardless of what others may say, then it wouldn't surprise many people if we turned out selfish and unwilling to commit to things and people. The solution? David has it right here: 'Surely you desire truth in the inner parts; you teach me wisdom in the inmost place' (Psalm 51:6).

That's it, we need wisdom. As the ultimate Creator, the all-seeing I am, God knows us like no one else ever could. We need his wisdom and his insight. Ask him why and where you might fall down. Ask him for help in readjusting some of your beliefs and values. Like David, ask for a total overhaul: 'Cleanse me with hyssop, and I shall be clean; wash me, and I shall be whiter than snow' (Psalm 51:7).

This is a key truth for us as Christians. Only Jesus' blood can wash us clean, only forgiveness that comes direct from the Father can wipe away our guilt. If we turn to him and genuinely ask for forgiveness, acknowledging what we have done wrong, then he will restore us, he will bring us back on home to the place where we . . .

... hear joy and gladness; let the bones you have crushed rejoice. Hide your face from my sins and blot out all my iniquity. Create in me a pure heart, O God, and renew a steadfast spirit within me. Do not cast me from your presence or take your Holy Spirit from me. Restore to me the joy of your salvation and grant me a willing spirit, to sustain me.

(Psalm 51:8–12)

One of the most obvious signs that we've messed up is that we lose the 'joy of our salvation'; things can become stale and dry as we drift further away from God (although when they do it doesn't automatically mean that we've sinned). The good news is that God can restore that joy, nothing is irredeemable.

It may be that you're going through a period where you're dealing with disappointment and doubt at the moment, not because your dreams have been wasted and not because your potential has been left stranded at the roadside. It may simply be that things are tough because you've messed up. Well, join the club. Get back up and run the race; make your apologies – you may need someone to help you – and start again. With God, there's always a second chance.

'If you look for truth, you may
find comfort in the end: if you
look for comfort, you will not get
either comfort or truth.'

C.S. Lewis

'Heroes are not
the ones that never fail, but the
ones that never give up.'

Ed Cole

6

When You're
Just Not Sure

Thomas's Story

As a fresh-faced, wide-eyed and innocent new Christian, I was hungry for knowledge. Sitting in my room I worked my way through countless books on different aspects of faith – you know the sort of thing: *How to Annoy Satan in Three Easy Steps* and *Why God Makes Good Christians Wealthy Overnight*. These were all very nice and entertaining, but something about them didn't quite hit the spot, something wasn't quite right.

It all made sense as soon as I returned from my local Christian bookshop with an entirely new type of book under my arm. It was an autobiography of some perfectly dentured American pastor, and little did I know that it would change things for me big time. Within minutes of starting to read this wonderful tome, I was captivated; all those other books had been so impersonal but here was a real-life person I could look up to and place on a pedestal. With the turning of each page came stories of spiritual battles fought and won, of trials and disasters which Pastor X sailed through with flying colours, faith and perfect smile well and truly intact. Whatever the devil threw at him – illness, bankruptcy, bereavement or faulty air-conditioning in his hotel suite – he fought back with steroid faith and the sure knowledge that he was able to give Satan's butt a right royal kicking.

This was the start of something new for me, and over the following months I became fascinated by this kind of Christian autobiography. I must have read hundreds of examples of it, each one giving me a new hero to follow, a new pin-up flexing his spiritual muscles to be admired. At first they made me feel great about myself; if they could sail through life's difficulties, perhaps I could too. Peering into the future I wondered what mine might contain; sure, there would be tough times, but there I'd be, striding along its highway, full of faith. Who knows, perhaps I'd even get to write books about my own victories one day.

After almost a year of this stuff it all started to go wrong. I had come across some kind of spiritual obstacle (can't remember what, exactly, but it was probably something to do with wondering whether God actually liked me) and nothing seemed to make sense. According to the world of Pastor X and friends, there was no room for doubt in the Victorious Christian Life. Life was for living, and doing it right meant believing 100 per cent that God was on your side and that everything was going to be A-OK.

Unfortunately things didn't seem like they were going to work out all right, and I certainly didn't feel full of faith. There had been a miracle on every page of the famous Christian minister's books, nothing had seemed to phase him and life had been one big advert for how the Lord sorted his mates out with a nice life. After months of lapping it up, I realised a profound truth about these authors. There was no denying the fact that my life just wasn't like theirs. I wanted to kill them.

Now that I get to write books and look serious whenever I'm on stage at a meeting, I need to be honest about a few things. My life still isn't like that of Pastor X and all the other faith warriors. It seems that even more than ever I'm plagued by doubt and confusion, and there certainly isn't a miracle on every page. I've got a feeling that yours is probably a bit like mine too, with there being more mess-ups than miracles, more confusion than canonisation. Above all, I bet there's been plenty of one thing that always seemed to have been flushed away by Pastor X et al: doubt.

But how do we do this Christian thing, then? How do we make sure that what we have holds together when all around us things seem to be crashing down? How do we deal with it when we aren't sure if God cares or even whether he exists? Is it fair to preach that we should never doubt our God? Whatever the cause – whether it's bereavement, redundancy, the breakdown of a relationship or the realisation that what seemed to be a plan with God's seal of approval on it has turned out to be a dud – life is full of reasons for us to question and to doubt our beliefs.

My own doubts come in various forms. At times I lie in bed wondering whether God really exists. At times I lie in bed wondering whether I really exist. Then there are the occasions when I have no problem whatsoever believing that God exists; what I struggle with is the question of whether or not he is *good*. I mean, there's so much evil in the world, can he really overcome it all? There are even times when I wonder whether he cares at all. Sometimes we Christians can put another spin on it, agreeing that God does exist and that he is good and loving, but that he doesn't actually love me. Then there are the other times when we're off on a mission that we may feel has been inspired by God himself when in creep those nagging doubts into our minds. The possibilities for doubt are endless, and I don't believe there's a Christian out there who doesn't go through it from time to time.

This is where it all gets confusing; you see I'm convinced – by my own life and others – that it is possible to have faith in God as well as to doubt. But here are the big questions: Does the doubt undermine the faith? Does the fact that we question God cancel out our belief in him? Is doubt like a virus, systematically destroying us and sapping our strength?

Surprisingly, my answer is: 'Well, it depends.' It all depends on how you define faith. Let me explain – you see, in my book, faith is more than an 'intellectual ascent to a set of propositions' (actually, I found that in somebody else's book, but I thought it sounded clever so I nicked it). It's not just about building up your knowledge of history and understanding of the Bible to a point where you can deliver a sixty-minute lecture on why Jesus existed. Faith is not about spewing facts or understanding words like 'eschatological' and 'God'. Don't get me wrong, though. I believe that it is important that we grapple with the facts and exercise our God-given intellect in these matters, but there's more to faith than that.

Faith is also more than a nice gooey feeling. Simply relying on the emotional highs that go with the rhythms of the Christian life is not enough. Becoming a Spirit junky, desperate for the next dose of Holy Ghost up the front at church will never breed real faith. But of course, ignoring the fact that Christianity works on an emotional as well as an intellectual level will surely lead to trouble further on down the road.

The solution is to look in the Bible, where you will find something interesting about the word 'faith'. In my opinion, the Scriptures paint a picture of faith being a verb – a doing word – rather than a static noun. We'll do some digging around in a bit, and throughout we will see that faith is far more something that you do, something to be practised and worked on rather than something that is merely acquired, like a jumper or a set of bath salts.

For what it's worth, my experience tells me that faith is the ability to keep on heading towards God, trusting in him, when we are surrounded by doubts. Some people say that faith is the opposite of doubt, that you cannot have faith and be in doubt at the same time. I don't agree; just remember the time when Peter and friends were out fishing one night and saw Jesus come towards them walking on the water. 'Come on, sunshine,' he said to Pete. 'Let's go for a stroll.' Peter duly climbs out of the boat and does a bit of the old no-sinking routine. All seems to be going well until Peter sees the wind and is reminded of the fact that by rights, he should be sinking fast. He begins to doubt and starts to sink, fast. Jesus wanders over, picks him up and delivers the line about 'you of little faith'.

This story at first glance can seem to have a pretty clear message on the subject of faith. Many have used it in the past to back up their claim that doubt is the opposite of faith. The truth, however, is far more exciting. Ask yourself, who had the faith? Was it Peter, the one who walked on the water, sank and then got rescued by Jesus, or was it the disciples sat in the boat with their tails between their legs, refusing to budge? I think it was Peter who got the pat on the back in this case; surely God wants us to have the faith to get out of the boat, to take that initial bold step to trust him. We should be like Peter who, when Jesus told him to come for a non-dip, asked, 'If that's you out there, tell me and I'll come.' The other disciples could have sat there muttering to themselves about how convinced they were that it was Jesus out there, or perhaps they might have been whooping and high-fiving each other, pumped up by how good they felt about the whole thing. Only Peter got out of the boat. He was the only one that *did*; the others simply *were*.

Like Peter, we too can often end up surrounded by doubts once we've taken a step of faith. But like Peter too, having taken that step towards him, we give Jesus the opportunity to come and pick us up. This leads us nicely up to the front door of an essential truth; faith is an adventure. What's more, I am convinced that instead of being the opposite of faith, doubt is the journey we take to come to faith.

The key to this side of the Christian life is keeping going with God despite the inevitable doubts and hiccups that colour our insecure moments. Right now as I write, in December 1999, I'm going through one of those insecure moments. Actually, 'insecure moment' doesn't quite do it justice; I think 'month of blind panic' would be more precise. You see, in precisely seven months, three weeks and four days, Soul Survivor will open the doors on its biggest event yet, just as this book gets published. The summer of 2000 will see us all hike up to Manchester for two week-long missions that aim to make a serious impact on a generation in and around the city. The Message 2000 is all about getting ordinary people to put their faith into practice by taking part in this massive mission, which needs almost 20,000 people to make it work. I firmly believe that the idea has come from God himself. I'm convinced he's into it, that he has said that he will honour and bless it.

Sitting here in my flat, staring out at the grey skies, I'm beginning to get a little worried. We have 104 people booked in for the first week and 43 for the second. Did I mention that we needed 20,000 to make it work? That's *19,853* left to go. Oh dear. Right now I wake up at 2 a.m., rigid with fear and cold with worry. Faced with the potential of losing hundreds of thousands of pounds I conjure up elaborate rescue plans. First I sell my flat, then I record a novelty single that goes straight in at number one. It uses the 'I feel like chicken tonight' melody and contains the following lyrics:

> I quite like bacon for tea
> Oinky oinky oinky oink
> I quite like lamb chops for lunch
> Baa baa baa baa baa baa.
> I quite like chocolate for afters . . .

I'm having trouble finding the noise that chocolate makes, but I'm pretty sure that the rest of it's a winner. With such a sure-fire hit as this up my sleeve, you may be surprised to hear that there are times when even 'Bacon for Tea' doesn't seem quite enough to banish worry and doubt from my mind. I'm left with feelings of doubt, and we are old friends. When our church decided to buy and refurbish a derelict warehouse, there were doubts about whether we could afford it. When we put on our first Soul Survivor festival there were doubts about whether anyone would come along. When I accepted the offer of running a youth group in my old church, there they were again, the doubts that asked whether I really could do it. But as well as the doubt, in each of these situations there was faith, made visible by the decision to keep on keeping on, no matter how wobbly or insecure I felt at the time.

I'm convinced that this thing called doubt is a gift from God, there to help us carry out quality-control checks on our faith. After all, faith was never meant to be a blind thing, something that was either on or off, present or absent. Faith is organic, needing to be fed, nurtured and tested. Without the opportunity to say, 'Yup, there are a few doubts around but I'm pressing on', what you're left with is untested and unproved. What use is that?

'Faith comes by hearing, and hearing by the word of God,' says the Bible. That means that our faith grows when we hear God's voice. It's easy enough to have a type of faith in all sorts of things which is little more than bravado or hype. The secret to picking yourself up off your knees in front of the empty tomb is having a tried and tested faith.

There's a character in the Bible who is spot on when it comes to any discussion of faith and doubt. No prizes for guessing that I'm talking about Thomas, AKA the Doubting Disciple. Where other disciples have been characterised as struggling with anger, fear or stupidity, history has recorded Thomas as the eternal pessimist. In John 14 we read about Jesus giving the people his 'in my father's house there are many rooms . . .' speech. He concludes with the most amazing promise anyone could ever ask for:

> I am going there to prepare a place for you. And if I go and prepare a place for you, I will come back and take you to be with me that you also may be where I am. You know the way to the place where I am going.
>
> (John 14:3–4)

If you ask me, it's pure dynamite. Apparently Thomas, however, didn't agree.

> Thomas said to him, 'Lord, we don't know where you are going, so how can we know the way?'
>
> Jesus answered, 'I am the way and the truth and the life. No-one comes to the Father except through me.'
>
> (John 14:5–6)

It's bizarre; Jesus is giving them such an encouragement yet you can almost hear Thomas whining above the rest of them as they murmured their appreciation. I think I would have been a lot less gracious with him than Jesus. After all the time they'd spent together, for Thomas to question such a fundamental truth would certainly have earned him a quick slap from me.

There's another story featuring Thomas which crops up when Jesus heard that his friend Lazarus had died:

> After he had said this, he went on to tell them, 'Our friend Lazarus has fallen asleep; but I am going there to wake him up.'
>
> His disciples replied, 'Lord, if he sleeps, he will get

better.' Jesus had been speaking of his death, but his disciples thought he meant natural sleep.

So then he told them plainly, 'Lazarus is dead, and for your sake I am glad I was not there, so that you may believe. But let us go to him.'

Then Thomas (called Didymus) said to the rest of the disciples, 'Let us also go, that we may die with him.'

(John 11:11–16)

You can't get much bleaker than that. Dear old Tom, while Jesus was about to perform one of his most spectacular miracles, was preparing to die himself. Jesus had even prompted them that they were about to see something inspiring (when he said that he was glad that he 'was not there, so that [they] may believe'). Thomas couldn't have got it more wrong if he tried.

Finally we have the absolute classic as Jesus catches up with his followers after he was raised from the dead. Here Thomas takes full advantage of the opportunity and makes himself look like an utter fool.

Now Thomas (called Didymus), one of the Twelve, was not with the disciples when Jesus came. So the other disciples told him, 'We have seen the Lord!'

But he said to them, 'Unless I see the nail marks in his hands and put my finger where the nails were, and put my hand into his side, I will not believe it.'

A week later his disciples were in the house again, and Thomas was with them. Though the doors were locked, Jesus came and stood among them and said, 'Peace be with you!' Then he said to Thomas, 'Put your finger here; see my hands. Reach out your hand and put it into my side. Stop doubting and believe.'

Thomas said to him, 'My Lord and my God!'

Then Jesus told him, 'Because you have seen me, you

have believed; blessed are those who have not seen and yet
have believed.'

(John 20:24-9)

Thomas's cries of 'unless I see/touch/feel' almost seem like
more than simple doubt, but a wilful stubbornness and a
desire not to get caught out. Having made him wait a week,
Jesus is kind to his dubious disciple, agreeing to his own
conditions by encouraging Thomas to feel his wounds for
himself. Suddenly Thomas the doubter speaks the words of
faith: 'My Lord and my God!'

So what is the antidote to doubt? First up we shouldn't
feel guilty that we question things. Everybody has doubts
and there isn't a human among us who hasn't questioned
their values and beliefs at some point. It's what separates us
from the fish, and being able to question and press on in the
face of opposition is a key step towards spiritual maturity.
But more than that, the antidote for us is the same as it was
for Peter and Thomas: to see Jesus. Jesus' words to Thomas
were pure acceptance and encouragement – 'Come on home,
son. It's OK to test me and have doubts. Feel these wounds
and let them ease your doubts. Now follow me.'

For many of us, each time we have a crisis in our lives and
everything seems to be going wrong we have the ideal
opportunity to put our faith into action. That doesn't mean
applying the fake tan and pearly white smile denying the
existence of doubt. Instead it's time to admit the fears and
take them back to the Lord. It's not failure, it's the
opportunity to find a deeper understanding of God.

'However bleak
events may be, we cannot
interpret them as telling us that
God has ceased to be the loving,
all-powerful, fair and extravagant
heavenly Father that he is. Instead,
because he is like that, it means
our difficulties are in his
control and his purposes
for us are good.'

Peter Meadows

7

Beyond the Tomb
Paul's Story

I'm always amazed by the way that Jesus can turn lives around. No matter how far away or how determined we may have been to keep the distance between ourselves and our Creator, Jesus always holds the power to bring us back. You may be wondering where this power comes from; the answer is plain and simple, it comes from Jesus' death and resurrection. We've gone into it in much more detail in the first book of this series (*Walking with a Stranger*), but the fact that Jesus chose not only to die on the cross (taking the punishment that we deserve for all our sin) but then rose from the dead means that the message of Christianity is the most potent around. Because of Jesus we have a future in heaven and the power to overcome all obstacles. In his letter to the church in Rome, Paul suggested that if the resurrection was a hoax, then we Christians are to be pitied. You see, the resurrection is absolutely central to what we believe and without it our faith falls down.

With that kind of ammunition, it's not surprising that lives get turned around as people encounter Jesus one on one. There are hundreds of stories told by people who have had their own lives turned around, but if you ask me, there's one particular tale that stands head and shoulders above the rest: that man Paul. Way back in the days of the early church, throughout the years following Jesus' life on earth, Saul (as he was known back then) was a persecutor. Not only was he a pure grade, 100 per cent zealous Pharisee, but he was also a particularly nasty piece of work. He hated the sect of new Christians, and used his time productively by killing, persecuting or imprisoning as many of them as he could find. In fact, we read that when Stephen made it into the history books as the first Christian martyr, it was dear old Saul who was helpfully holding the coats of those who were stoning him to death. It was a tragedy for the early church (known as 'the people of the Way'), made even worse by the fact that Stephen was widely recognised as being a good man, full of faith and the Holy Spirit. He even echoed his Saviour, asking with his final words that his killers be forgiven.

This side of heaven we will probably never know what sort of impact this inspiring display of Christianity in action made on Saul, but by the time we reach Acts 9, we get to know him a whole lot better:

> Meanwhile, Saul was still breathing out murderous threats against the Lord's disciples. He went to the high priest and asked him for letters to the synagogues in Damascus, so that if he found any there who belonged to the Way, whether men or women, he might take them as prisoners to Jerusalem. As he neared Damascus on his journey, suddenly a light from heaven flashed around him. He fell to the ground and heard a voice say to him, 'Saul, Saul, why do you persecute me?'
>
> 'Who are you, Lord?' Saul asked.
>
> 'I am Jesus, whom you are persecuting,' he replied.

'Now get up and go into the city, and you will be told
what you must do.'

(Acts 9:1–6)

So, blinded and probably just a little confused, Saul makes
his way to the city where he hooks up with a fine man by the
name of Ananias. Within a few verses the story covers his
conversion and we begin to glimpse the extent to which he
has been transformed. Like many millions of others throughout time, Saul's transformation came when he met the risen
Jesus. So extreme was this change that because of Paul's life,
the rest of the Bible – in fact, the rest of Christianity – would
never be quite the same again. Instead of knocking it down,
he went on to build up the early church, making sure that it
had strength and wisdom enough to see it through.

But it wasn't all plain sailing. If you thought that once he
changed his name to Paul everything went smoothly, unfortunately you'd be wrong. For Paul, life was full of trials and
tribulations; he was beaten, shipwrecked, arrested and put in
jail. He was run out of town and faced death and opposition
almost wherever he went. Yet he was fired up, fully committed to doing whatever it took to ensure the good progress
of the message of Jesus Christ.

With such an impressive CV it's not surprising that he was
responsible for depositing more than a few pearls of wisdom
in his time. Of all his wise words, I reckon that some of the
best can be found in his letter to the church at Philippi. It was
no ordinary letter; not only is it stuffed full of reasons why
his friends the Philippians ought to be rejoicing, but it was
written while Paul was locked up in a Roman jail. He was
permanently chained to a guard who was changed every six
hours. Now there's an obvious reason why these guards were
given six-hour shifts, but reading between the lines I'm
convinced that it wasn't just the call of nature that had them
bursting to unlock themselves and leave Paul's company. Paul,

it would seem, saw the arrangement of chaining a guard to him as a perfect opportunity for evangelism, and he told his readers that . . .

> Now I want you to know, brothers, that what has happened to me has really served to advance the gospel. As a result, it has become clear throughout the whole palace guard and to everyone else that I am in chains for Christ. Because of my chains, most of the brothers in the Lord have been encouraged to speak the word of God more courageously and fearlessly.
>
> (Philippians 1:12–13)

He told his jailers all about his faith, and I bet for many of them it was one of the most taxing shifts going; I almost feel sorry for them. In the end there were believing Christians at the heart of Roman power – in the palace guard – all because of one Christian who just couldn't keep his gob shut.

This love of God-chat was so strong in Paul because he so profoundly realised that he had been saved. What is even more exciting is the fact that by many measures, he was doing pretty well in society's eyes before he met Jesus. As he puts it, his pedigree was near perfect:

> If anyone else thinks he has reasons to put confidence in the flesh, I have more: circumcised on the eighth day, of the people of Israel, of the tribe of Benjamin, a Hebrew of Hebrews; in regard to the law, a Pharisee; as for zeal, persecuting the church; as for legalistic righteousness, faultless.
>
> (Philippians 3:4b–6)

Not only was he a Jew, but he was a member of one of the better tribes. He was not only religious, he was professionally religious, and very good at it too. He was a top-notch social climber with a bright future in the persecution business. As he said, he had every reason to 'put confidence in the flesh', to rely on his own strengths, talents and abilities without turning elsewhere for assistance. He had it all, until he met Jesus:

> But whatever was to my profit I now consider loss for the sake of Christ. What is more, I consider everything a loss compared to the surpassing greatness of knowing Christ Jesus my Lord, for whose sake I have lost all things. I consider them rubbish, that I may gain Christ and be found in him, not having a righteousness of my own that comes from the law, but that which is through faith in Christ – the righteousness that comes from God and is by faith.
>
> (Philippians 3:7–9)

Bible translators tend to be fairly polite people, and so their choice of the word 'rubbish' here should not be taken too seriously. Instead, Paul's original letter in Greek would have contained something more like 'I consider all these things *dog dung* compared to knowing Christ'. He makes it clear that he found something far more worthwhile and exciting than the human talents and religious rituals that he was previously so reliant upon. Instead he shouts it from the rooftops that it was Jesus who made all the difference in his life. And like those attempts to get into the *Guinness Book of Records* for toppling dominoes, there's always a spectacular ending. Paul's argument leads up to this, one of my favourite verses in the Bible:

> I want to know Christ and the power of his resurrection and the fellowship of sharing in his sufferings, becoming like him in his death, and so, somehow, to attain to the resurrection from the dead.
>
> (Philippians 3:10)

Face facts; that verse rocks. Take the first bit, I mean, who wouldn't want to couple up with the Lord Almighty and share in some of his amazing power? But in the same way that God doesn't separate the twin elements of victory and pain in the cross, Paul keeps things in order. It can be all too easy for us Christians to get off on a happy 'n' holy trip, enjoying the good stuff of blessings and spiritual sunny days. As soon as the merest cloud appears on the horizon, as soon as there's a hint that things aren't going to be quite the picnic we had planned, we find it all too tempting to get in a big strop with God and refuse to keep moving on with him. But loving God truly means loving the tough stuff as well as the blessings. When Ananias was given his instructions about hosting Saul after his meeting with God along the road to Damascus, Ananias was understandably hesitant – I mean, wouldn't you be if faced with a similar proposition? Yet the Lord told Ananias that he was going to show Saul exactly how much he was going to suffer for him. Resurrection and suffering go hand in hand and, for our sake, Jesus went through the pain of the cross in order to reach the resurrection on the other side.

Being like Christ means being like Paul in the sense that sometimes we have to travel the harder path instead of enjoying the chauffeured limo. I believe suffering falls into two categories. First, there's the type of suffering that is dictated by circumstance – the illness, the poverty and the tragedy. Second, there's the type that we choose – the decision not to follow our own wills all the time but to sacrifice for the will of God. Like a parent getting up to answer the cries of a baby at night, or a lover clearing up after someone has been ill, this type of sacrifice sends a message loud and clear about how love is twinned with sacrifice.

I'm certainly not saying that if faced with a choice between a pleasurable and an unpleasant situation that it would be God's will that we automatically opt for the worst. We're not supposed to be miserable gits in hair shirts, but for all of us, surely it makes sense that if we really are following the God who laid down his life for us, then our lives will show reflections of that same spirit. There must be some situations when God's will and our will are in opposition and we end up choosing to go for his. Even Jesus in the Garden of Gethsemane went through this one. 'May this cup pass from me,' he pleaded with his father. The agony of the cross was just hours away, yet he followed on by saying, 'Not my will but yours be done.' That's the suffering that comes from obediently following.

And so we end up once again with Mary Magdalene, weeping before the empty tomb. The central message of Christianity comes in the death and the resurrection of Jesus Christ. He actually came in order to die. A man on a mission, he came to face death – the ultimate enemy of us all. He came to fight it and to conquer it, to announce a victory that is on offer to us all. Because Jesus died we don't need to weep before the tomb; it's empty and Jesus is long gone. He has risen, leaving the tomb and returning in glorious victory back to heaven. We don't need to mourn; the resurrection gives us hope. When life is tough like it was for Job or Joseph, when we have doubts like Thomas, mess up like David or Samson, in the end there's hope for us precisely because there's no one in the tomb. Because he rose our lives *can* change, they *can* be different. That's the hope which is available to us all, and that's what we will be going on to look at in the last of these four little books; the great hope of life after death.

'Never give in, never give in,
never, never, never – in nothing,
great or small, large or petty –
never give in except to convictions
of honour and good sense.'
Winston Churchill

Afterlife

Facing the Future with God

Mike Pilavachi with Craig Borlase

Hodder & Stoughton
LONDON SYDNEY AUCKLAND

To Elvira and Janet, our mothers.
We would not be here without you!

Contents

	Introduction	289
1	The D Word	295
2	Life Is Made Up of Little Deaths	307
3	Dealing with Grief	317
4	The Second Coming	327
5	How to Die a Good Death	339
6	Heaven, Angels and All That	349

Introduction

In preparing to write this book I've read two books on angels, three books on Jesus' Second Coming, two more on death and various other leaflets, articles and backs of cereal packets. In the hope of coming up with something interesting to say about this most peculiar of subjects I trawled through such a variety of texts that I wound up not only confused, but enlightened, amazed and queasy all at the same time. You see, when it comes to death, not only are the vast majority of us in the West a bit slow when it comes to thinking about it, but we Christians also have the peculiar habit of embracing between us the most astoundingly diverse set of beliefs. Recently within the space of a couple of days I heard two Christian speakers give passionate yet totally opposing arguments about the very heart of Christian thought on the afterlife and things eternal: one believed that the Second Coming was just around the corner while the other was convinced that it could take both many events to unfurl and countless decades to pass before Jesus' return.

Now, of course the fact that there's a whole load of debate and difference of opinion within the Church shouldn't really be much of a surprise to anyone who has spent more than five minutes in a church council meeting, but something about this situation struck me as interesting. It's not that our beliefs can be so different that got me; it was the fact that when I stopped to ask myself what I thought about it, I realised that I really wasn't sure. In fact, when it comes to the whole thing of the Second Coming, the make-up of heaven and the future of mankind – and I probably ought to be embarrassed to admit this – it had been a while since I'd really got stuck into it. We'll go into reasons why this might be so later on in the book, but for now – to start things off gently – let's check out the landscape.

When it comes to what happens when we die, there's a wholesale fascination that runs through almost every aspect of contemporary culture like 'BRIGHTON' through a stick of rock. As with my two opposing speakers, for us Christians, things can begin to get a little muddy, but for the average bloke in the pub, the picture that enters their mind when the word *heaven* is mentioned might be reasonably clear: harps, clouds and all that. Others might opt for a fairly firm belief that what follows death is nothing more than nothingness. Christians, on the other hand, have it tough. We've got a book stuffed full of images that occasionally would seem more at home in a *Dungeons and Dragons* game, with material that has prompted theories and beliefs as diverse and confused as you could possibly imagine. Depending on what church you visit you might hear that heaven is a physical place, a spiritual state or that it exists already. Some choose to play it down while others like nothing better than to spice up a bland sermon with a few trouser-soiling examples about just exactly how you might be spending eternity should you fail to get things right this time around. It's confusing. I'm confused, and even after all my research, I think I'm only slightly better off. Never having let a little ignorance get in the way of things, however, I shall continue.

As the final book in the series, *Afterlife* takes a look at death. We'll examine theories and ideas about what things will look like for us once we're on the other side, as well as taking a slightly more sideways glance at how the concept of 'dying' translates into one of the most important aspects of the Christian life – sacrifice. We'll split the subject down the middle, with the literal biblical stuff on one side and the more personal lot on the other. There's far more to death than meets the eye, and hopefully we'll end up living stronger – if not longer – lives at the end of it.

While I'm not one for rules, we need to get a couple of things straight before beginning, particularly with regard to the concept of what happens to each of us after we've shuffled off this mortal coil. The key to any study/argument about life after death is not to get bogged down in speculation about whether it will take place on earth or in heaven or whether there will be sex there. Forget whether Jesus will be blond, black or fond of thrash-metal-hardcore-country dancing, the key is to remember that afterlife is life with God in all its fullness. It means seeing him face to face and, as Paul says in 1 Corinthians 13, now we see in part, then we will see face to face and we will know as we are known. If we really want to prepare for the kingdom to come the best thing we can do is to get used to living that way now. We all need to get to know the author of life while we're here. After all, he's the one who transcends and overpowers death.

One of my favourite countries to visit is South Africa. In fact, I'm going there in just two weeks' time and I can't wait. I haven't always felt this way, though; before my first visit to South Africa I was quite apprehensive and uncertain, mainly because I knew no one from that country. Now I have many friends there. My friends are waiting for me. It's the same with heaven. My friend Jesus is waiting for me. The more I get to know him the less apprehensive I will be. I have often found that those who know God the best are those who fear death the least.

We often can get our focus wrong, both when it comes to

heaven and God in general. Because we're fond of entertainment and shy of hard graft with little reward, we can often find ourselves getting well into seeing God work or having him do something spectacular in our lives but switching off at the thought of working at getting to know him better. We often would rather be a spectator than a player, and when it comes to God this can lead to an unfortunate lack of balance in our relationship with him.

The same can be said of our approach to the afterlife; we love the thought of all that time and goodness, but are unprepared for the prospect of being quite that close to him. If we really are keen to think about and prepare for the next life, I would suggest that instead of worrying about the travel arrangements it's far better to get on with continually building on our relationship with God. Instead of merely coming to him like children, eagerly looking in his hands to see what gifts he has for us today, we need to be prepared to look into his face, to learn to recognise and appreciate him. The more we learn about Jesus, getting to know him, absorbing ourselves in him and gazing into his face, the more we will long not for death, but for what comes after it.

As Christians we get glimpses of the afterlife right here on earth. At one stage some people asked Jesus where the kingdom of heaven was. He told them that to try and plot it on a map was pointless for the simple reason that the kingdom of heaven is to be found within us. What did he mean? The kingdom of heaven is within us when Jesus, the king of heaven, makes his home in us. When I became a Christian, Jesus by his Holy Spirit came to live in me. Jesus was saying that the first thing we need to look for when we are searching for the kingdom, is not a physical place but a person (see Luke 17:20–1). You simply cannot define heaven without focusing on Jesus, for he is what it is all about.

We're fond of teasing ourselves by wondering whether we will recognise each other in heaven. For what it's worth I think we will be able to; we will have resurrection bodies just in the same way that Jesus does and did when he rose in bodily form from the dead. It does seem as though we will live on a new earth, one that will be redeemed and reclaimed, where all the effects of pollution and unnatural corrosion will be wiped clean. We will live as we were meant to live, on the earth as God intended it.

Much of this comes from the book of Revelation, and alongside these facts can be found the most obscure and figurative pieces of prose in the whole Bible. But if you manage to get to the end of the book you will see that more than it being about beasts covered in eyes or scrolls, horsemen and virgins, it is actually about Jesus. There is the most wonderful passage in chapter 22 verses 4 and 5:

> They [the servants of the Lord] will see his face, and his name will be on their foreheads. There will be no more night. They will not need the light of a lamp or the light of the sun, for the Lord God will give them light.

God himself is light, and he will call us home. It matters less where that home is or how it will look, and matters more who will permeate its every corner; the answer is God himself. He is the afterlife.

1

The D Word

Death: the final frontier. Our bravest have conquered Everest, our most intelligent have placed their fellow humans on the moon. Our most beautiful are celebrated the world over and our history books are littered with tales of excellence and exception. Scientists have broken through medical barriers that only a handful of years ago were considered immovable. Barely a week goes by without an announcement of a new development that promises to shape the way the world will be tomorrow. 'The future is now' we tell ourselves, chests swollen with pride as we sample the air of the new dawn of the millennium. Evolution or not, there are plenty of us who believe that we are one seriously impressive species. 'Well done, human beings,' we say to ourselves, 'you're coming along nicely.'

But deep down we know that all the perfect smiles and jaw-droppingly impressive achievements in the world cannot alter the fact that there is still one thing that we cannot overcome. The clock is ticking for each of us, and while the diets and exercise may be able to slow it down, none of us can put off the inevitable: one day we will die, and what happens after that is something many of us would rather not think about.

At the end of the day, each of us will face an ending. It doesn't matter about wealth, health or social standing, death is the final frontier we simply cannot avoid. It unites us all, bringing together the rich and the poor, the famous and the forgotten, the foolish and the wise.

The fundamentally democratic rule of 'one person, one death' applies today as much as it did when life expectancy was well below fifty years and a common cold could be fatal. No matter how hard we try to drag things out, in the long run our death rate is 100 per cent; we're all going to die.

It's kind of odd then, that such an important and universal subject should be such a taboo. After all, if we're all going to end up the same, shouldn't we be able to talk about it a little more? But we can't quite seem to be able to manage to overcome our fear and find out how others feel. As far as conversation goes, death is off the menu. It's the 'd' word; the subject that's best avoided, like politics and religion.

I found this out for myself when I was seven years old. My first pet had just died – an obese hamster by the name of Gunter (I was into German football when I named him). Gunter was great and his death was a bit of a blow. However, not being told otherwise, I saw no reason why the mere fact that he had stopped breathing should separate us. As a matter of fact, now that his body had stopped working, carrying him around in my pocket during the day was far less trouble than when he was alive (he had had a very weak bladder, you see). And so he remained in my coat pocket for the first few days after his passing. I would stroke him as I walked along and he, well, he would just lie there, eyes wide open and claws outstretched as if contemplating the very make-up of the universe itself.

One day – a while later – it was my turn to step up to the front of the class and grasp my fifteen minutes of fame in a round of Show and Tell. I was excited and couldn't wait to bring Gunter out and tell the whole class about our new-found friendship. I stood at the front – chest out, shoulders back – and went into intricate detail about my life with Gunter. I told them about the day that I bought him, about the naming ceremony, the joy of playing with him every day and the trauma of seeing him get caught in the food processor while my mother was making bread. (Thankfully he stood out well against the flour and a near crisis had been averted.) I must admit I was doing pretty well and could tell from the faces beaming back at me that they knew exactly how great a hamster Gunter was.

I was therefore surprised that when I came on to the subject of his death that my fellow classmates failed to share my excitement. For me, Gunter's passing had been a wonderful thing. To them, it was a horror story. As I plunged into ever more intricate detail about how Gunter breathed his last (no time to tell it now, but it involved a trail of Brazil nuts and a faulty sandwich toaster) the tears began to flow from my audience. In a desperate attempt to convey that it had not been a tragedy but a wonderful new dawn, I pulled Gunter from out of my coat pocket and ran around the room waving his flat, branded and criss-crossed body under my colleagues' noses. There was chaos. I ended up with lines and Miss Jones's nerves never did seem quite the same again. Death, I found out, is not best introduced to the classroom.

Of course, over the years I developed a much more suitable and anglicised approach to death. Not only did I stop talking about it but I also stopped thinking about it. Like most of us I put it to the back of my mind, quarantined from the rest, buried deep down until it had to be faced when some other Gunter met the grand sandwich toaster of life.

Apart from my hamster story, there aren't many better examples of how keen we are to avoid the subject of death than in our language. We wrap it up in all sorts of fluffy phrases in a desperate attempt to make it easier to swallow. 'He's passed away' we gently sigh or talk about how 'she's gone to a better place'. People are 'at rest' or have 'moved on'. We even apply the same rule to our animals, choosing to declare that they are 'put to sleep' instead of killed or put to death.

Today we have less experience of death than we ever did. While there might be fewer people being born in the Western world, we're managing to hang on that little bit longer before we finally do get around to kicking the bucket. These days it's getting increasingly unusual for young people to experience the death of a close friend or family member; one hundred years ago a teenager may well not only have lost the odd grandparent, but perhaps a parent and a sibling or two. Back in the twenty-first century it is precisely because of this lack of experience that many of us are becoming increasingly ill-equipped to deal with death.

At the same time we're fascinated by it; from TV to the cinema, fiction to art, we just cannot seem to keep away from it. For many of us this is the nearest that we get to death. Whether it's comic book violence or morbid fascination, the 'd' word has also become a billion-dollar industry, and the tills keep on ringing. But this type of approach to death has changed things for us. It has sanitised it, cleaned it up and made it far easier to swallow. In films it's not unusual to get into double figures with on-screen deaths during the duration of a picture – but this is nothing new; after all, Shakespeare was well into a bit of bloodbath in his day, as the final moments of *Hamlet* make clear. It's not just about quantity, it's about attitude. When James Bond pumps a slug from his Walter PPK into a baddie, we don't think twice about the significance of the event. In the film *Austin Powers, International Man of Mystery* it is put so well as the wife of a recently killed henchman of Dr Evil turns to camera and suggests that no one stops to think about the family of an evil tyrant's henchman. Freshly cleaned up and rendered suitable for family viewing, we clock up an astonishing number of on-screen deaths, and by the time they are sixteen, the average American has seen 18,000 murders on TV. Among a UK audience, the figures are equally shocking.

Our cartoon attitude to violence spills over to our perspective on war and human tragedy. The pictures that were beamed back from Kosovo and Chechnya held our attention for about as long as they could, but sooner or later the channel got flicked, the kettle put on and we returned to the business of getting on with our lives. It's such a familiar sight to all of us that death these days doesn't seem to be quite what it was, and viewing the end of someone's life just doesn't seem to be enough to hold our attention.

But despite this easy attitude there have been many studies that have pointed to death as being the main source of worry among young people today. The thought of a premature death, of dying before our time, is often almost too much to bear. It's not hard to get your head around it either, as with the proliferation of nuclear weapons, the reports of advances in chemical and biological warfare and the ease with which conflicts flare up into full-scale stand-offs, death can sometimes seem just around the corner. We have the capacity to destroy ourselves many times over, and with the breakdown of the Soviet Union, the arrival of India and Pakistan to the list of nuclear countries and the likelihood that the same applies to Israel, Iran and others in the area, many are worried that it is only a matter of time before some nutter finds his finger on the trigger.

Not only that, but there's the very real prospect that it won't even take a nuclear holocaust to finish our planet off; that we're doing quite a nice job of destroying the planet ourselves, thank you very much. The slow progress of ozone depreciation, pollution and global warming march us on towards a fate the full horror of which few of us have even begun to comprehend.

Then there are the new diseases that have come onto the

scene over the last few years. Despite the warnings, HIV/ AIDS is on the increase and cancer looks set to continue to baffle scientists well into the next couple of decades. A recent report by the Cancer Research Campaign suggested that cancer now hits four in every ten of the British population. Ironically doctors put this down partly to the fact that we are living longer. Instead of getting struck down by the killers of old such as pneumonia and septicaemia, we face an old age punctuated by the horrors of lung, breast, bowel and prostate cancer. Despite this, however, the death rates from cancer are dropping, thanks to advances in technology for treatment and detection. Still, the fact that many of us might be able to rate our own chances of making it through to a peaceful and natural death at the end of a long life may be some comfort, but what about our children; do they really stand a chance from all the rest of the killers that look set to darken future horizons?

Yet many of us seem to have such interesting and occasionally bizarre views on death that sometimes I find it hard to see the connection between what we imagine happens to us on the other side of life and the increasingly desperate-looking reality that has been described above. It wasn't that long ago that we all were treated to Mr Glenn Hoddle's views on exactly what was what and who would be in line for what in the life after this one. Thanks, Glenn. He's not alone, though, as there are plenty of others out there who share equally sanity-free ideas on the afterlife. Often a fine blend of Eastern mysticism, New Age focus and morality-lite pleasantries about 'being a good person', these views often touch on reincarnation, and for many it comes down to believing in something that simply makes them feel good.

Of course, these people are not in the minority; there's a huge hunger out there for understanding and a sense of purpose. From spiritualists and mediums to the use of Ouija boards and Tarot cards, people are prepared to go to great lengths to find out how the story ends.

In 1999 cinema-goers were treated to the ultimate horror movie, *The Blair Witch Project*. There was no blood, no on-screen violence and no traditional horror – just suspense as the film lived out our most common anxieties; that there is an unseen force out there which we don't understand, a force that will end our lives. The fear of the unknown is so great that for many viewers, the film was almost too much to bear. Interestingly the film was praised for its astonishingly low budget – costing just US$60,000 to make. The marketing bill wasn't quite as slimmed down, however, as in excess of $20 million was spent promoting the film.

Lots of us are scared about death and few could claim to fully understand it. Many are searching for answers, and I believe that the Christian faith provides something that is worth more than all the answers and all the theories on offer. It's called *hope*, but don't think I mean some kind of flimsy, fluffy hope, the sort based more on nice and cuddly feelings. The hope that comes prepacked for everyone who turns towards Christ is firm, based on reality and rooted in the eternal goodness that is God. Just take a look through the Bible and you will see how Jesus preaches a message that explains what it means to live a life that is not affected by death. Jesus redefined life and death, bringing them back on track and helping us to view them not as polar opposites, with life at the good end and death at the bad. Instead he taught us that life is made up of little deaths, that in learning how to follow him we would look beyond our own lives. At the heart of Christianity is the most upside-down death of all; Jesus on a cross. In dying Jesus took on himself the punishment for our sin. In rising from the dead three days later, he rewrote the rule book; death has lost its sting. We'll find out just how right this is throughout this book, but first it might be wise to take a stroll around the grand supermarket of life and see what they've got on a special offer in the death department.

Life and death can be hit-and-miss affairs. No matter how grand our lives, how great our achievements or well-known our exploits, death can often turn the tables. Of the great thinkers of the last century, Albert Einstein was probably the greatest. But when he died, his final words died with him. His nurses didn't speak German and so the final chapter of the man's story was left incomplete. Then there was Alfred Nobel; his life was dedicated to the discovery and perfection of dynamite. When by accident someone published his obituary before his death, Mr Nobel came face to face with the stark reality that his life had been about nothing more than perfecting the art of killing people. This sparked a full-on 180 degree turn and he altered his will to set up the Nobel Peace Prize, rewarding those who made great contributions to prolonging and enhancing life instead of destroying it.

Rock-and-roll's speeding highway is littered with stories of fast-living stars and celebs. 'Live fast, die young, leave a good looking corpse' so they say, and there are plenty taking the advice. From James Dean's fatal ride to Kurt Cobain's descent into the world of heroin and guns, we've developed a taste for this type of ending. We like our teen idols to go out in a blaze of glory. I mean, who hasn't felt a twinge of embarrassment as yet another dinosaur of rock fails to age gracefully on a trout farm but chooses instead to rock out with their zimmer frame in public? Mick Jagger's still at it, as are the front half of Led Zeppelin and dear old Cliff Richard. Generally these ageing hipsters don't have an easy ride of it in the public eye, and perhaps there is something about their highly visible struggle to be considered young way beyond the time when their grandchildren have learnt to drive that we all find vaguely embarrassing. Ending your career the way of Jimi Hendrix, Janis Joplin, Richie Manic or Jim Morrison helps keep you forever young in the land of pin-ups and rock legends.

But there's one who was the daddy of them all, out-consuming the others while alive and upstaging the rest after death. Of course I'm talking about Elvis, the man who was reported to have more drugs than Superdrug inside his body when the post mortem was carried out. He had a taste for burgers, pills, bourbon and handguns, not to mention the cat suits, capes and ballooning physique. In his heyday he was absolutely massive, but the exploitation of a crooked manager and a number of bad career choices left him facing a mixed reaction. Only a reincarnation as 'the Comeback Kid' and a string of gigs in Vegas helped him end on something of a high note. In terms of status, however, things got better for Elvis once he was dead. These days it seems like he cannot put a foot wrong.

Across the globe fans believe that his passing was their cue to celebrate his life in all manner of ways. First came the obsessive collectors, people who turned rooms and houses over to shrines of the man they called *The King*. Of course, this was helped by the fact that every money-minded souvenir producer jumped on the bandwagon after the singer's death, flooding the market with everything from Elvis plates and Elvis rugs to Elvis toilet-roll holders and Elvis condoms (I kid you not). Then came the impersonators, crooning and 'thangyouvermuch'-ing their way through the grand sequinned jump suit life. Here in the UK, Elvis-look-alike Gary Jay broke the world record for non-stop singing of Elvis's hits. He managed to score a whopping ten hours without a break, swivelling his way through more than a hundred of the greatest numbers.

For others, merely looking and sounding like their hero isn't enough, and every year fans gather at various locations (Graceland in Memphis being the main one) to celebrate the anniversary of Mr Presley's death. Putting their own unique twist on the man's style, it's not uncommon to witness all manner of Elvis impersonators on 16 August. There are

Viking Elvises, Japanese Elvises, even an Indian Elvis, named Elvis Singh. This fine chap wearing a turban and excessively long sideburns has been known to croon: 'I don't do drugs, I don't drink bourbon, all I wanna do is shake my turban.'

But being an icon after death doesn't get much better than the lengths to which some Elvis fans have gone to; setting up their own church, The First Presleyterian Church of Elvis the Divine. Most aren't quite sure what they believe, but rumour has it that communion comes in the form of a Big Mac and double chocolate shake.

Moving back to reality, one of the great messages of Christianity is that in Jesus Christ we can have eternal life, made possible through Jesus' triumph over death. Yet, it strikes me as being quite odd that we use this message of eternal life as a selling point for people in and around our contemporary culture. Take a look around and it's plain to see that there are plenty of people within society who are continually debating how to end this life. Euthanasia, excess and a single-minded commitment to live for the moment don't seem to be particularly strong indications that news of a next life after this will go down too well.

Despite that, I believe that the eternal life Jesus offers is worth focusing on. I don't believe it's right to focus on quantity (after all, most people would agree that an infinity of anything is bound to get boring after a while), but instead we ought to be chatting about the quality of eternal life. You see, what Jesus offers is a life free from pain, and a life that goes even further; a life in the presence of God himself. Now that's got to be a hit.

'It's not that I'm afraid
to die. I just don't want to be
there when it happens.'
Woody Allen

'I am ready to
meet my maker, but whether my
maker is prepared for the great
ordeal of meeting me
is another matter.'
Winston Churchill

'I don't mind dying, it's just that
one is a little stiff the next
morning.'
Woody Allen

'I thank my God
for graciously granting me the
opportunity of learning that death
is the key which unlocks the door
to our true happiness.'
Wolfgang Amadeus Mozart

2

Life Is Made Up of
Little Deaths

Before we get on to having a look at what lies in store for us on the other side of the funeral parlour, I propose we take a couple of chapters out to have a look at how death plays a part for each of us while we are very much alive. Looking at the subject, it seems clear to me that it isn't just limited to the obvious. Sure, on the one hand death is all about a decomposing/eternal life/plaque on a park bench type of thing. On the other hand, however, surely there's a bit of it that also affects life itself. We'll look at how to deal with grief and bereavement in the next chapter, but it also occurs to me that life itself – strangely – is made up of deaths; there is death at the end of life and there are deaths throughout it. It's not only when we breathe our last that we come face to face with death, but throughout our time on earth, almost from day one.

Each of us has a genetic blueprint, right? Well, in each of those blueprints can be found the code that may point to the closing chapters of our earthly destiny – high blood pressure, cholesterol or whatever. It's long been known that once we enter our third decade our bodies begin their slow decline as the creation of new cells is outnumbered by the level at which the others are dropping off. Sorry if all this sounds a bit depressing, but there is a point to it all. There's more to life being made up of death than merely cell-degradation and all that; death is much more than a physical thing, it is an emotional one as well. To say goodbye to a friend is to die a little death, to see an ambition finally become an impossibility is a little death. To lose a job or to move house will take us along the path of separation and ending, even if it might not necessarily include grief.

But for Christians there's something even more significant about a life full of small deaths. Following Christ means walking in his footsteps, and it doesn't take a genius to work out that his was a story marked at every turn by acts of selflessness and humility. Throughout his life, Jesus communicated a potent message about the need for people to follow his lead and put their own priorities and preferences second to his greater will. If you're fond of Christian jargon you could call this *dying to self*. What a repulsive term. I can hardly think of anything less attractive. Thankfully Jesus fleshed the idea out a little, exclaiming at one point: 'If anyone would follow me, let him deny himself, take up his cross and follow me.' At another instant he suggested that 'if anyone seeks to gain his life he will lose it, but he who loses his life, for my sake and the gospel, will find it'. Maybe calling 'dying to self' repulsive was a bit strong; Jesus was pretty clear about things and it's obvious even from these two verses that he has a slightly different take on death from ours. Where we might get offended at the thought of having to die to anything – after all, we're *alive*, aren't we? – Jesus saw life as something different. Actually, he saw death as something different; not the horrendous ending that many of us fear. Instead death was something to be welcomed, to be embraced and ultimately to be conquered. For Jesus, death was a way of life.

Considering that we are a generation who live for the moment, seek pleasure wherever it might be found and who hope to extend life to the max, Jesus' words are strangely relevant. You might think me a fool for suggesting such a thing; after all, how on earth can two such opposite ideas ever be compatible? But I tell you that they can, that it is possible to get the most out of life at the same time as embracing the idea of self-sacrifice. The answer to a 100 per cent full life is not found in a pill, a boutique or that authentic East Asian travelling experience. The answer – according to God – is death. It's not only possible, it's vital.

Just the day before writing this chapter I visited my sister-in-law in hospital. She'd just given birth to her first child, a beautiful 3.5 kg girl called Emily. To be honest my sister-in-law was fairly spaced out from all the emotional and physical demands placed on her by the birth, and I knew that she was wondering about how she would cope as a first-time mother. She told me that she was scared that she wouldn't turn out to be a good mother, that she wasn't ready for all the challenges and changes that lay ahead. She knows even now that from the birth onwards – as well as being filled with an immeasurable joy – she will have to make some hefty sacrifices for little Emily. She might put to death perhaps the idea of buying that better house, going on that holiday or having that leisure time. For the first year or two she's most definitely going to have to put to death any idea of getting a regular and complete night's sleep. How can she do this? Because she loves her baby. The conclusion that we can draw from this is obvious; we are all happy to make sacrifices – even big ones that scare us senseless – for someone that we love.

There are plenty of other examples of sacrificial love leading on to little deaths, the ultimate being Jesus himself. His life as described in the first four books of the New Testament is an astounding display of a series of smaller deaths and sacrifices leading to the most costly and important death of all. Following him means that we Christians need to understand that there's a tasty little paradox existing at the heart of life: the way to find real life, real joy and real fulfilment is to let go the fierce grip which we have on our own lives. The way to find fulfilment is through sacrifice for God and for others. Easy to say, hard to do.

When it comes to God that might mean – as we have covered in other books – offering him a sacrifice of praise, giving him our best and loving him even when it hurts. Living a life for God means realising that our life actually belongs to him rather than ourselves. Paul got it so right when he wrote in Philippians 1:21 'for me to live is Christ and to die is gain'. What does that mean? Paul had discovered that his life had been turned upside down and inside out by God himself. It was no longer about his own ambitions but being ambitious for the kingdom. He learnt to put his own motives and desires second, choosing instead to put God's agenda in front of his own. Millions of Christians have come across the same truth: that there's more to life than the here and now. Living it for God means that we are able to make the kind of sacrifices that would be almost unthinkable if we believed that there was nothing to come after this life. We Christians can see it all in context – God has created us, is calling us home and wants us to bring along as many guests as we can find.

As Paul discovered, we all need to live a lifestyle that's in step with the rest of the kingdom, consulting God and following him every step of the way. Living a kingdom lifestyle means recognising that he is God of our wallets as well as of our hearts. Surely the man who gave everything for us, the one who laid down his life for ours and who demonstrated how to live, deserves not only our full attention but our most radical commitment as well. We need to ask Jesus how he wants us to live in the light of the poverty that blights the majority of the world's population. How does he want us to live in response to the state of the environment? Perhaps we ought to be thinking about spending that little bit more on fairly traded products rather than the sometimes cheaper produce of less ethical companies. Perhaps we ought to think about where we bank in the light of the issues surrounding Third World debt. Perhaps we ought to consider the power of the vote and start mobilising those around us to influence those in a position to bring about change.

The other side of living a sacrificial life is to follow Jesus' model and live it for others. Take Mother Teresa of Calcutta, for example. She lived for the poor, turning from fame and wealth and choosing instead to care for those too poor to secure for themselves a dignified death. She found Jesus in the poor, following the trail of poverty, chastity and obedience. Then there's Jackie Pullinger – a British woman who spent years working alongside drug addicts and gang members inside Hong Kong's Walled City. She boarded a ship from England with a one-way ticket and left behind her family, friends and financial security purely because she believed that God had told her to. There are hundreds, even thousands, of these stories about people who have given up all they had simply to follow Jesus, some even taking it to the point of death, giving their lives for the cause of the King. Many of them can be found in Foxe's *Book of Martyrs*, a fat book listing many of those who died for their belief in Christ in Europe up to the middle of the sixteenth century. Sacrifice, it would seem, is not dead and buried, but alive and well.

Here in the comfy West, being martyred can seem to us like a distinctly remote possibility, but it happens – if not on our doorstep then at least in other parts of the world. Would we be willing to take it all the way? Would we be willing to make the ultimate sacrifice? For most of us these questions are so far removed from our reality that they seem totally hypothetical. After all, how can we truly answer if the nearest we might come to death for a cause is stubbing our toe when rushing to turn the TV on?

But there is one way to find out whether we're on the right track. Are we living a life that is more than just peppered with little deaths? Are we giving up our will for God's? Jesus in the Garden of Gethsemane went through a deliberation prior to a sacrifice: 'May this cup pass from me . . . but not my will but yours be done.' That was him denying himself, taking up his cross, big time. Will we do the same? Chances are that it will be a less dramatic and final act that we are agreeing to, but will we go along with it all the same? It might be some cash that we would rather keep a hold on for ourselves – will we give it away? It might be someone that we really don't like hanging out with but who values our company nevertheless – will we put our own discomfort second and have them round?

There are all sorts of possibilities for sacrifices, yet sometimes it can be easier to imagine ourselves making the large heroic sacrifices – the ones that bring us widespread praise and attention – than it is to actually say yes to making the little, anonymous and unglamorous sacrifices that we face on an almost daily basis. Face facts, nobody's going to want to read a book made up of gloriously victorious stories of how we managed to listen to someone who bugged us or cleaned up after someone was ill. No, we much prefer the grand, flashing lights of 'I Drove a Truck to Sierra Leone with No Fuel or Food and Saved 25,000 Grateful People'. We like sacrifice best when it is big, bouncy and happens once with a quick and noticeable amount of recognition. We're a tad slower to sign up for the long-term slog that accompanies the type of sacrifices that come our way more often.

I need to be careful with this next bit as I don't want to put anyone's name up in lights and turn their acts of sacrifice into fodder for cheap books. Still, there are a few people I know whose sacrifice has paid off, despite the fact that they felt ill-equipped to carry it through from the start. The church to which I belong (Soul Survivor Watford) has many faults, many of which have been conceived, nurtured and developed by me, the pastor. But in the summer of 1999, I was amazed; so many of the members gave themselves in all sorts of ways – small and not so small – to see that the Soul Survivor festivals ran smoothly. We put on three of them, back to back, and hosted over 16,000 people from around the world for almost three weeks. Sounds impressive? You should see the team; you couldn't imagine a more ordinary bunch. Yet they worked hard – often through the night – many giving up their holidays and sacrificing precious time just to be there to help other people get closer to their heavenly Father.

There was one time when those of us from the church who were down on site met up to chat and to pray. We were all tired and I watched the others shuffle in and settle down. One of the speakers was there to pray for and talk to us, and he came up with just the right words. 'You know,' he said, 'God's proud of you. He knows what you've given up and have sacrificed to put this on and he knows that as a church you have chosen to make this commitment.' Nearly everyone was quietly weeping and it suddenly hit me just what a sacrifice it was that they had made. You see, I love the festivals because I love showing off; I love being up on stage and seeing what God's doing around the place. But there would never have been any of the Soul Survivor festivals if it wasn't for an army of people quietly getting on with the dull, frustrating and downright difficult jobs that go on away from the public eye. It's like what Jesus said: 'When a grain of wheat falls into the ground and dies there is much fruit.' He was talking of himself, the grain that came to earth, died and in so doing produced the fruit of eternal life. I think he was also talking about something else. In the summer of 1999 I saw plenty of little grains of wheat, dying their own little deaths so that there might be plenty of fruit. Nearly 1,000 people became Christians that summer. None of it would have been possible if there weren't a group of struggling Christians from Soul Survivor Watford, getting tired, wet and fed up for the sake of people they had never met.

There's no limit to what God can do through a person who is totally dedicated to him. The one thing that God is looking for when he searches among his people are those who are willing to give up their lives for his sake and for that of the gospel. You know what? When we answer 'yes' to that question we find more life, joy and fulfilment than we could ever imagine.

I remember when I was leading the youth group at St Andrew's, Chorleywood. Among the number was an immaculately coiffured Matt Redman who, despite his obsession with combing and conditioning his hair, was developing an understanding of God's love of sacrifice. His school's drama department was very prestigious and he had been involved in productions for quite a while, doing increasingly well, even directing some of his friends in one particular production. One day we were travelling to a houseparty when he told me that he had decided to quit the boards and leave the drama behind. He said that God had told him he faced a choice, with the theatre on one side and worship on the other. 'Don't be ridiculous', came my spiritually enlightened reply. 'Of course you can carry on doing both.' Knowing that God had spoken to him and wanting to follow it through, Matt quit drama a while later. It proved to be an incredibly costly decision; not only did his friends not understand him but his teachers thought him a fool. He had to watch as productions came and went without him, something that was at times almost agonising. The point is that it was drama that he enjoyed the most – he came alive when he did it – but God had asked him whether he was prepared to lay it down for him.

There's a story in the Bible that takes the idea of sacrifice to a far greater level; God asks Abraham if he is prepared to give up the thing he values most, his son Isaac. It turns out that he is and he prepares to sacrifice him, literally. In the end God gave Isaac back to Abraham, but not before he had been ready to let him go. Matt never got drama back, except that in a strange way that I will never fully understand, out of that willingness to sacrifice came a blessing. These examples may be poles apart in terms of what was given up, but Matt was sure that God had told him to make his sacrifice, as was Abraham and as were the people who helped out at Soul Survivor 99. We might not be able to be confident that we can follow Jesus all the way along the road of sacrifice, but we can all start out with: 'Lord, I'd rather not do this, but it's not my will, but yours that I want to see done.' Out of that comes power; the sort that can change a world.

In our all-new consumer brand of Christianity we're so keen to find the latest quick fix, the most shiny tool that will make us feel better. The power of the sacrificial life – the sort that Jesus taught us how to live – is the key to rising above this unchristian state and to move on to becoming the type of people who really will make a difference where it matters.

'Submit yourself to
death, death of your ambitions
and favourite wishes every day
and death of your whole body in
the end: submit every fibre
of your being, and you
will find eternal life.'
C.S. Lewis, *Mere Christianity*

'I look upon life
as a gift from God. I did nothing
to earn it. Now the time is coming
for me to give it back, I have
no right to complain.'
Joyce Cary

3

Dealing with Grief

So far in my life I've only had to face one major bereavement. About sixteen years ago my father had a heart attack. He managed to recover and for a while we all thought that he was getting better, but he soon seemed to get worse again. It never occurred to me at the time that this deterioration might signal the end, and I can remember being at work one day while my mother had gone to the hospital to pick him up after some tests. I got the phone call from her, the most horrendous phone call I've ever had. She told me to come to the hospital as the doctor had just told her that he had a week to live. Then she cried.

I can remember collecting my sister and rushing to the hospital. That last week was terrible; we all knew that he was going and all that we could do was to watch him slip away. The night he died I sat next to him as his breathing got slower and slower. There were bigger and bigger gaps between breaths and my mind was racing. At about 3 a.m. there was one particular gap between breaths that was so drawn out that I stiffened, thinking that it was all over. Then he breathed again and I went back to waiting. I had held it all together until then – for days I hadn't cried or broken down – but that moment changed things and I started weeping. In the morning

317

I was exhausted and my family told me to go home to get a little sleep. They stayed with him while I returned home.

As soon as the phone rang I knew what I was about to find out. I rushed back to the hospital to join the rest of my family in saying goodbye to the father and husband who had just died. It was the most bizarre feeling as we gathered round his bed, each giving him a kiss. The idea that that was it, he had gone and that we wouldn't see him again on this earth was the start of much more grief that was to follow. I'd find myself breaking down as I saw and experienced new things, reminded that he would never share any of them with me. It lasted a while. There were moments within the period of grief when it was easier, and there were moments (particularly for my mum) when it was much, much worse. I'll never forget the agony of the first Christmas without him. My sister's second child had just been born and the fact that he was not there, the fact that in our hands lay the beginnings of a life which he would never know and who would never know him, was almost too much to take.

All of us will go through periods of grief in our lives. We will all taste it – some sooner than others – and without exception we will all encounter different levels of it as we experience the passing of those close and others not so close to us. We are all going to lose a loved one – that much we know for sure – but how should we (as Christians) deal with it? What help can we find from the Bible and what we know of God that can be of assistance as we work our way through?

Losing my father brought about a big change in the way I felt about things as a Christian. Previously I had thought about death and grief in strict theological terms. I knew the theory and I applied it to my conscious mind deliberately and with some degree of precision. Once I had collided head on with the agony of grief, all that theological rhetoric went out of the window and left me not so much thinking about things but feeling them in the most intense way imaginable. I was ruled by the emotions and pleaded with God for an answer to the biggest question that we can ask; why?

The truth is that just in the same way that my questions came from the guts, bypassing logic, so too does God's answer make little sense to our minds. It is something that exists beyond the limits of our limited rational thinking. We cannot place God in a box and we cannot explain with words many of the things he does. Accepting death at any time is bound to be hard, but when it involves someone who has been taken way before their time, working through the grief can almost seem impossible. Where is logic for the mother who mourns her teenage daughter knocked down by a drunk driver? Where is rational argument for the partner who mourns the loss of their loved one, left alone to bring up a family?

So we cannot reduce grief to a set of rules and regulations, giving directions, reasons and arguments to ensure that all come out of it unscathed. Grief is emotional, it is important, and we do ourselves wrong if we try to bottle it up, ignore it or pretend that we can get by without it.

But just as we spent the last chapter looking at the way that life is made up of little deaths, of sacrifices that mark our Christian path, so too it is made up of little griefs. Grief is not just limited to the death of a loved one; we all go through a similar process of mourning at many other points in our lives, often ones quite separate from actual physical death. For example, realising that a relationship is over, that an ambition may never be fulfilled or that a hope is empty, all these will take us through a grieving process. Through it we will begin to reconstruct our lives around the gap of something we had always assumed was – or would eventually be – there.

One of the first things that happens when we grieve is to face disbelief. It's common for people to deny the death of a person soon after it has happened. Just the other day I was getting towed back from Wales listening to the AA man tell me about some of the experiences he had collected in over twenty-one years of service. He told me about one time that he had been called out by the police to attend to a car with a broken windscreen. It had broken when the driver had knocked down a child one hundred yards down the road. Despite the fact that the man had just killed this child, the AA guy told me how the driver was talking away as if nothing had happened, making jokes and small talk all the way to the garage. There was something almost sickening about the story, as if the man was going too far in his denial, and the AA man never found out what happened to him later. I'm sure that it came home in a big way but, nevertheless, even if it isn't quite so dramatic for us, it's not unusual to find that the reality of death takes a while to sink in.

When I realised that no one was going to wave a magic wand and stop the inevitable from happening to my father, as I waited between his breathing in and breathing out in the middle of the night, the tears came. I didn't want to do it, but something told me that I had to begin to believe that this was the end. As the days followed the struggle between denial and acceptance carried on, not so much as an all-out war that was over at any specific point, but as a series of battles and skirmishes as I realised that he would no longer be around in a whole variety of different scenarios.

In many ways this picture of grief as a series of random events rather than set stages is one that I find helpful. I think it's highly unlikely that any two people's experiences of grief will be absolutely identical. So we need to be easy on ourselves and others, finding the balance between allowing the process to follow its own path and pace, and encouraging a general movement through the stages we're outlining here.

One of the things that many people find they experience during a grieving process is anger. Sometimes the anger can be directed at God himself as questions are fired at him in the midst of the confusion. How could he let that person die?

How could he let that dream fall through? How could he let that relationship break up? Often we can spend some time in this stage, something which can in itself cause us to feel guilty about harbouring such thoughts and resentments towards God.

Through the film *Shadowlands* many of us have found out more about C.S. Lewis's life. He married late and had a wonderful marriage to Joy, who contracted cancer and died long before 'her time'. He wrote about his feelings after her death in a little book called *A Grief Observed* (Faber, 1961). There's one paragraph that stands out from the rest:

> Not that I am, I think, in much danger of ceasing to believe in God. The real danger is to coming to believe such dreadful things about him. The conclusion I dread is not 'so there's no God after all' but 'this is what God is really like; deceive yourself no longer'.

That seems to echo something that I and many others have been through: a period of despair. I've known people who, because of some tragedy in their lives, have tried to say 'there is no God' and question how he could exist in the face of such cruelty. After the First World War there was a significant drop in belief in God throughout Britain which many put down to the horrors witnessed on the battlefields and the grief of those at home. The trenches at Flanders sent people back with the question, 'How can there be a God if this can happen?' I've known other people who have kept up their belief but have doubted his character, just as C.S. Lewis feared.

On the other side there are those who are aware of these two possibilities, and who try to avoid them by denying the existence of any such feelings at all. Call it what you want – stiff upper lip or religious repression – there are plenty who have struggled bravely on, accepting death but denying that grief has any part in their own lives. Of course a desire to hold on to God is to be applauded, but in fact this repression can often cause far more long-term harm than good.

It's also completely unbiblical. I love to read the psalms; they are raw emotion. The psalmist appears to be totally at ease with the extremes of his heart. Not only is he able to praise God for his infinite goodness, but he is able to express the darker side of things. 'Where are you?' he asks. 'I weep on my bed all night . . . my enemies have me surrounded . . . you've deserted me.' It seems to me that he has permission to pray prayers that are so close to the edge that they almost appear to be blasphemous. He has permission to express the doubt, the horror and the pain, just as we do. Through the honest expression of such difficult feelings we – like David – end up at peace with God. First there's the denial, then the anger and the despair, and finally there comes the restoration of peace.

On the other side of grief is a wonderful thing called acceptance. Not only do we find that we can accept things as they are, but we can feel accepted by God, that he both understands and shares our feelings, from the beginning to the end. C.S. Lewis finally knew that God was with him throughout the time he mourned the death of his wife, despite the fact that for much of the time Lewis was not aware of God. Even when his desperation was so great that without realising it he pushed God away, God was still there, with him, sharing his grief.

As I've said we can grieve over all sorts of things, but before we get too analytical about things, we need to get back to basics. We need to learn to express our grief, to give it a voice and allow it to be heard. Nothing is too bad to be brought before God; no despair or anger is too much to be laid before him. If we don't express it, we bury it. Once buried it can eat away at us, decaying the good that once was there.

We come back to the cross once again. After all, who better to let it all out on than Almighty God – the one who gave up most, who sacrificed more than anyone else? Jesus shares in the experience of humanity on a level that we will never understand when he says, 'My God, my God, why have you forsaken me?' The words can be such a comfort to us as they are proof positive of the fact that he has been there, to the darkest place. Jesus has been there ahead of us, separated from God where things simply don't get any worse.

When things go wrong each of us faces a choice. It might seem like bad timing, but this choice is a vitally important one. It proves the maturity of our relationship with God. Either we turn from him and get bitter or we turn to him, express the pain, call out to him and get better. Either we can be like the little child who will not receive comfort but who keeps running away in floods of tears, or we can be like the child who cries and cries in its parent's arms. Sometimes we may need to do a little wriggling, sometimes we may need to punch out, but the arms of a parent are strong, strong enough to take the blows.

Coming to the end of grief also brings us face to face with a choice. As Christians we all face the option of whether or not we will trust God and all his goodness. With the psalmist we can paint it as black as we really see it and still find it in us to wind up saying, 'Yet will I rejoice and trust in you.' We can be honest about the circumstances much as Habakkuk was:

> Though the fig-tree does not bud
>   and there are no grapes on the vines,
> though the olive crop fails
>   and the fields produce no food,
> though there are no sheep in the pen
>   and no cattle in the stalls,

>yet I will rejoice in the Lord,
>I will be joyful in God my saviour.
>
> (Habakkuk 3:17–18)

Basically, Habby got to the place where even if everything went wrong – even something totally disastrous like the olive crop failing – he wouldn't let his own pain and anxiety get in the way of his faith in God. But crucially, he didn't fall into the trap of pretending that the pain was not there.

Choosing to put our faith in God is itself a healing act, and we emerge the other side with a strengthened faith and a relationship one step closer towards maturity. This reminds me of the story of the disciples in the boat as Jesus walked towards them one stormy night on the Sea of Galilee. They were all afraid, yet Peter sussed that it might be the Lord. 'If that's you,' he said 'just show me that it's you and I'll come.' We can walk on the water, through the storms of life, when we know that it's Jesus in front of us and him we are heading towards. What I take from this story when looked at in the context of grief is that when there are storms all around us, when the waves look too big and the grief and pain threaten to overpower us, there is just one question that matters: will we follow Jesus? When we hear his voice, will we be brave enough to step out from the fragile security constructed around us and make ourselves even more vulnerable by trusting Jesus and turning towards him? We're very fond of overcomplicating our faith, yet it really is that simple, and – depending on how the storms of life are treating you at the moment – it really is that easy/hard.

Having said that we need to be honest as we move through the grieving process, there also comes a place where an expression of trust in God acts as praise, even in the midst of pain. Some of the most amazing times of worship that we can have on earth this side of heaven are the times when we worship when it hurts, when it's a sacrifice. It happened to

King David, who mourned the death of the son born out of his extramarital affair with Bathsheba. As soon as he heard that the child had died he washed his face and went to rejoice and praise his heavenly Father, the one who had forgiven him so much.

There is an aspect of that determination which we can see in Paul's letter to the Philippians. Even though he was writing from a jail and circumstances really could not have been worse, he wrote a letter about rejoicing in the Lord. We know that on one particular occasion while in jail he was having such a storming late-night worship session that the very doors that kept him captive flew open.

But we need to be careful. This is not about using worship as a means of escape from reality – the Christian faith is certainly not an escapist one – but there is a rejoicing that comes in the acknowledgement of the fact that life hurts yet praise can still take place. This is not because we're defective or bottling things up; it is because God is good. Not only does he deserve a sacrifice of praise – the sort that costs something, that takes place even when we don't particularly feel like it – but worship of him is also infinitely compatible with our pain. As we have seen, he's been through it all already.

Romans 8:28 brings us a truth that: 'we know that in all things God works for the good of those who love him, who have been called according to his purposes.' There is a very real sense that some of the things that we cannot see this side of heaven cannot be understood. All we see is the pain and the grief, yet from heaven's perspective there is an answer, there is a bigger picture into which all these things fit. To rejoice is to trust heaven's perspective. Believing in that bigger picture and the absolute goodness of the artist behind it requires nothing less than a leap of faith.

'All who have faith
in Jesus Christ can know the
strength of his presence, helping
them to deal with grief and, when
the time comes, to face
death itself.'

Harold Bauman, *Living Through Grief*

'Until our Master summons
us, not a hair on our head can
perish, not a moment of our life
can be snatched away from us.
When he sends for us, it should
seem but the message that the
child is wanted at home.'

Anthony Thorold

4

The Second Coming

In a book this size I have decided not to look at the issues surrounding Jesus' return, such as will he come before the earth goes through a tribulation which will last a thousand years, or will he return after? What are the signs we should look for? Some of these questions have kept Christian theologians arguing happily for years as to what the Bible actually says. The purpose of this chapter is limited to unpacking the consequences of the wonderful truth that he will return!

This book has been oozing its way out of my subconscious as the calendar has rolled from 1999 into 2000. So far Millennium Night Fever appears to have been rather a lot of fuss about nothing, and right now people around the world are busy trying to justify the US$328 billion spent on 'fixing' the Y2K bug. While the prophecies of planes falling out of the sky and toasters refusing to co-operate seem to have been a little over the top, the cause for millennial madness wasn't only restricted to computers. As expected there were a few people predicting the return of Jesus, and security was tight around Jerusalem and other key sites in the Holy Land. There were fears that wacky Christians would carry out threats to do their bit for revival by planting bombs, but again, everything seemed to pass smoothly.

While the trees and tinsel have gone, I'm still left thinking about things; it wasn't just the nutters who thought about Armageddon. I spoke to plenty of friends about this over the period, and many of them were surprised to admit that they too had ended up thinking about things eternal. So what was it that made so many of us turn our minds – however briefly – to the subject of the Second Coming? What makes me so sure that I would recognise it if it did come in my lifetime? Am I thinking about it because I'm bored or can I really be so arrogant to believe that Jesus would choose my time over any other to pay up on his promise and come back for his people?

Why should we even bother considering the Second Coming? Isn't it best left to those with a passion for home-made explosives and a gift for losing the plot? I hope not, and I'm sure that to do so would be to throw the baby out with the bath water. Whenever I start to feel confused about things I generally try and remind myself of the importance of looking back as well as looking forward. After all, it seemed to work for the Israelites; every so often they would stop and go over all the good things that God had done. In reminding themselves of their history and unique relationship with God, they would get all fired up about their future. Viewed in context of God's always being there and being continually gracious and mighty to save, it's not surprising that God's people after Jesus' life on earth have looked forward to his return.

Part of my confusion comes from the fact that the Second Coming is one of those subjects that hasn't been talked about in the Church much over the last couple of decades. We might have dusted it off at a couple of points in the calendar, but in general the return of Christ has been left on the unpreached sermon pile, somewhere between homosexuality and Leviticus. I think that's a shame. Of course we don't want to end up being too heavenly minded to be any earthly good, but I firmly believe that there is a whole stack of lessons waiting to be learnt from taking a good hard look at the return of our Lord Jesus Christ.

When I was a frighteningly fresh Christian I was keen. I was also intensely sensitive, slow to think things through for myself and prone to getting scared easily. Together these character traits led me into a head-on collision with the most disturbing film I have ever seen. As part of the RE curriculum the teacher decided to do a little evangelism on the sly and make some fresh recruits for the cause by scaring them senseless. He chose to show a film called *A Thief in the Night* – a dramatic representation of the Second Coming as depicted in the Bible. Along with a few of my mates who had also become Christians a month before, I watched as the film played out. With some seriously awful 1970s photography and some acting the likes of which are usually reserved for public information films on the dangers of leaving the gas on, the film worked its way through a number of scenes. A regular family were sat at home when all of a sudden two were taken away and three were left. A group were walking along the road one minute, and one of them had vanished the next. The film went on to show other aspects of what might happen when Jesus returns, and as it finished the whole class sat in a stunned silence. A friend of mine refused to sleep for almost three nights, choosing instead to be like one of the wise virgins and stare out of his bedroom window in case Jesus made a sneak return to Harrow in the wee small hours. I managed to spend almost a year avoiding fields and cosy family situations where the total number of those present equalled five.

Despite the fact that many of us acted a little strangely after the film, looking back now I'm convinced that it did us some good in the long term. Not only did it get us excited about a central truth of Christianity – that Jesus will return –

but it also got us into reading our Bibles in a way that we hadn't quite done before.

Perhaps a film like *A Thief in the Night* would not get made today precisely because of the new millennium. During the years sandwiching the start of the twenty-first century it has almost become a bit of a cliché to talk about things of an apocalyptic nature. After all, everyone knows that there are plenty of nutters out there preaching hellfire and impending destruction, why give the rest of the population the satisfaction of playing up to the stereotype? Yet I think we can go too far in shying away from the subject. Perhaps we need to have restored to us a sense of biblical balance about the whole thing.

OK, so we might have sussed that this whole Second Coming thing is worth the chat, but that brings us neatly on to the next confusing issue: what will it look like? The New Testament church had a far better hold on this than we do. They managed to believe passionately in Jesus' promise and allow it to fire them up to live radical lives at the same time as managing not to appear like dribbling loonies. Quite an achievement.

Acts 1 shows them all hanging around as Jesus returns to heaven. He tells them to hold back in Jerusalem where they are to wait for his Holy Spirit to introduce himself and fill them up.

> After he said this, he was taken up before their very eyes, and a cloud hid him from their sight. They were looking intently up into the sky as he was going, when suddenly two men dressed in white stood beside them. 'Men of Galilee,' they said, 'why do you stand there looking into the sky? This same Jesus, who has been taken from you into heaven, will come back in the same way you have seen him go into heaven.'
>
> (Acts 1:9–11)

Do you get that? Jesus is coming back in the same way he returned to heaven. It's astounding stuff, but we miss the point if we don't pay proper attention. Jesus may have left on the clouds, but his first arrival was very different. He came to earth – God made flesh – as a baby. He was both impoverished and unrecognised – to many people he would even have been unremarkable. Only if you were in the know would you have had a clue about the future that lay in front of him. But the Second Coming won't be marked by secrecy or stealth; as the angels said, Jesus will come again in the clouds. This time there will be no doubt about whether he really has arrived or not, and his return will be accompanied by him bringing justice and the rule of heaven in all its fullness. As with those in the early church, we too are living in the in-between times, straddling time from the point that Jesus left the earth to the moment of his return. His final trip will be to end the established order and bring about a new heaven and a new earth.

> Then I saw a new heaven and a new earth, for the first heaven and the first earth had passed away, and there was no longer any sea. I saw the Holy City, the new Jerusalem, coming down out of heaven from God, prepared as the bride beautifully dressed for her husband. And I heard a loud voice from the throne saying, 'Now the dwelling of God is with men, and he will live with them. They will be his people, and God himself will be with them and be their God. He will wipe every tear from their eyes. There will be no more death or mourning or crying or pain, for the old order of things has passed away.'
>
> (Revelation 21:1–4)

We know from Scripture that Jesus will return to look for the Church – his bride – whom he expects to find waiting for him. His longing is that we will be looking forward to his arrival, and for that reason I'm convinced that we need to spend more time looking into every aspect of the Second Coming.

The fact that Jesus is returning has certain implications for us. What exactly does it mean when the Bible says that he will bring his rule, authority and justice completely to us? Yes, we may have a taste of it already – we may think we know a little of his kingdom and the way things should be – but do we really know what it will look like in the flesh? True, the kingdom of God is here in part, but it is incomplete. 'Creation,' as Paul writes in Romans 8:19, 'waits in eager expectation for the sons of God to be revealed.' The phrase 'creation waits' can easily be translated as 'creation groans'. I believe that part of this groaning is the waiting for the story to be completed, for the prophecies to be fulfilled.

The Bible tells us that eventually we will receive our resurrection bodies – the Mike Pilavachi I was created to be – and we will live on the new earth – the planet as God intended, free from pollution, corruption and the effects of hatred. We won't be going to Mars and turning left; the new earth will be very much right here.

The presence of justice as a key factor in the Second Coming brings us on to the slightly less attractive subject of judgement. While many of us might prefer it if we all could go on happily ever after regardless of how we lived our lives, it is impossible to separate justice from judgement. When the Lord returns he will be angrier than any of us could ever imagine. Before you start contemplating a career change to Buddhism, don't forget that our interpretations of anger should not be confused with God's. His isn't an indiscriminate, broken-bottle-in-hand type of rage, unfairly mowing down all who dare to cross his path. His is a righteous anger, putting things back the way they should be; those who have done wrong receiving what they deserve. Don't we hate it when crimes go unpunished? God's judgement is the best there is, and unlike many of the poor imitations we see on earth, it is something to be looked forward to.

So then, what about hell? As the point of heaven is not so much about angels, harps and clouds as it is about eternal relationship with God, so the point of hell is not about the fire, brimstone and lakes of sulphur. Hell is eternal separation from God. If someone who has heard the gospel in this life but has died rejecting Jesus – and therefore rejecting relationship with God as Father – then the Bible makes clear that their choice lasts for ever. That's hard on the person concerned, but we need to remember that it's even harder on God. It's the sort of pain any parent would feel as their kid walks out on them, wanting no more to do with them. So what about babies who die before they've had a chance to hear about Jesus? Surely it isn't fair for them to be hell-bound too? The Bible doesn't make itself incredibly clear on this point, except that we are told to trust in God's mercy, grace and love. I don't think that for a moment a baby in this situation would go to hell. This is a tough subject, perhaps even the toughest. It's good for us to realise though, that the choices we human beings make now have eternal consequences. We all deserve eternal separation from God because of our sin. The cross is God's way of bridging the gap. Jesus did the horrendous bit by dying for us; all we have to do is come to the cross. Is that really such a bad deal?

I find Peter's second letter to the Church at large to be essential reading when it comes to the end of time. He takes the reader through some fairly fundamental stuff, spelling it out clearly.

First of all, you must understand that in the last days scoffers will come, scoffing and following their own evil desires. They will say, 'Where is this "coming" he promised? Ever since our fathers died, everything goes on as it has since the beginning of creation.' But they deliberately forget that long ago by God's word the heavens existed and the earth was formed out of water and by water. By these waters also the world of that time was deluged and destroyed. By the same word the present heavens and earth are reserved for fire, being kept for the day of judgment and destruction of ungodly men. But do not forget this one thing, dear friends: With the Lord a day is like a thousand years and a thousand years are like a day.

(2 Peter 3:3–8)

When it comes to God, time is relative. Just because we have a few scoffers doing their scoffing thing around us, just because theories of evolution may appear to some to rule out God's hand, we must never forget that God's timing is not ours. 'The Lord is not slow in keeping his promise, as some understand slowness. He is patient with you, not wanting anyone to perish, but everyone to come to repentance' (2 Peter 3:9).

So here we have it; the core of this issue of God's timing. We might be thinking that 2,000 years is pushing it as far as waiting for Jesus' return might be – we share those confusions and frustrations with the people around Peter who had waited just thirty-seven years since Jesus returned to heaven. The delay is easily explained; God wants everyone to be saved and in relationship with him before he returns in judgement. His 'slowness' is only there because of his goodness. In a sense, the more years that pass without his return, the more reason we have to praise and worship him as he holds back from final judgement for the sake of those who might not make it through.

But the day of the Lord will come like a thief. The heavens will disappear with a roar; the elements will be destroyed by fire, and the earth and everything in it will be laid bare. Since everything will be destroyed in this way, what kind of people ought you to be? You ought to live holy and godly lives as you look forward to the day of God and speed its coming.

(2 Peter 3:10–12)

And here is the key: why should we be looking forward to the Second Coming of Jesus? Because when we have him as our focus and our hope, when we understand that one day he will return in bodily form, we will live the type of lives that reflect his nature, and in doing so quicken his return. The Church is called the bride of Christ in the Bible, and one day when Jesus returns there is going to be the mother of all weddings. As people who love him, we can look forward to his return in hope, not in anxiety.

That day will bring about the destruction of the heavens by fire, and the elements will melt in the heat. But in keeping with his promise we are looking forward to a new heaven and a new earth, the home of righteousness. So then, dear friends, since you are looking forward to this, make every effort to be found spotless, blameless and at peace with him.

(2 Peter 3:12–14)

The Second Coming is definitely bad news for certain people. For those who have lived selfish and self-centred lives, for those who have been greedy, immoral and who have made themselves comfortable and rich at the expense of the poor, and who have completely rejected him, the return of Jesus will not be something to celebrate, to put it mildly. But for the Church, it's what we're living for.

But hey, guys, let's not get smug about it. The knowledge of Jesus' return should spur us on to tell as many people about him as possible in the meantime. Just as the first Christians – who expected Jesus' return at any time – were urgent in their evangelism, so should we be.

'Eternal life is a
gift from God, and the key that
releases it to us is faith.'
David Winter, *What Happens after Death*

5

How to Die a
Good Death

My friend Matt Redman has a younger brother named Thomas. I've known him and the rest of the family for years and have seen them all go through various phases as they have grown up. One phase that Thomas would probably rather forget is his Flopsy-the-Bunny stage. He was ten and decided to get himself a rabbit. He and his mother made a hutch and a run in the garden and Thomas went out and bought Flopsy, a large white thing with – you may have guessed – floppy ears. Days came and went and all Thomas ever seemed keen to talk about was Flopsy; the reports came almost hourly and I counted it a splendid privilege to know exactly how many bites of her carrot the dear thing had taken at any specific time.

A few weeks after Flopsy's arrival I dropped by unannounced to catch up on the latest instalment of 'Flopsy Eats a Cucumber', when I was greeted at the door by the entire family, ashen-faced and deadly quiet. I came in and joined them in staring across the hall, where I could see Flopsy lying on a radiator. I count myself an expert in neither rabbits nor death, but I could tell that something was most definitely wrong. My question about whether the rabbit was dead was met by denials and murmurings about how Flopsy wasn't dead, she was simply cold and needed a little warming up. None of them wanted to admit the truth and for a while I too joined them in telling myself that just a few more minutes on the scorching radiator would bring her back to life. It didn't last and after a while I could stand it no more.

'I think she's dead, guys,' I said.

Thomas burst into tears. I felt awful and wished I was wrong, but it was no use. Flopsy was a gonner and slowly the rest of the family began to come round to the idea. Somehow I ended up with the job of burying the rabbit in the back garden. Now, I'm about as good at gardening as I am at figure skating, so when I saw how frosty and frozen over the ground was, I began to panic. After what seemed like hours of digging I admitted defeat and announced that the grave would simply have to do, unconventional as it was. Where most graves are long and thin, allowing the body to be laid horizontally, Flopsy's final resting place was deep and narrow, requiring her to be buried vertically. After a considerable struggle I managed to get her in – using a technique approximately the opposite to removing a cork from a bottle with a corkscrew – and sat back to admire my handiwork. Thomas looked on aghast from his bedroom window.

The whole episode made me think about how keen we all are to skirt around the subject of death, regarding it as a wholly bad thing. But is that really the truth? Are we destined to be dragged kicking and screaming towards an undignified and horrendous ending of our days on earth? I don't really know anyone who I would say has had a particularly good death – at least I haven't seen any first hand – but reading the account of Jesus' death as told in the New Testament, I'm convinced that death has plenty of potential. Jesus' death was a lot more than just simply 'good'; it was brilliant.

In November 1999 I had some pains in my chest and stomach. Instead of being the usual side effects of one late-night curry too many, these seemed sharper and altogether more intense. Of course I thought I was dying – I usually do whenever I'm bored and slightly ill – but this time my convictions that I was about to meet my maker were altogether more real. Instead of being the usual call for attention and entertainment, I actually felt as though I was telling the truth. I was shocked; usually I use the 'I think I'm dying' as a way of passing the time and whipping up a little extra sympathy or a free dinner. It never stops me from carrying on my daily routine. This time things were different; the pains got worse and were refusing to go away, and it looked as though I was even going to have to cancel a fast-approaching trip to Holland. The day before we were due to leave I finally gave in and blew the trip out, retiring to lie curled up beneath my dining-room table, moaning quietly to myself. This had me worried, because usually I would choose a far more public place (like the office) in which to do my moaning.

Soon afterwards some friends came round to check up on me. They took one look and called the doctor who asked to have my symptoms described to him over the phone in greater detail. His response didn't exactly do my confidence much good as he suggested that an ambulance be phoned immediately as he suspected a heart attack.

It wasn't a heart attack, in case you're wondering. It was something far less glamorous (gall stones), but for a moment I can honestly say that I thought my time was up. Waiting for the ambulance, wondering whether the heart attack was about to kick in for real and finish me off, I went through a bizarre selection of thoughts. As well as worrying about who was going to pick up my shoes from the menders, my mind was filled with the sense that I couldn't die just yet as there was so much more that I wanted to do. I'm sure most of us would feel something similar.

For Jesus it was different. Sure he died young – younger than me when I thought I was on my way out – but it's clear from the Bible that there was not one ounce of regret, not a hint of remorse that time had been wasted or that there was still more to be done. Jesus' whole life was a lead-up to his death. When he came to earth he began a journey that didn't end, but that culminated in the cross. Death was not a cruel and early stop to a match in progress; it was the perfect goal after the perfect build-up that won the match. We see that Jesus' life was a preparation for his death, and his death was a vital part of his coming to earth. In Jesus' case, death and life were perfect partners, each one dependent on the other, combining to alter the course of history for ever.

As Christians, Jesus' death should make us look at death in a very different way. Instead of murmuring under the table we should recognise that through the cross we have a power that blows death out of the water. 'Death, thou shalt die', wrote John Donne, and he was right. In a one-on-one fight Jesus kicked death's butt royally. There simply isn't a contest any more and through Jesus – his mighty power and glorious resurrection – we have nothing to fear.

For me, the very core of Jesus' death being a good one is that he actually chose it. He was prepared for it and knew that he was dying for a purpose; to bring us life and allow us to know God. As he was dying on the cross, Jesus made seven statements that I'm convinced are the most incredible statements that a person could make as they are dying. While it's not precisely clear from the Bible which order they were said in – different Gospels give you different versions – I've put them in an order that makes sense to me. What is clear though, is that these are words which will live for ever.

In Luke 23:34 Jesus says, 'Father, forgive them, for they do not know what they are doing.' What had they done? Together with the occupying Roman forces, his fellow Jews had falsely accused him, lied about him, beaten, tormented and tortured him. He could have rained down fire on them, poured out a string of verbal abuse and threats or called down all manner of curses upon them. Instead he forgave them, making sure that the Jesus we see on the cross acts 100 per cent in line with the Jesus that we have read about beforehand.

His death on the cross becomes even more amazing when we realise exactly who the 'they' were that Jesus was referring to when he asked his Father to grant forgiveness. It wasn't just the authorities or the soldiers that Jesus was talking about, it was us. Jesus' death was caused by us; we sent him there. My sin and yours were the ticket that led him to the place where he paid for all our sin. Make no mistake, when it comes to our wrongdoing and habit of living our lives away from God, there was only one true sacrifice that could have been made to secure our relationship with him. As a just God, our heavenly Father could not let our sin pass without a just punishment, and Jesus paid the price on our behalf when he took our place on the cross.

In his holiness God judged that the payback for sin is death, but in his love he also decided that he would send the most precious thing that he had to pay the price so that he might have us back. Jesus, as he hung on the cross, said through the pain and the agony, 'Father, forgive Mike Pilavachi as he doesn't know what he is doing.'

Moving to Mark's version of the life of Jesus we come across these words in chapter 15 verse 34: 'My God, my God, why have you forsaken me?' To understand the true horror of these words it is vital that we understand how for eternity, God the Son and God the Father were continually united. For the time that he hung on the cross God the Son knew the agony of separation from his Father. It was a key part of the punishment for sin that simply could not be avoided.

Sadly, the idea of being separated from God for a time probably does not fill us with the same sense of fear and dread as it did Jesus. But for many of us, as we die our little deaths or agonise over the death of a loved one, this sense of loss is a vaguely familiar taste to our lips. When things go wrong in our lives we can often feel something of what Jesus felt, as though God is a million miles away and nothing can seem to bring him back. Jesus not only shared but felt more deeply than we could ever feel that sense of forsakenness.

Third, in John 19:26–7 we read that Jesus sees John the apostle and Mary his mother standing together around the cross, watching him die. Can you imagine what it must have been like for Jesus' own mother to watch her firstborn son die on the cross, crucified like a common criminal? Jesus says to his mother: 'Dear woman, here is your son.' And to John: 'Here is your mother.'

What is he saying here? He brings home the message that his death makes us family. Because he died we not only have reconciliation with God the Father, but we can also have reconciliation as a human race. In fact, that is precisely what the Church is supposed to be; the family of Jesus here on earth.

All this might read very well on paper, but you may be wondering whether it actually works out there in reality. I can honestly say that I've seen people – and I'm thinking of two in particular – who have hated each other with such passion and bitterness that the prospect of any form of forgiveness passing between them has been about as remote as remote can be. Having met with Jesus and understood what he did for them on the cross they have been filled with the power to be reconciled to each other. Amazing.

John 19:28 shows that at one point Jesus cried out, 'I am thirsty.' Once he did that the guards offered him a sponge dipped in vinegar, a cruel act as there was no way that such a drink would quench his thirst. But Jesus' thirst was not limited only to the physical; it was as if he wanted more of God. The thirst that was in Jesus, his desire to return home, went hand in hand with a knowledge that it was God and God alone who could satisfy him. And so we have a picture of Jesus on the cross, alone and separated from his Father yet still holding on to the fact that he is utterly dependent on him for sustenance and support.

The next saying can be found in Luke 23:42–3. Luke tells us that Jesus was crucified in between two criminals, possibly thieves. One of them joined in the mocking of Jesus, challenging him to save himself if he really was who he said he was. The other quietened him down and pointed out that while the two of them deserved what they were getting, Jesus had done nothing whatsoever to warrant crucifixion.

> Then he said, 'Jesus, remember me when you come into your kingdom.'
> Jesus answered him, 'I tell you the truth, today you will be with me in paradise.'

And that was the reason that Jesus came: to save repentant criminals like the thief, like me and like you. 'Today you will be with me in paradise' is the word of hope that not only would have turned that man's life upside down, but which can alter the course of our lives for ever. For all of us who ask his forgiveness Jesus' reply is the same.

This takes us back to another thing that Jesus said long before he died, this time reported in John 14:1–3:

> Do not let your hearts be troubled. Trust in God; trust also in me. In my Father's house are many rooms; if it were not so, I would have told you. I am going there to prepare a place for you. And if I go and prepare a place for you, I will come back and take you to be with me so that you also may be where I am.

Jesus' earlier encouragement for us not to focus on death as an ultimate end but as a gateway between now and something wonderful should not be forgotten. The profound truth that he has even gone on ahead to prepare things for us is enough to blow my mind.

Sometimes I wonder what heaven will be like; boring, perhaps. Endless angels twanging their flippin' harps as eternity whiles itself away in some kind of easy-listening pastiche. I hope not. If Jesus is preparing a place for me, that means it is a place that will fit me. I don't mean physically, but spiritually I know that I shall be at peace, that I will have come home to a paradise of all-embracing love.

The sixth saying of Jesus on the cross can be found in John 19:30, made up of three simple words: 'It is finished.' Jesus came to suffer for us, to pay a price and settle the issue of our approach to God once and for ever. Moments before death he knew that the job was complete and that we had been bought back with his life.

Lastly, Luke 23:46 gives us the final words he uttered on the cross: 'Father, into your hands I commit my spirit.' I'd like to think that I could, but I'm not sure that I would have either the grace or the certainty to be able to mark the end of my life with any sort of comment about how sure I was of my place with God. For Jesus it was different; not only did he know that he had done enough, but he also trusted his Father at what is for most people the most terrifying moment of their lives. The amazing thing for us as Christians is that even with death staring us in our face, we can trust our heavenly Father, we can be sure that his goodness and power will win out, even beyond the grave.

'Death — the last sleep?
No, it's the final awakening.'
Walter Scott

'What the caterpillar calls
the end of the world, the master
calls a butterfly.'
Richard Bach

'If man hasn't discovered
something that he will die for,
he isn't fit to live.'
Martin Luther King

'The valley of the
shadow of death holds no
darkness for the child of God.
There must be light, else there
would be no shadow. Jesus is the
light. He has overcome death.'
Dwight L. Moody

6

Heaven, Angels and All That

I've heard it said – in fact, I've even written it myself – that some people are too heavenly minded to be of any earthly use. This critique usually gets levelled at people fond of ranting about doomsday on street corners or suggesting that behind every nasty cough or piece of criticism is an army of demons. Like all soundbites it has a pleasant ring to it and acts as a brilliant put-down in defence of the type of Christian who tries to break free of the 'nutty Christian' label. But there's a problem with it, one that betrays our severe lack of understanding about heaven, angels and all that. You see, I don't think that heaven is all white clouds, fairies and harps. I think it's real, practical, passionate, relevant and good. To be truly heavenly-minded is not something I think we should be ashamed of; instead it is to catch hold of the pulse that courses through God's veins (if he has veins), to be in tune with his heart. God is no tweed-wearing-elbow-patched-grandpa, scared of us humans and unable to comprehend what makes us tick. Let's not forget that it is us who are made in *his* image, us who carry some of his genes. If anything is going to be of use on this earth it's getting suitably topped up with a continual dose of heavenly-mindedness, catching hold of God's thoughts, passions and plans. Let's not do heaven the disservice of assuming that it's all flowing robes and no substance; instead it might be of help if we could find out a little more about exactly what it is like.

To have a vision of heaven and a clearer picture of what the future holds is the best form of equipment we could ask for to serve God in this life. It's no coincidence that some of the people who have had the surest knowledge of how things are going to work out for us have gone on to serve God in the most wonderful of ways. It simply is not true that we can get away with putting up our feet and taking it easy while on earth, brushing aside the question of heaven and eternity with the flimsy argument that it can all be dealt with once we've moved on to that next level. *Wrong!* Eternal life starts now; as soon as you've been granted a glimpse of it, as soon as you've hooked up with Jesus then heaven is an active concern in your life.

When Jesus came to earth for the first time, it seemed that everybody was expecting him to turn up with the kingdom of God in tow. They thought that his arrival would mark the beginnings of heaven on earth, ending poverty, misery and all forms of oppression. In a way they were right; the kingdom did come, but not in all its fullness. We might see parts of the kingdom of God – his rule and authority – scattered here and there, but the day will come when we see it break out across the whole earth in all its life-changing fullness.

We often seem to struggle to comprehend the eternal. We get hung up on the fact that we cannot seem to understand the invisible nature of God. The temptation to sign up to the forces of materialism – as well as giving fuel to the injustice of poverty – can lead us even further down the path of 'if I can see it, I'll believe it'. We learn how to rely on the physical rather than the spiritual.

There's a great story in 2 Kings 6 where Elisha and his servant are surrounded by a tribe named the Aramaens. There are far more of these Aramaens than there are Israelites, and verse 15 brings us to the verge of battle:

> When the servant of the man of God [Elisha] got up and
> went out early the next morning, an army with horses and
> chariots had surrounded the city. 'Oh, my lord, what shall
> we do?' the servant asked.
>
> 'Don't be afraid,' the prophet answered. 'Those who
> are with us are more than those who are with them.'
>
> And Elisha prayed, 'O Lord, open his eyes so that he
> may see.' Then the Lord opened the servant's eyes, and he
> looked and saw the hills full of horses and chariots of fire
> all around Elisha.
>
> (2 Kings 6:15–17)

After that the enemy came to attack Elisha and the rest of his
crew and, due to some sneaky manoeuvres, the enemy wound
up well and truly beaten. So often our problem is that – like
Elisha's servant – we only see the physical problems. We get
bogged down with details of money, people or circumstance.
Instead we need to echo Elisha's prayer, asking the Lord to
open our eyes so that we too can see that 'those who are with
us are more than those who are against us'. As wacky and as
thoroughly unpostmodern as it may sound, there is a spiritual
world, a realm invisible to us where forces are at work that
affect and direct our lives.

'God is spirit', says the Scripture, and it might be good for
us to get back into the habit of thinking about just what that
means. The Bible tells us that before he even created human
beings he created *spiritual* beings, called angels. There are
almost 300 references to either angels or angelic visitations
throughout the Bible.

They are created by God not as something nice for us to
put on the front of Christmas cards or trees, but to be – as
they are called in the Bible – 'ministering spirits' (see Hebrews
1:14). They exist to serve us, to communicate to us at certain

key times as well as to protect us when things sometimes get a little shaky.

Angels are invisible as they don't possess physical bodies, although they appear to human beings every now and then, often taking a physical form. What's more, despite the fact that we may not see them every day, they are hardly what you would call an endangered species. Hebrews 12:22 mentions 'thousands upon thousands' of them.

They were created – just as we were created – and so are not meant to be worshipped. They exist to serve God as well as us. They are not to be confused with the Holy Spirit – he is God, after all – despite the fact that they often appear to be carrying out God's wishes, much in the same way that some have characterised the Holy Spirit.

They appear throughout both the Old and the New Testaments, which both have some absolutely classic examples of angelic intervention and interaction with humans. When he was shoved in the lions' den, Daniel found himself joined by an angel who 'shut the mouths of the lions' (Daniel 6:22). Then there was the time (you can read about it in Luke 2) when the angel Gabriel appeared to the shepherds and told them not to be afraid. Other angels showed up and started to worship God. The shepherds were, perhaps understandably, petrified.

Throughout the book of Revelation angels play a key role in John's description of heaven. Even though I find the book fairly confusing, there is so much in it that is helpful and inspiring. Through it the new heaven and the new earth seem to come alive, as the angels who have been at God's side doing his will are going to be joined in their worship by us.

The difference between angels and us is that while we both are created beings, it was into us that God breathed his breath. That means he gave us something of himself, that we have been made in his image and likeness. That's why we and we alone are redeemed and can be called the children of

God. We've been adopted and are his offspring. Angels – on the other hand – are simply God's creation, not his children. When God created them he created something outside of himself, like making a computer, a piece of art or a building. They are inspiring and impressive, but ultimately they serve a function. When God created us it was more like giving birth.

There have been plenty of reports in recent times of people having seen angels. Some have seen them just the once while others have notched up a few glimpses. Often it seems that people see them as they are ministering to us, helping us out. I'm sure that this is what they are doing most of the time, and that for various reasons it is us who don't see them rather than them who aren't playing a part in our lives. I think that it's right that we spend most of our time ignorant of their deeds and assistance. They are not there to be worshipped or even noticed; their role is to get God noticed.

When it comes down to it, there are some key truths that lie behind the subject of angels, as well as behind the afterlife and the Second Coming of Jesus. We can take a highly dispassionate stance, approaching in study with a mind to fit it all into our own parameters of logic and reasoning. We can bend the forces of God to try and fit the rules of rational thought. Unfortunately it never truly satisfies and, after all, what kind of God would he be if we could so easily explain and define, predict and comprehend? In the end the whole point about looking at the subject of life after death is to realise that it is filled with Jesus. Eternal life makes no sense unless not only viewed alongside his life but through his words, through his eyes. Sometimes we humans have latched on to a desire to live for ever, to shrug off the weakness of mortality and emerge from the chrysalis of humanity. From the ancient legends about the elixir of life to the contemporary possibilities offered by drugs and oxygen tanks, the idea has captured the attention of almost every generation. But you know, we make a mess of this life, time and time again. As much as we may crave immortality, we have a natural talent for imposing horror and oppression on our fellow humans. The nightmares that punctuated the twentieth century were not unusual – genocide, greed and godlessness appeared in every century that went before it. Left to our own devices the chances are they'll crop up in the ones that follow it too. Who wants to live for ever when this is the best we can do? Who wants an eternity of greed, corruption and hatred? Sure, we might get better, but get better at what? Refine the ways of practising our sin, hone the ability to turn our backs on God?

As Christians we believe that God – the ultimate higher power – can put things right. We also believe that he has set aside a time for each of us as well as for the planet when life as we know it will come to an end. Replacing it will be a time when 'the lion will lie down with the lamb', when all the wars, pain and misery will cease. At that time we will be so caught up with the Father and his Son that we will join with the angels and the twenty-four elders of Revelation. That's when we will live and reign with him for ever. At the end of the Bible it says 'Amen. Come, Lord Jesus' (Revelation 22:20). Those are the words that we need to be echoing. We need to be praying for Jesus to come back and end this pain and suffering, to come in power and rule with justice, toppling the wicked and destructive. As we live our life here on earth in the light of heaven, becoming increasingly heavenly-minded, we will find for ourselves a whole series of earthly uses of which we never had a clue before. I believe that the thing that God is calling us to do in these days is to go deeper into him. As his people in the West we're so busy doing things that we have forgotten that in the end it's all about finding him, pursuing a relationship with him like a dog after his master. It's about resting in him, worshipping him and placing him above everything else that screams for our attention.

Whenever God's people have tried to get closer to him, reaching a new place of intimacy with their Creator, they have always encountered opposition. Sometimes it has even come from within the family of God, but certainly it has not been unusual for it to come from outside. When you think of King David being so excited at bringing the Ark of the Covenant back into Jerusalem that he danced before the Lord with all his might, there was his wife Michal despising his foolishness. 'Oh, yeah?' he replied. 'And I'll become even more undignified than this.' He refused to let his passion for God be diluted by someone who failed to understand exactly what it meant to him.

In the Gospels we read about Mary, sitting at Jesus' feet, listening to him while her sister Martha kept herself busy in the kitchen. 'Why don't you tell Mary to give us a hand?' Martha asked Jesus. He had to explain how she herself had become distracted and had missed the point of it all; the best thing is to hang out with him. Everything flows out of the relationship.

There's a hymn that we used to sing at school:

> Immortal, invisible, God only wise,
> In light inaccessible hid from our eyes,
> Most blessed, most glorious, the Ancient of Days,
> Almighty, victorious, thy great name we praise.

OK, so the language might seem a tad out of place in the twenty-first century, but the sentiment is timeless, as well as being something that we perhaps have lost. The sense of God's wonder, his otherness, his size. It is as we get a glimpse of eternity that we become fully fit to serve in this life. When we take time to explore the eternal God of heaven, invisible as he is, things change for us. There's an amazing part in the Gospel of John when Jesus prays: 'Now this is eternal life: that they may know you, the only true God, and Jesus Christ whom you have sent' (John 17:3). That's the definition of eternal life; the more we get to know Jesus, the more we get to know heaven. The more we know Jesus, the more we live in the kingdom. The more we live with Jesus in the present, the more we get a glimpse of the future.

That's why worship should take such a high priority in our life here on earth. Worship is the activity of heaven; intimate relationship with God. That's our timetable for eternity. Worship. Worship. More worship. Heaven is going to be saturated with the power, love and goodness of Jesus. Our response will be to love him for it. Fear not though, heaven will not be an eternal church service, it will be unlike anything we have known. We simply will not be able to help ourselves as the passion inside will force its way out as we give God his worth. I'm sure we'll have things to do in heaven – all to do with ruling over the new heaven and the new earth – but it's all going to come from the base of our relationship with God. He created us for himself and for ever he will have us for himself. Our heart's true home is him.

The gift of God is
eternal life, not the gift from God,
as if eternal life were a present
given by God: it is Himself.'
Oswald Chambers

'Aim at heaven
and you will get earth
thrown in. Aim at earth and
you will get neither.'
C.S. Lewis

'We shall not sit on
wispy clouds playing harps,
but we shall have good, fruitful,
satisfying activity. We shall
perfectly, at last — serve him.'
David Winter, *What Happens after Death*

Also by Mike Pilavachi with Craig Borlase:

Live the Life
A Soul Survivor Guide to Doing It

Life the Life doesn't pretend that being a Christian is easy, but points the way to a walk with God that impacts the whole of our lives, tackling questions such as: 'How do we deal with temptation and guilt?'; 'Can we hear God speak?'; 'How can we share our faith?'; and 'How do we know what to do with our lives?'. Now published as a new edition with a new 'study-guide-style' life application section and illustrative cartoons.

'This really is crucial teaching: read it and be well blessed!'
ANDY HAWTHORNE, WORLD WIDE MESSAGE TRIBE

'Working on our relationship with God is the most valuable thing we can do. Live the Life is going to be a great help to anyone wanting to go deeper.'
DELIRIOUS?

Published by Hodder & Stoughton
ISBN 0 340 78591 8

By Craig Borlase:

Soul Survivor Presents
The Naked Christian
Getting Real with God

Picture yourself as the Naked Christian, stripped of
the trappings and comforts of cosy church life.
Just you and God.

This is a book about what it really means to be a Christian
– not what your mates tell you, not what your parents
tell you, not even what the Church tells you – but what
God wants you to be. It is about honesty, integrity,
learning to respect who you are and to value the
unique gifts God has given you.

Be warned: this groundbreaking book is unlike any
Christian book you have ever read before.

Published by Hodder & Stoughton
ISBN 0 340 78529 2

By Beth Redman:

Soul Survivor Presents
Soul Sista
How to be a Girl of God!

Ever get the feeling:

- you spend most of your life trying to be someone you don't really want to be?
- there are too many boys in the world, and not enough men?
- being a Christian shouldn't be half as difficult as everyone tells you it is?
- you want to know God, but you're not sure if he wants to know you?

It's time to fight back! *Soul Sista* is the definitive survival guide for every girl who's ever wondered why the holy life sometimes seems to be just one bad hair day after another. It's about becoming a Girl of God: proud to be a Christian, proud to be a woman.

Beth Redman is an evangelist and schools worker, and former member of the World Wide Message Tribe.

Published by Hodder & Stoughton
ISBN 0 340 75677 2

By David Westlake:

Soul Survivor Presents

Upwardly Mobile
How to Live a Life of Significance

The glossy mags will give you all the advice you need for a
fast-track route to flash cars, crisp suits and a seat on the
board. But God's blueprint for life has rather different goals:
feeding the hungry, sheltering the poor and loosening
the chains of injustice. Despite any feeling of apathy or
inadequacy you may have, *Upwardly Mobile* will help you
discover your God-given potential to make a real difference
in the world in which we live.

Soul Survivor Presents

Outwardly Active
Evangelism as Jesus Did It

On the day you realise you're never going to make it into the
Evangelist All-Stars Hall of Fame, it might be worth taking a
fresh look at what evangelism is really about. How did Jesus
himself do it? It's not all about bums on pews or lightning-
flash revelations. The example Jesus set is a little more
realistic: an authentic balance of relationship building,
showing faith through actions and words, and seeking the
guidance of the Holy Spirit.

David Westlake is Youth Director of Tearfund.

Published by Hodder & Stoughton
Upwardly Mobile: ISBN 0 340 75654 3
Outwardly Active: ISBN 0 340 78556 X